*DOLLAR CRISIS, POUND DROPS, GOLD RUSH*—these newspaper headlines have flashed out at us with alarming frequency over the last ten years. But most of us are unable to understand the implications of these monetary panics. Now *The Gold War* explains what has been happening on the international monetary front in simple, accessible, and highly readable terms.

"Behind the economic and monetary complexities lies a fairly simple story of political and diplomatic conflict, and it is this political drama which is our main theme," explain the authors. Starting with the founding of the International Monetary Fund in 1944, they expose the rules of the game played among the leading nations of the West—the so-called Group of Ten. The effect of the decline of the dollar, the devaluation of the pound sterling, the uncertainty of the slippery franc, the consequent rise of the Deutschemark, the speculative rush on gold, and the creation of new gold reserves, or "paper gold," are all highlights of a political story fought out on a monetary background. Highly critical of de Gaulle's willful stand and

# THE GOLD WAR

taking to task the official U.S. attitude of maintaining a *status quo*, the authors tell a dramatic, if controversial, tale which may raise eyebrows but is highly relevant to how many dollars are left in our pockets.

With their international working backgrounds and a fresh, balanced outlook, the authors are in an ideal position to evaluate much of the firsthand source information resulting from recent financial negotiations in Europe. For quick and easy reference, basic topics such as speculation, the balance of payments, and Euro-dollars are pinpointed in succinct summary form at various points throughout the book. This is a book everyone will need to read.

Gordon L. Weil, an American, was formerly the Common Market correspondent for *The Washington Post*. Ian Davidson, an Englishman, is a senior reporter for *The Financial Times* of London. Their paths first crossed when both were working in Brussels and Paris covering international financial negotiations.

# The story of the World's Monetary Crisis

# THE GOLD WAR

## GORDON L. WEIL
## & IAN DAVIDSON

HOLT, RINEHART and WINSTON
New York   Chicago   San Francisco

# Contents

# Preface

Most people think that international monetary problems are hopelessly complex. They are not, and this is one reason why we wrote this book. They also think that these problems are best left to the technicians and are of little concern to the average person. They are not, and this is the other reason why we wrote this book.

Behind the apparently complex economic and monetary events of the past decade lies a fairly simple story of political and diplomatic conflict—a story affecting more people than may have realized it. In order to highlight the political story, we have simplified the economic issues, perhaps putting them into a perspective somewhat shocking to purists and largely unknown to those who could only follow the story in the newspapers.

We appreciate the opportunity that the *Financial Times* and the *Washington Post* gave us to follow this story.

G.L.W.
I.D.

Cushing Island, Maine
*January, 1970*

**Money is like muck,
not good except it be spread.**

—*Francis Bacon*

**H**e is a black man and a miner. He works long hours and lives far from his family under the suspicious watch of the Afrikaner. He digs for gold in South Africa.

She is a French housewife. She has been finding that German household appliances are irresistibly good bargains, especially in comparison with competing French products.

He is a Zurich banker. He knows that some call him a "gnome," but far from being a mysterious elf, all he really does is buy and sell gold and foreign currencies for his customers, just as some brokers buy and sell wheat.

He is an American investor. He likes a speculative fling now and then. He has just seen an ad in *The New York Times* for gold stocks, and he makes a mental note to ask his broker if there is any chance of a quick killing.

He is an Englishman and works at the Bank of England—the Old Lady of Threadneedle Street. He notices that many people are selling pounds for other currencies and wonders if today the Bank will have to step into the market to buy pounds in order to keep up their price.

He is the American representative at NATO. His government wants him to bargain with its

CHAPTER **1**

# The Rules of the Game

allies for the withdrawal of some American troops from Europe in order to reduce U.S. expenditures abroad, but he knows that his German colleague is going to fight hard to prevent any pullout.

She is a tourist staying at the Paris Hilton on August 9, 1969. She has just heard that the French franc has been devalued and thinks she should be getting more francs for her dollars at the cashier's office. But she is told to come back in two days if she wants to obtain cheaper francs, because the hotel is uncertain what the new exchange rate will be.

These people have never met one another. Their daily lives, their problems, their hopes, are probably quite different. Yet they are all playing out their roles in the international monetary system, and their actions and those of millions of people like them have a powerful influence on the economic health of most of the nations of the world and even on questions of war and peace.

The one thing these seven people have in common is that they are worried (or should be worried) about whether gold and the scraps of paper called currency will have the same value tomorrow as they do today. Will the franc, the dollar, or the pound be worth less, thus requiring more currency to buy the same goods? Will gold be assigned an even higher value by most countries—or no value at all? Although they may never ask themselves such questions, their actions and decisions reflect their underlying uncertainty about the monetary system in which they are participants. If they and their governments lose confidence in the ability of that system to serve the world's financial needs, the system may collapse. In fact some of these seven symbolic figures and almost all governments do now have serious doubts about the world's monetary system.

Most of us understand the role money plays in our lives. Dollars, pounds, francs—they are all tokens which are accepted within a country in order to permit each person to transform the fruits of his labors into things that he needs and wants. They represent value—for example, the number of hours of work required to earn them—and they are accepted as a medium of exchange. Indeed, in each country the government makes sure that the officially issued currency is the only medium of exchange.

Just as individuals must have money to pay for their transactions with other people, nations must have money to pay for their transactions with other nations. But the international community is not as well organized as most countries. There is no authority that can determine what money will be acceptable to all nations in settling their debts to each other. Instead, the governments must negotiate and agree upon an international monetary system. This system must be able to meet their nations' needs so that governments and individuals will have confidence in it. Without an international authority able to enforce the will of the majority, the monetary system will work only if people believe in it. And as we shall see, the international monetary system—the world's greatest confidence game—affects all people, and they all affect it.

Confidence is a fragile flower; it withers whenever there is the slightest change of temperature in the monetary atmosphere. A country must in the long run break even in its transactions with other countries or people will begin to doubt its ability to maintain the value of its money and its economic place in the world. Its government has to make sure, through the national economic policy, and in fact through every other policy ranging from trade through defense, that it is not a chronic debtor. Many governments believe it is also their job to say things are going just fine, even when they are not. This approach only makes the fall from grace harder when it comes, as it inevitably does.

Governments can often get themselves into financial difficulties without any help. Usually they cannot get themselves out without help from other governments. This is why there is an international monetary system: it is a kind of international mutual-aid society, as well as a mutual discipline society. But, as we shall see, it doesn't always work as intended and has even been deteriorating in recent years. Partly this is due to the failure of some countries—the United States and Britain are the best known—to put their houses in order and partly because international confidence in the system has been purposely undermined for political reasons —most clearly by France.

The story of the world's monetary system shows a steady decline in confidence in it since its creation in 1944. This state of affairs is probably not the fault of the system, which is fairly ingenious. But the changing fortunes of the United States and Britain, the French and German attitudes as they regained economic strength, the succeeding waves of speculation, have been causes of the decline of the system and at the same time results of that decline. This is a fascinating story, because, under the veneer of monetary affairs, it is a story of "high politics."

As long ago as 1815 the major European powers gave their seal of approval to a set of rules for international financial conduct—known as the "rules of the game"—which is the foundation of the present monetary system. The basic rule provided that if one country wished to purchase the goods of another, it either could barter some of its own products for them or could pay for them with gold. This relatively rare metal, long regarded as having great intrinsic value and, incidentally, beauty, was accepted as a medium of exchange by all countries.

No country could afford to spend more money abroad than it received from abroad over any extended period. If it persisted in running up international debts, it soon would have insufficient gold to pay for its purchases. Thus, in the long run, each country was expected to attempt to spend about the same amount abroad as it received from other countries.* A number of supplementary "rules of the game" were adopted to enable nations to use a wide variety of domestic and international tools to help keep credits and debits in the foreign accounts of all countries in relatively even balance.

By the end of World War I the system was, however, functioning badly, and not much as European leaders, meeting at the Congress of Vienna in 1815, had intended. By the end of World War II the system was in shambles and was not working at all.

The collapse of this relatively simple monetary system, known as the gold standard, can be explained in almost as many ways as there were countries participating in the system. But three of the most important causes are beyond question.

For one thing, there has not been enough gold available for many years to finance all international transactions. In 1815 it has been estimated that about two-thirds of the money in circulation in the major nations had been made up of gold and silver (this metal was, at the time, also acceptable in international transactions). Governments began to print paper money which could be used to supplement gold in making both domestic and interna-

* See "The Balance of Payments," pp. 16-19.

tional payments. By the eve of World War I, gold and, to a small extent, silver represented only about fifteen percent of the money available; the rest was paper money. In absolute terms, the amount of gold used as money had actually increased, but the need for money had increased even faster. To fill in the gap, people were willing to use paper money so long as they believed that they could get gold for their dollars or pounds or other currency. As a result, international trade and investment grew rapidly. But if and when people lost confidence in the value of their money, because they doubted it could be turned into gold at any time, this paper money became useless for international dealings. In such a case, the world immediately faced a shortage of funds, known as a liquidity crisis.

When the "rules of the game" were properly applied, and a nation found itself in the position of a chronic debtor, it would reduce the amount of money available to its citizens in order to curtail their purchase of goods from abroad (and, incidentally, also domestic products). By cutting foreign purchases, a government could strive to bring them below the total value of its own country's sales abroad. But workers and farmers could not be counted on to accept without protest a drastic reduction in their purchasing power. They wanted "easier money" and supported candidates like the legendary William Jennings Bryan, whose historic and histrionic 1896 speech warned that "you shall not crucify mankind on a cross of gold." Politicians could not afford to ignore the demands of the working classes and still hope to remain in office. As a result, they often preferred not to play by the "rules of the game."

Another reason the "rules" failed to work as they should have was the practice of almost all countries of exporting their economic difficulties. By so-called "beggar-my-neighbor" policies, countries would try to solve their domestic economic problems by drastically reducing imports or by other measures which had the effect of slowing down the economy of other nations as well. A government might deem it wiser to try to solve its problems this way than to urge belt-tightening at home. The net result was gradual collapse of international cooperation and confidence.

The twentieth century is the century of total war. A country can no longer pit its armies against those of another nation while continuing to permit trade and investments to flow between the two. In wartime it has not been a question of the monetary system working badly; it has not worked at all. And in the wake of the world wars, most countries were far too weak simply to pick up where they had left off in their international economic relations. By the waning days of World War II it had become obvious that a new international monetary system was needed to ensure that transactions among nations could take place in an atmosphere of stability and certainty—the ingredients necessary to guarantee confidence. The responsibility for building and preserving such a system belongs to governments, and their policies and decisions are as much "political" as they are "monetary." Indeed, monetary policy takes its place beside other foreign policies, as we shall see.

Thus, for these three reasons—insufficient gold, failure to play by the "rules of the game," and the disruption of international relations by two world wars—a new monetary system had to be built. Gone forever were the days of the golden vanity, when that precious yellow metal was the arbiter of the world's monetary system. Almost imperceptibly, all that had seemed so simple and so permanent in the nineteenth century disappeared, and a new game and new rules had to be devised.

## THE PARITY OF THE NATIONS

A country's currency is like its flag—an object which symbolizes the nation's economic strength, embodies part of its prestige abroad, and attracts a large measure of patriotic veneration. Most governments will not trifle with the national currency, and seek to maintain it at a fixed value so that their own citizens and other countries can have confidence in it.

Because there is not enough gold to pay for all the trading deals, foreign investments, military and foreign-aid programs, and other international transactions, national currencies must also be used. Gold is essentially unchangeable, but money can be transformed in value by a mere stroke of the pen. Thus before paper money can be made acceptable in international transactions, it must be assigned a fixed value. Currency may be defined in terms of gold—the amount of gold that may be obtained, for example, for one dollar; or it may be defined in terms of another currency which is itself redeemable in gold—the number of dollars that may be obtained, for example, for a Deutschemark. Because the ultimate value of almost all major currencies has, until now, been set in terms of gold, each currency also has what amounts to a fixed relationship with every other currency.

One of the objectives of any monetary system must be to ensure that the exchange rates among the currencies of the participating nations are sufficiently stable or at least predictable enough to allow them to be easily traded for each other when necessary. The relationship between national currencies is known as their parity. If, for example, a German manufacturer sells widgets to an American consumer, the American can normally pay only in dollars, while the German can use only Deutschemarks. Before he makes the sale, the German must therefore be certain that he will be able to obtain the proper amount of Deutschemarks for the dollars he will receive in payment for his widgets.

When the parities among the currencies of countries participating in the international monetary system are set at the appropriate rates, commerce and other transactions can take place among them on the basis of the real value of the transaction (as in barter) and not simply because one currency is cheaper than another. If a currency is undervalued or too cheap, this means that an artificially low price tag is being put, perhaps deliberately, on its products when they are sold in world markets. Consequently, governments regularly cut the value of their currencies in comparison with those of other nations in the period between the two world wars; a new monetary system had to be so built as to discourage them from continuing to do so.

Directly related to the fixing of parities among the world's currencies is convertibility—the opportunity actually to exchange one currency for another whenever necessary. The new monetary system also had to encourage governments to allow their currencies to be convertible. Before any government would agree to allow its money to become freely convertible to other currencies, it had to make sure that the international community had confidence in the value of its money. For international purposes, the value of a currency is dependent on the amount of the country's holdings of gold and currencies that are readily acceptable by all nations and on its ability to earn more gold and acceptable currencies.

### RESERVES, OR KEEPING THE WOLF FROM THE DOOR

A country cannot always spend more abroad than it receives from foreign countries. If it did so, it would soon go broke. A government might try, of course, to print more currency in hopes of using it to finance additional foreign purchases, but as soon as other nations found out that they were being paid with worthless "printing-press money," they would refuse to accept any more. On the other hand, they would accept any currency if they were convinced that they could always turn it in for gold, in the value of which they had complete confidence, or for other currencies which themselves could be converted easily to gold. Such convertible currencies and gold thus constitute the international reserves of any country. By holding a sufficient stock of these reserves, a country can maintain its solvency and the credibility of its own currency if it is convertible in transactions with other nations. When a nation's reserves are gone, so is international faith in its ability to pay for what it wants from abroad.

A country's success or failure in keeping an adequate reserve which can be used to pay for international transactions is measured in its balance of payments. In simple terms, the balance of payments is the regular accounting which indicates whether more reserves are flowing out than are coming in, making the country a "deficit" nation; or if more gold and convertible currencies are being acquired than being spent, making the country a "surplus" nation. Ideally, each nation would have a long-run balance in its international transactions with all other nations.

A major task of the monetary system is to define, for the benefit of all participants, just what reserves are. Certainly gold is an acceptable reserve for all countries. But we have seen that there is not enough gold to go around, and thus the monetary system must define what currencies, and under what conditions, may serve as supplementary reserves.

Naturally, no country can count on being a "surplus" nation or on being in balance all the time, even if its economy is basically sound. A country may need to tap additional reserves from time to time when it is in debt and may be quite willing to repay these reserves when it becomes a "surplus" nation. A new international monetary system would provide needed reserves temporarily if the nation borrowing them can make a commitment to repay them within a short time. If a country is chronically in debt and shows no evidence of being able to repay reserves borrowed from the system, it should not be able to acquire such loans. Instead, the system should provide a way to allow it to change the parity of its currency—in effect to make it cheaper—so that its products can be competitively priced with those of other countries. As a result of such a cut in the parity of its currency, known as devaluation, a country can expect to become once again a "surplus" nation.

A new international monetary system has important tasks to perform: the fixing of parities among currencies, including a framework for devaluation or revaluation (increasing the value of the currency of a chronic "surplus" nation), defining reserves, and providing a means of borrowing and lending these reserves to countries experiencing short-term difficulties in achieving a surplus in their balance of payments.

The problem of creating such a system is what economic experts thrive on. These certainly appear to be technical problems which can best be solved by technicians. But they are also highly political. Parities involve prestige; is it respectable for France to allow there to be five francs for every dollar? And every nation would like its currency to be as good as gold. A "surplus" nation likes to remain that way; its government is almost certain to gain the approval of the domestic electorate for performing this feat. A country with a balance-of-payments surplus has funds available to pursue foreign policies which may cost money, in a way that a chronic debtor, who must try to live well within its means, cannot. Thus the decisions on the creation and operation of the monetary system may seem economic; they are essentially political.

## IN THE BEGINNING, MAN CREATED BRETTON WOODS

For most of the month of July, 1944, one thousand men, representing forty-four countries, struggled to devise the new postwar monetary system which would bring order out of chaos and provide the stability considered essential to economic reconstruction. They met at the Mount Washington Hotel, a resort nestled in the Presidential Mountain range at Bretton Woods, New Hampshire. For the first time since 1815, an international conference was to create a new monetary system. In 1944 the job took just twenty-two days.

As early as April, 1943, the United States and Britain had simultaneously issued plans for the new monetary system. The American plan drafted by Treasury Undersecretary Harry D. White and the British plan of John Maynard Keynes, perhaps the leading economic theorist of this century, laid the groundwork for the final agreement. But the negotiations between the two countries were not easy. The British hadn't altogether received the message that the United States had taken over its prized position of leadership in the management of the world's monetary affairs. The Americans were more cautious than Keynes, and while they were in favor of the creation of an international currency pool, they were reluctant to accept his bolder proposals for an independent and powerful international bank.

Finally the Americans and Keynes came to terms (mostly American), and their proposals were turned over to the Bretton Woods conferees. Among the forty-four delegations were representatives of most of the Allies, including the Soviet Union and other East European countries; nations of the British Empire; and Western European and Latin American countries. Jammed into the Mount Washington and working day and night, they debated the plans submitted to them. During the course of the talks they decided to create two new international organizations, not one, as had been originally suggested. Many of the countries were unhappy with Anglo-American domination of the proceedings, and the Soviets let it be known that they would not participate in the new system. The French delegation threatened to hedge its signature of the agreement with so many reservations that other delegations said they would have to do the same. At the last minute, the entire agreement seemed to be falling apart. Then Fred M. Vinson, vice-chairman of the U.S. delegation, made a supreme effort to flatter the French—a classic case of diplomatic apple-polishing. The ploy worked, the French withdrew their formal objections, and the way was clear for the creation of a single new monetary system.

The embodiment of the new system is an organization called the International Monetary Fund, commonly known as the IMF or simply as the Fund. The Bretton Woods negotiators assigned to it a number of duties which would ensure that the new monetary system would meet the most critical needs—the establishment of a fixed relationship among currencies, convertibility of currencies, the definition of reserves, and financial assistance to nations experiencing short-term difficulties in their balance of payments.

Each member of the Fund—there are now 111—should declare the par value of its currency—its value in terms of gold or dollars. The value of the U.S. dollar is set in terms of gold—at thirty-five dollars an ounce—and other currencies may be defined in terms either of gold or of dollars.

When a government sets the par value of its currency, it is not just going through the motions; it is pledged to maintain that parity. It must make sure that in exchange transactions the rates used are kept within one percent either side of the fixed rate. This creates a sort of "band" around the official exchange rate:

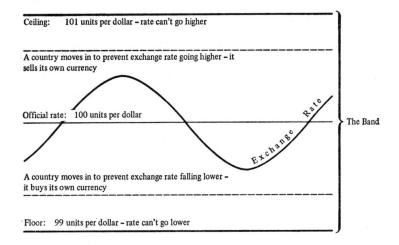

Ceiling:    101 units per dollar – rate can't go higher

A country moves in to prevent exchange rate going higher – it sells its own currency

Official rate:   100 units per dollar

Exchange Rate

A country moves in to prevent exchange rate falling lower – it buys its own currency

Floor:   99 units per dollar – rate can't go lower

The Band

An exchange rate within these permissible limits is used for transactions in the international currency market for immediate delivery of currency. A tourist cashing traveler's cheques will get a quite different, but still legal, rate because the bank may change money at the so-called "forward" rate—based on an actual currency, one to three months later. If the currency is being traded near the "floor," the tourist may in fact get a rate below the floor because there is at least some expectation that the currency may soon be devalued. In addition, he will have to pay a healthy bank service charge. The net result is that the official rate and the band are for the banks—but not for the average person.

Although the great majority of IMF members have assigned exchange rates to their currencies, only thirty-four countries have made their currencies convertible—freely exchangeable with other moneys for current transactions. These convertible currencies are what is sometimes known as "hard" currency. Other countries which are usually poor, and often have precarious or at least unstable economies, do not dare take the risk of allowing their currencies to be freely converted.

Another task for the IMF was the definition of reserves—means of payments among nations which would be readily acceptable. Naturally, gold could be counted as part of a country's reserves. In addition, any convertible currency could, theoretically, form part of a nation's reserves, because it could ultimately be turned into gold. A convertible currency could be exchanged for dollars, and the U.S. Treasury was committed to selling gold at thirty-five dollars an ounce. (It will also buy any gold offered to it at the same price.) In practice, however, only two currencies were ever considered as being roughly equivalent to gold as part of a country's reserves. They were the dollar and the pound sterling. Other currencies were declared fully convertible early in the Fund's history, but were not widely enough used in international transactions. Thus, though the Guatemalan quetzal was made convertible long before the pound, there just were not many nations interested in holding quetzals. Even the pound never really attained a status of equality with gold and the dollar, as we shall see. As a result, only the dollar, widely accepted and deemed to be easily redeemable in gold, took its place beside that metal as an international reserve that almost all nations were willing to hold. Twenty years after the IMF was created, some countries began to have their doubts about the dollar as well, and in 1969 the IMF created a new reserve, popularly called "paper gold," which we shall describe later.

The ability to use currencies which could be exchanged for gold, rather than gold alone as international reserves, spelled the formal end of the gold standard. Though the practice of using currencies as well as gold had been widely used in the interwar period, it was not until 1944 and the IMF agreement that the gold standard was formally interred, only to be resurrected in a modified form as the "gold exchange standard."

The key element of the IMF agreement was the creation of an international monetary pool to help tide nations over when they ran into short-term balance-of-payments difficulties. The idea of a money pool had been proposed by both Keynes and White. It meant that a country in trouble would not have to depend exclusively on the willingness of other nations to bail it out, but could turn to an international agency especially created for this purpose. Not that the IMF was to become a foreign-aid organization, because all drawings from the Fund would have to be repaid.

The Fund's working capital is contributed by its members according to a schedule of quotas which may be changed once every five years. The formula for calculating the quota is as complicated as the technicians could devise, but it really doesn't mean much. The contributions are mainly based on the political importance and the wealth of each country—which can hardly be measured accurately. Each member pays in some gold and some of its own national currency. In return it will be able to draw out of the IMF pool currencies of other countries. Its so-called "drawing rights" may go as high as two hundred percent of its contribution, but with each succeeding withdrawal, the IMF attaches tougher conditions.

Drawings last for no more than three to five years, because the currency aid is supposed to be used only to help a country get over temporary difficulties. If a nation is running a balance-of-payments deficit continually, the short-term aid will probably not be enough to help restore a surplus. In this case, its balance of payments is said to be in "fundamental disequilibrium," and it may be wise for the country in question to devalue its currency.

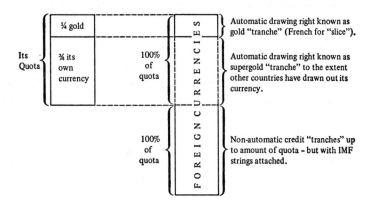

What a country pays into IMF · What a country can draw out of IMF

| | | | | |
|---|---|---|---|---|
| Its Quota | ¼ gold | | | Automatic drawing right known as gold "tranche" (French for "slice"). |
| | ¾ its own currency | 100% of quota | | Automatic drawing right known as supergold "tranche" to the extent other countries have drawn out its currency. |
| | | 100% of quota | | Non-automatic credit "tranches" up to amount of quota – but with IMF strings attached. |

The Fund is supposed to declare whether the proposed devaluation decided by one country is acceptable or not, in accordance with the IMF rules of the game. In actual practice, the IMF has not been able to do much about devaluations; usually a government will make its decision unilaterally and will try to act quickly in order to discourage speculators from undercutting the maneuver by selling their holdings of the currency and thus further depressing its value. As a result, the Fund's opinion will not sway the government once it has made its decision. But the mere existence of the IMF rules has discouraged governments from competitive devaluations, designed to make their countries' goods cheaper in world trade, but not justified by their balance of payments.

At the Bretton Woods conference, both White and Keynes made proposals which would have supplemented the basic currency-pool idea. White wanted to authorize the Fund to carry out its credit operations, in response to requests for drawings by members, by using a new international currency not altogether fortuitously named the *unitas*. This unit would, like the dollar, be defined in gold. The Bretton Woods conferees showed little enthusiasm for the idea.

Keynes made a much bolder proposal. In addition to the currency pool, he suggested the creation of an international bank, which could grant credits to its members. The credits, in the form of a new international currency called the *bancor* (Keynes was slightly more modest in naming his proposed currency than were the Americans), would be doled out to nations on the basis of their prewar share of world trade. Though the *bancors* would be defined in terms of gold, their value could be adjusted from time to time in order to meet increasing international needs for reserves. Not surprisingly, the country that stood to benefit most from the British plan was Britain. On the basis of its prewar trade, it would have had a right to more *bancors* than the United States. Naturally, the Americans vetoed the Keynes proposal.

The Bretton Woods conference yielded two new organizations. One was given the tongue-twisting title of the International Bank for Reconstruction and Development, which has since come to be known as the World Bank. This institution was based in part on Keynes's proposals and was designed to provide loans to war-torn and to developing nations to help them build up their economies. With capital contributed by its members, the World Bank would operate much like a commercial bank, making loans to countries in need and raising additional funds by floating loans. Thus the World Bank did meet some of Keynes's requirements that the new international economic order provide help to the less fortunate nations. But the World Bank disposes of no *bancors* and is not the regulator of the international monetary system.

Chief responsibility for the monetary system was eventually given to the International Monetary Fund. The IMF is both a system and an organization. The organization has the job of making sure the system works. Like the World Bank, it is a member of the United Nations family, but more similar to a distant cousin than an offspring. The task of helping countries to stabilize their currency-exchange rates and to keep their international payments in balance is far less dramatic and politically less volatile than the peace-keeping duties of the United Nations. In addition, the IMF was spared the logjam of cold-war controversy, because the Soviet Union and its allies are not members.

Operational decisions in the IMF are made by its executive directors, who meet weekly. They need not decide unanimously; a majority will do. The voting rights of each member country are determined by the size of its quota—which means that the United States has always had a large enough bloc of votes to veto any decision of which it disapproves.

The IMF staff is traditionally headed by a European managing director, now France's Pierre-Paul Schweitzer. Both the managing director and the staff have acquired worldwide reputations for objectivity and intelligence. But neither the governing boards nor the managing director and staff are truly political institutions. As a result, the most important decisions affecting the IMF and the Bretton Woods system are made elsewhere.

The Bretton Woods system and the IMF were devised without much thought being given to a situation in which the United States itself would have a "fundamental disequilibrium" in its balance of payments—in other words, when the United States would be continually in the red. The "rules of the game" were based on the belief that the dollar would always be as good as gold, so therefore all nations would be as willing to accept it as gold. Fifteen years later, when the number of dollars held by foreigners came to far outstrip the American ability to redeem them all for gold, confidence in the dollar was undermined. In 1944, however, the United States seemed far from a situation when more dollars would be flowing out than were flowing in. The vast American economy had much to offer and the other nations of the world had little to offer it in return, either because of the war's devastation or because of colonial poverty. Yet, thanks to the speedy economic recovery of Europe, to which the United States made an enormous contribution, the tables were turned far faster than had been expected.

The monetary system worked well until and even for some time after America's role as the world's benevolent creditor was altered. But eventually political pressures and decreasing confidence were to bring an end to the halcyon days of the IMF.

## THE BALANCE OF PAYMENTS

In every government there is a man who has the job of toting up all of the money that has come in and all of the money that has flowed out during the year. He is a sort of national accountant. Each year he reports whether the country has shown a surplus or a deficit.

The results will show one or the other; balance-of-payments figures never balance. Thus what he is really working out is the nation's imbalance of payments.

The balance of payments is the main barometer used to gauge a country's performance in the world economy. If a country has a deficit year after year, it may be in serious trouble. If it has a surplus year after year, it may come under pressure to take steps to cut its profits.

The balance of payments looks like this:

A. Goods and services

    1. Merchandise
    2. Nonmonetary gold } These figures show the trade balance
    3. Services—some of which are sometimes called "invisibles" (such as freight and insurance on goods, travel, investment income)

B. Transfer payments

    These include grants by the government and funds sent to and received from other countries by private companies and individuals.

C. Capital and monetary gold

    These include direct investment (for example, funds used to purchase plants abroad), private short- and long-term movements of capital, similar movements of funds by the government, and the international liabilities and assets of private institutions (like banks) and the central bank.

The national accountant keeps all these statistics, using a double-entry system, which shows the inflows and outflows for each item. The net result for each item, when added to all other net results, should agree with the country's total surplus or deficit. If a country has a surplus—a profit for the year—its reserves of gold and convertible currencies will have gone up. If it has a deficit—a loss for the year—these reserves will have declined.

The only problem is that the balance of payments never works out that neatly, and the national accountant is therefore allowed, under what are politely called "accounting conventions," to use a "finagle factor," which makes the sum of the net performances for each item equal to the overall balance-of-payments figure. This factor is called "errors and omissions"—a most useful and often very large item in the balance of payments which a government is never required (and may be unable) to explain.

If a country has a temporary deficit, the IMF may help tide it over with reserves from its own pool. If the payments balance is in chronic deficit, the country is in trouble and may devalue its currency to make its own goods cheaper when sold abroad and foreign products more expensive for its residents. If the payments balance is in chronic surplus, the country may be asked to revalue its currency by increasing the value of each unit (Deutschemark, guilder, etc.). By doing so, it will make its own goods more expensive for foreigners and imports from abroad cheaper for its own residents. Willingness to revalue is often considered a contribution to international cooperation.

Who makes the decision whether there is a surplus or deficit and whether it is chronic? The government itself.

Now, balance-of-payments figures can be interpreted in almost any way a government chooses. Usually deficit countries try to minimize the extent of their troubles, and surplus countries try to appear in worse shape than they really are. Both can use that old favorite, "errors and omissions," as a cosmetic to serve almost any purpose, and the official statistics may get some "window dressing" by last-minute transfers of funds which make a country look better on the last day of the year, though it quickly returns to form once the books for the year are closed.

One way for a government to achieve its desired result when it talks about its balance of payments is to focus on a specific balance of payments different from the overall figure. It may simply stress the trade balance, particularly if it is making a profit there and losing reserves on most other items. Or it may talk about "current account," defined to mean the balance of goods, services, and transfers (some nations exclude government transfers from this concept). Or it may count the overall balance with the exception of short-term capital movements, which are extremely volatile and may not help provide an accurate picture of the country's international performance.

All this juggling of the figures makes it difficult to compare how countries are doing. A further complicating factor is the differing ways governments count various flows. The United States, for example, considers foreign economic and military-aid programs as part of the current account, but almost all other developed countries count them among capital movements. As a result, the American balance on current account looks worse than it needs to by other people's standards.

Not all the difficulties in getting a clear idea of the balance-of-payments figures result from selective reading by governments. It is no mean task for national accountants to come up with accurate figures. Britain, which has had trouble with its balance of payments, twice in 1969 found mathematical errors in the way it had been calculating its statistics. In one case the error had been carried over for years, and in another an independent-minded computer had gone astray. Fortunately for the British, when both mistakes were straightened out, the balance of payments looked better: there was less of a deficit.

The way of calculating the overall balance of payments which we have been discussing is called the balance of payments on the liquidity basis—in terms of the inflows and outflows of currency from a country. But not all of the money-flows pass through the central banks. For example, a dollar sent abroad may be used abroad and never turned in to a central bank. When these dollars are left out of the government's calculations and only transfers of reserves among central banks are counted, the result is the balance of payments on the official-settlements basis. This figure may present an entirely different picture from the liquidity balance. In 1969, for example, the United States had a 7 billion dollar liquidity deficit, but a 2.8 billion dollar surplus on the official-settlements basis.

But this way of measuring a country's international performance is probably even less accurate than the liquidity basis. If a country has a convertible currency, and if most of that currency is held by people in other countries, this money represents an ever-present threat to the reserves of the country in question. The United States and Britain, for example, show sizable reserves of gold and foreign exchange. Yet if all the short-term claims on their reserves —in the form of dollars and pounds held by foreigners—were redeemed, their reserves would be wiped out and they would find themselves deeply in debt. In addition, part of their holdings may at any time be made up of reserves lent them by the IMF or other countries to discourage a run on the dollar or the pound. These confidence-building reserves are not, however, really part of the reserves of the United States or Britain. A mere glance at the widely fluctuating reserve position of these countries throughout the year will show that not much can be learned from the balance of payments on the official-settlements basis.

The ins and outs of the balance of payments prove (though it may be impolite to say so of sovereign nations) that figures don't lie, but liars figure. In any case, that most important of indicators— the balance of payments—has probably come to indicate nothing more than what the government wants the statistics to show. In fact, some experts now say it is totally meaningless, because, thanks to the two-tier gold price system and the effects of inflation, the United States can have a balance-of-payments deficit and still increase its gold holdings.

**A**ny American tourist setting out for Europe in the late 1940's or early 1950's would equip himself with a fistful of dollar bills. He knew that he could buy all kinds of small favors from everyone—porters to prostitutes—merely by sweetening the payment with a dollar or two. If he felt like the king of all he surveyed, his American passport and his wad of dollars heralding his way, he was not far from wrong. But he probably did not fully comprehend the way in which his dollars worked to assure not only his comfort but a large degree of grudging respect.

Europe was hungry for dollars. The United States had the heavy equipment, consumer goods, and even food that war-torn Europe desperately needed. But Uncle Sam would accept only dollars for his goods, which made good sense to him but provided little hope for the Europeans. The American economy, which had almost doubled in size during World War II, was booming, and the Truman administration wanted above all to avoid the seemingly inevitable depression that set in after each major war effort as the economy geared down from producing weapons to making more mundane goods. In large part, demand for American products

CHAPTER **2**

# The Decline of the Dollar

would come from Americans themselves, for they unleashed a pent-up desire for refrigerators, automobiles, telephones, shoes, and thousands of other consumer goods. The rest of the world produced little that could not be obtained at home, and since the primary need was to keep the American economy booming, the government would not, in any case, have been anxious to encourage purchases from abroad.

The situation looked hopeless. The Americans would have little need for European products, so Europe would never have a sufficiently large stock of dollars to buy the American goods it needed so badly. It looked like a classic case of "the rich get richer, while the poor get hungry." This was the period of the so-called "dollar gap," far more real and far more frightening than any missile gap or credibility gap of later years. In their eagerness to acquire dollars, European governments paid a high premium for them above the official exchange rate. Thus Europeans who managed to obtain a few dollars could turn them in for a big packet of domestic currency, which helped ease their way in the hard postwar years. As a result, they were willing to jump through hoops for the American tourist dollar.

Almost alone, Britain tried from the outset to operate on something above mendicant level. The British still recalled the interwar years, when their nation had been the world's leading monetary and trading power. They were anxious to give the pound the same privileged position as the dollar, in line with the Bretton Woods agreement. This meant that the pound was to be made fully acceptable as an international medium of exchange, with confidence in its ability to perform this role based on the right of any holder of pounds to turn them in at the Bank of England for gold. Only if Britain could maintain a sizable surplus in its international accounts (because others wanted to purchase British goods with pounds rather than turning them in), and thus maintain confidence in its solvency as a banking country, could the pound play this role.

But Britain had been severely damaged by the war and could hardly compare with the United States as the prime source of goods for Europe. This lesson was, however, to be learned the hard way. The British insisted on declaring that their currency was fully convertible, that it could be freely exchanged for other currencies and for gold. In order to give other nations confidence in Britain's ability to make good on its claims for the pound sterling, in 1946 the American government made a 3.75 billion-dollar loan to the Bank of England. Presumably, other countries would believe that since Britain could rely on such a large stock of dollars to back the pound, they would be willing to use pounds in international transactions without actually testing its strength by trying to redeem them at the Bank of England. But this expectation seriously underestimated the diminished standing of the pound in the rest of the world. The dollars poured out of the Bank of England's coffers at a dizzying pace after the pound was declared convertible on July 15, 1947. Though a handful of courageous aviators had been able to save Britain from a German invasion in 1940, all the dollars in the world could not save the British economy from the rude and belated discovery that Britain, though spared from conquest, had in fact been one of the big losers of the war. On August 20, 1947, the pound was once again made nonconvertible. Britain found that all European countries were equal and that, sadly, she was now more equal in her dependence on America than any other. The dollars which had been her grubstake quickly flowed back to the United States, leaving the British sadder but wiser, and saddled with a whopping new debt to the United States. The only salve to Britain was that, in theory at least, the pound was an international-reserve currency just like the dollar. At least the Bretton Woods agreement said so.

The "dollar gap" was an unhealthy situation. It meant that the United States could look forward to endless years of Europe's living on the American dole. Dollars would have to be given to the Europeans, who could then spend them in the United States for American goods. And because there could never be enough goods to meet all the American and European demands at the same time, despair was sure to set in among the European nations. The Soviet Union could be expected to try to cash in on such disappointment by urging that nations spurn American "imperialism" and by subverting their democratic governments.

The American response—the Marshall Plan—has been called a prime example of enlightened self-interest. Enlightened because the Truman administration saw that World War II had finished Europe unless somebody extended it a helping hand. Self-interest because an economically restored Europe would be the best customer for American goods and would keep the American economy turning at a steadily accelerating rate.

Under the Marshall Plan the United States channeled over sixteen billion dollars into Western Europe between 1948 and 1952. This was the most massive aid program the world has ever seen. It was unselfish in its extent; much less American aid made available over a longer period might have done the job. But Truman was anxious to get the job done and, to his great credit, he did it. The Marshall Plan, representing the breakthrough out of the vicious cycle of the "dollar gap," was a major factor in preventing the spread of Soviet influence into Western Europe, while at the same time it contributed to the end of Europe's economic dependence on the United States. The little haberdasher from Kansas City and Marshall, his patrician general-cum-Secretary of State, had reason to be proud of their efforts.

But America was still Europe's creditor, as indeed the Bretton Woods agreement had foreseen. With demand remaining high for dollars, there was no threat to its international role. The international monetary system functioned smoothly. In fact, it worked so well, not because of its own largely untested merits, but because the dollar was in such good health and the United States held most of the world's gold. If there was ever a period of *Pax Americana*, this was it. In 1945 the situation looked permanent and unchangeable; but it changed radically within fifteen years. The only way to go was down, and down the dollar would go, due, not to the Soviets or the Europeans, but to the United States itself.

And it all came from doing what comes naturally. Military programs abroad, foreign aid, international commerce, and investment in other countries—all were normal enough activities for the United States and its citizens. But when the net effect of these activities was calculated, the result was red ink in the balance of payments for eighteen out of the last twenty years. Here's how it happened.

## THE PRAETORIAN AND PREDATORY GUARD

The Americans came to Europe to put down dictatorship; they stayed to put down roots. Having learned the lesson from the aftermath of World War I, that a nation must not only win the war but also stay to maintain the peace, the United States readily accepted the commitment to maintain a large standing army in Europe. Gone were the days when the American armed forces would dwindle to a handful of professional troops, while their civilian cousins rushed headlong home to enjoy the rewards of peace. The draft never disappeared, and American forces remained to occupy Germany and Italy and to aid in the reconstruction of other countries of Western Europe. In the Far East, General Douglas MacArthur established a military government in Japan to replace the undeified and undignified Imperial government.

Most nations were glad to see the United States perform the sticky and difficult job of occupier. It spared their resources for other tasks. In Europe, the Soviet Union, hoping to expand its influence, accepted some occupation duties; Britain, hoping to play the role of the great power it once was, kept troops on the Continent; and France, hoping to keep up with the Joneses, insisted on being given the right to occupy some territory, though its troops could hardly live better than the people they had supposedly beaten. In Japan the United States handled the job alone.

By 1950, a full five years after the end of hostilities, Americans were still stationed abroad. But the old war had given way to the cold war. In 1947 a peace treaty was concluded with Italy. In 1949 a peace treaty of sorts was concluded with Germany (the Soviets refused to cooperate, since they had grown fond of having their own little Germany), and in 1951 a peace treaty was concluded with Japan (with the Soviets once again opting out, though here they really didn't matter). But the troops stayed on, because now they represented the American commitment to prevent any further Soviet expansion.

The Soviet blockade of Berlin in 1948–1949, following hard on the heels of the Communist coup d'état in Czechoslovakia, was a sure warning that military forces would have to be kept in place to ward off any new moves to redraw the map of Europe. The North Atlantic Treaty Organization, the first multilateral defense pact which the United States had ever joined, was founded in 1949 as a response to this challenge. It committed the United States to come to the aid of any Western European nation that was threatened by the Soviets. And short of immediate resort to atomic warfare (by 1949 the Soviets, too, had the bomb), land and sea forces had to be kept on the ready to repel any invasion and to signal the need, in case of an all-out attack, for the use of nuclear weapons. Under the terms of the NATO agreement, the United States was committed to maintain forces in Europe. At the same time, the Europeans were asked to shoulder part of the burden of their own defense. Germany, still not fully recovered from the abbreviated history of the Thousand Year Reich, was pushed, kicking and screaming (some said not loud enough), into re-creating a war machine. By one of those not too surprising ironies of fate, West Germany was to be the only European nation that fulfilled its military commitment to NATO. Otherwise, most of the European nations were content to let the United States do it, with only a relatively small contribution on their part, outside of the land made available for bases.

In the Far East, North Korean troops marched over the thirty-eighth parallel on July 25, 1950, to take over their brothers in the south. Once again the United States threw its manpower and firepower into the breach and eventually repelled the invaders. But the message that American troops might have to be stationed in Asia indefinitely came through loud and clear. As a result, the Eisenhower administration virtually locked the United States into mutual defense alliances with every nation of the non-Communist world (both in Asia and in Europe) through mini-NATOs. But everyone knew that they simply meant that the United States would have to be on the spot—and thank you, you can just leave your troops here as our insurance policy—in case the Russian hordes or any Soviet stooges should make their move.

The reason for wanting the most powerful nation in the world to give up hostages as insurance that it would intervene when necessary (a totally unprecedented state of affairs) was not purely military. It had not completely escaped the civilian planners in Washington that stationing troops abroad would mean a continuing expenditure of dollars abroad and that money was flowing out with nothing much coming in to show for it, except some intangible item called "security," which never appears in national balance sheets. It had also not escaped the notice of military planners, but they were strangely unconcerned by the resulting dollar outflow. Troops had to be housed, clothed, equipped, and paid when they were abroad. Not everything could be shipped from the United States, and the soldiers could not be kept in a kind of gilded solitary confinement. The host nations were quite pleased to note that not only were they getting protection, but they were making a profit.

Of course, this direct military aid to other countries could not go on forever, said the Washington sages. We must give them sufficient military equipment and training so that they can develop their own armed forces, capable of defending their own lands. Fine, said the recipient nations, as they saw more equipment and instructors pour across their borders, allowing them to spend their still-slim resources on building up their economies. These grants of military matériel represent a drain on the dollar, though they appear on the plus side of the ledger. As exports, they are listed on the profit side of the balance sheet. The only problem is that the money used to "purchase" these exports comes from the American exchequer. Uncle Sam is, in fact, his own best customer.

The costs will probably never be fully known. For one thing, to make them public would constitute giving aid and comfort to the enemy. For another, their publicity might also give aid and comfort to those who oppose the vast military programs. In addition, the money flowed so quickly, in some cases, that government statisticians had all they could do to keep up with it. But if we look at the years from 1946, the first full postwar year, to 1968, when Vietnam was a major national preoccupation, the numbers are impressive. In these twenty-three years the United States spent 57.7 billion dollars on military activities abroad and an additional 36.8 billion dollars on so-called "military grants of goods and services" designed to help other nations build their own national-defense programs.

The accompanying chart shows just how much the American foreign military program cost. As the years went by, the program seemed to be even more expensive, though its price appeared to be leveling off at the end of the period. But between 1965 and 1966, even a not-too-astute chartist can read the beginnings of the quest for security in a big way in Vietnam.

The figures all serve to show that the United States was making a determined effort to export dollars in a way that would give

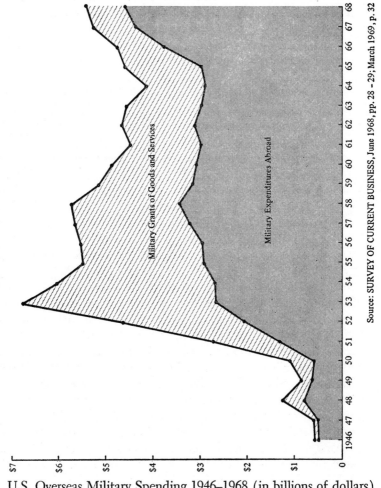

## U.S. OVERSEAS MILITARY SPENDING, 1946–1968

Military Grants of Goods and Services

Military Expenditures Abroad

Source: SURVEY OF CURRENT BUSINESS, June 1968, pp. 28 – 29; March 1969, p. 32

U.S. Overseas Military Spending 1946–1968 (in billions of dollars)

other nations all they wanted. But—and we shall sound this refrain again—when these nations had more dollars than they
wanted, they could turn them in for gold. Thus the American
troops abroad, a kind of twentieth-century praetorian guard, were,
at the same time, predators on the precious American gold stock.


## THE COST OF VIETNAM

Most of the dollars that the United States spends abroad on
its far-flung military programs eventually fall into the hands of
other countries—including some Communist states. If U.S. aid is
being given to a small nation, this country will almost certainly
use the dollars it accumulates to help finance its international
transactions. Indeed, the "hard-currency" income derived from an
American military-aid program may be its principal source of convertible money. Naturally, the country receiving U.S. military aid
will spend many of its dollars for American material, and the dollars will quickly find their way home. But it will also make purchases in Western Europe and Japan, thus building up the stock
of surplus dollars held by foreign countries. To the extent that
these nations hold on to the surplus dollars derived originally
from U.S. military-aid programs, they are supporting the Americans by enabling them to continue to pump out dollars for military purposes. If they cash in the dollars for gold, they are trying,
at least implicitly, to discourage the United States from extending
its foreign military operations. In addition, no monetary circuit is
leakproof, and somebody along the way may siphon off some of
the dollars into Communist hands. This is particularly easy in a
country like Vietnam, where it is virtually impossible to distin-
guish friend from foe. The Communists need dollars for their purchases, of course, and should they hold any surplus, they make
sure that it is used to drain away American gold. It was widely
believed that in the mid-sixties in Vietnam, dollars thus accumulated were promptly shipped to Paris, where the Communists
could be certain the French would use them in the most appropriate way to undermine the dollar.

The Communist dollar policy was a relatively minor annoyance
so long as non-Communist nations were willing to hold dollars

and not cash them in for gold at the U.S. Treasury, as is their right under the Bretton Woods agreement. Yet the American balance of payments suffered, statistically at least, by the constant outflow of dollars, which was not compensated by any tangible inflow. And the Americans could feel the pinch every time a foreign nation turned in some of these dollars and the gold supply at Fort Knox dwindled. With the Vietnam war, the United States found itself in serious trouble.

Many of America's allies disapprove of U.S. policy in Vietnam. Yet to continue to hold American dollars, whether obtained as a result of the military-aid program or by other means that we shall soon explore, amounted to support for the United States. The French, for example, who opposed both the American intervention in Vietnam and the Bretton Woods monetary system, which gave the dollar pride of place, certainly chose to cash in their dollars as a sign of disapproval of both. Others, who gradually shifted their international reserves toward gold—countries like Belgium, the Netherlands, and to some extent Germany—also indicated their implicit disfavor. Italy, Japan, Canada, and other nations which continued to hold a large stock of dollars could be considered firmer allies of the American policy. Experts began to talk of a "gold zone" and a "dollar zone." In the first were those who opposed American policy in Vietnam and perhaps elsewhere in the future and who preferred to hold gold as the major portion of their international reserves. Those who continued to hold dollars thus became members of a "dollar zone," a term which smacked of a satellite relationship to the United States.

In this way, monetary policy became inextricably wrapped up in Vietnam policy. Of course, the decision to hold dollars was not entirely or perhaps even principally based upon a government's attitude toward the war there, but any such nation was open to innuendos that it did in fact support the United States operations in the Far East. While it could be admitted by those critics who want to see American domination in everything that happens outside the Communist world, that any nation must have some dollars to finance its international trade, they could easily set their own standards of what was permissible and brand any country in the "dollar zone" as an overly faithful friend of the United States. More important, in fact, than the war in Vietnam was the implicit commitment supposedly made by "dollar-zone" nations to support any future American policy.

Official Washington has never made any claims that the supposed "dollar zone" was contributing to the American war effort. For one thing, the people who are mainly responsible for Vietnam operations—the White House, the State and Defense departments—are not widely famed for their grasp of international monetary problems, at least not until they threaten to get so far out of hand as to affect national security. Those who are responsible for monetary and fiscal policy—the Treasury Department and the Federal Reserve—have about as much influence over Vietnam policy as Senator Fulbright and certainly much less than Senator McCarthy. In addition, while foreign support for the U.S. intervention is welcomed, the American government certainly does not want to embarrass any foreign government before its own somewhat unenthusiastic public by claiming that through their monetary policies they are helping the United States in Vietnam.

Thus, the only answer to the "dollar-zone" thesis has come not from the ranks of officialdom but from Robert Roosa, the man who, as Undersecretary of the Treasury, played a leading role in the early sixties, just as the Vietnam war was building in intensity, in shoring up the fading strength of the dollar. Roosa maintains that the whole world is a "dollar zone" so long as nations are willing to use dollars instead of gold. And even the French, who would like to see the special international role of the dollar ended, admit that the greenback is still useful when one nation has to pay its bills to another.

In addition to the policy impact of the link between Vietnam and the dollar, we cannot overlook the simple fact that U.S. intervention is expensive. Not only has the American defense budget virtually exploded, but the annual drain on the dollar has increased far faster than the Defense Department can follow. Expenses for military operations abroad hit all-time post-World War II highs in 1966, 1967, and 1968. All of the increase was due to Vietnam. In addition, an overall reduction in military expenditures abroad simply never took place. The Defense Department has admitted that the net effect is a dollar drain of at least 1.5 billion dollars a year and has not opposed estimates that have gone as high as three or four billion dollars. As we shall see, this out-flow could not have come at a more inopportune time, although the Defense Department does not seem especially disturbed.

## FOREIGN AID: AMERICA THE MUNIFICENT

Quite apart from the financial, logistical, and instructional assistance the United States distributes in the form of military aid, it also provides foreign economic help to a host of countries from Afghanistan to Zambia. At one time or another since the end of World War II, almost every nation of the world has received American foreign aid. The reasons for giving foreign aid are probably as varied as the outlooks of members of the U.S. Senate or as numerous as the nations who have received the aid. In any case, the United States has adopted a policy of helping nations to strengthen their economies (or just simply to feed their people) with little reason to hope for a direct political payoff in terms of subservience or even friendship. But American policy has been based on the belief that if nations are better equipped to survive economically, they will contribute to the maintenance of political stability (devoutly to be desired in Washington's view) and hence the prevention of Communist "takeovers."

Unlike military expenditures or other policies, official or private, which result in a net outflow of American dollars, the American foreign-aid program has had a less harmful effect on the balance of payments as time has gone on. But virtually none of the reductions in foreign-aid appropriations (as distinct from actual expenditures, which reflect only the cuts after some delay) was made in order to defend the dollar. Many congressmen have simply come to believe that the foreign-aid program is designed to buy friends for the United States and that the past twenty-five years have only served to prove that a nation can't buy friends. This reasoning may seem overly simplistic (though Egypt proves the point with amazing regularity), but many congressmen may also seem so. Some countries, it should be noted, have actually surmounted their need for foreign aid. In general, however, U.S. foreign aid has been cut back because of a shortsighted view of its purpose, which has gradually replaced the belief that economic aid should be designed to help nations to decide their own futures.

The most successful part of the foreign-aid program was the Marshall Plan—and it was also the most costly. In the years from 1946 to 1951, when most U.S. aid was being channeled into Europe, American foreign-aid expenditures totaled 19.6 billion dollars, or 39 percent of the amount of all foreign-aid outlays in the twenty-three-year period of 1946–1968. The results of the European Recovery Program are generally regarded to have been an outstanding success.

Compared with the annual rates of expenditure of three billion dollars and four billion dollars in the late years of the Marshall Plan, recent annual outlays have been in the neighborhood of 1.9 billion dollars. In terms of the total American budget, which has been climbing to dizzying heights, foreign aid has become a smaller proportion with each passing year.

Many U.S. aid dollars find their way back to the United States, usually because strings are attached or simply because only American goods will meet the needs of the recipient nations. But these dollars can and do fall into the hands of other developed nations, much in the same way that military-aid funds do. Developing countries frequently ship the dollars off to the European nations (often former mother countries), thus adding to the stock of dollars that the rich nations accumulate in excess of their actual needs. These dollars are a threat to the American gold stock.

## MONEY MAKES MONEY—BUT FOR WHOM?

One of the main American exports in the last quarter-century has been money. Dollars have been sent abroad, not as military or economic assistance, but simply to make more money. American industry has, to a large extent, gone international, with traditional borders being ignored or politely hopped over. The real "one-worlders" of today, though one expects they might shudder at the thought, are American businessmen.

American business firms expanded abroad after World War II for a number of reasons, though they all boil down to a single word—profit. Many of the largest companies, fully able to compete in the vast American market, found that they were, in fact, equipped to take on the whole world. Even if profits from American sales were substantial and growing, managers came increasingly to believe that if their companies were not expanding, they were, in fact, falling behind in the competitive race. In addition, profits from investment abroad actually topped the return on investments at home. Thus, without really being forced into the international arena, as are many firms in the small and closely packed European nations, they decided to extend their operations abroad. Once a few among the top five-hundred corporations made their move, the tide swept the others along. It is safe to presume that virtually all of them have had their fling with foreign subsidiaries, although more than one hundred of them subsequently retreated, having found that they could do better by exporting from their home base in America.

The creation of new economic groupings, like the European Common Market, was a powerful stimulus to the overseas expansion of American firms. Begun in 1958, the Common Market was designed to create a single, integrated economy for its six member countries—France, West Germany, Italy, and the three Benelux nations. This initiative has resulted in the removal of trade barriers among its member nations and the creation of a single tariff for all of them in their trade relations with outsiders. Less ambitious projects, like the European Free Trade Area, of which Britain is a member, also provided for the removal of tariffs among members. U.S. business leaders reasoned that it would be wise to set up manufacturing plants on the territory of members of these groupings and thus be able to ship their output free of duty throughout the tariff area. They believed that sales resulting from production abroad would more than compensate for expected losses of exports resulting from the new external trade barriers being created by the Common Market in an effort to promote trade among members.

The general postwar improvement in the economies of many nations and the accelerated push for prosperity which resulted from the Common Market and similar groups also made the foreign market attractive to American business. Europeans were acquiring a taste for American consumer goods, for example, and it paid to package and merchandise these products in ways calculated to increase their appeal. Once again, the lure of a European-based operation, often staffed by Europeans rather than Americans, led to the creation of U.S. subsidiaries. Increased economic cooperation among governments and clear signs that they placed greater emphasis on promoting economic growth for all rather than beggar-my-neighbor policies, which were supposedly in the interest of one nation, also provided insurance to American businesses that, once established abroad, their subsidiaries would not have the rug pulled from under them by anti-American policies.

Investment in subsidiaries was also stimulated by the quest for new sources of raw materials. Once minerals were found in abundance in Australia, Canada, or Peru, plants were built to process them on the spot, often for export to neighboring countries.

Where did American firms go? Canada was and remains the prime target for American business, which usually considers the Canadian market simply part of a larger North American market. Of 59 billion dollars in direct U.S. investments abroad at the end of 1967, some 18 billion dollars was located in Canada. But the most rapid growth took place in Europe. The U.S. Department of Commerce reports that at the end of 1960 about twenty percent of U.S. direct investment was located in Europe, below the levels in both Latin America and Canada. Seven years later, Europe held thirty percent of all direct American investment abroad, twice as much as Latin America, and about the same as Canada. In the last few years the biggest upswing appears to have been in those countries providing mineral and chemical raw materials, including some developing nations. Venezuela, with its large oil deposits, was the big winner among these nations.

Where does U.S. foreign investment go? The answers (in billions) for 1968:*

| | |
|---|---|
| Canada | $19.5 |
| Latin America | 13.0 |
| European Common Market | 9.0 |
| Rest of Europe | 10.4 |
| Africa | 2.7 |
| Middle East | 1.8 |
| Far East | 2.9 |
| Oceania | 2.8 |
| Other | 2.7 |
| Total | $64.8 |

* Source: *Survey of Current Business*, October, 1969, p. 28.

As might be expected from the investment boom in Europe and Canada, most of the money shipped abroad goes into the manufacturing sector. American automobiles dominate the market or come close in Canada, West Germany, and Britain, though some of the brand names and models would be completely foreign to the average American auto purchaser. But an even faster-growing sector is petroleum. Total cash outflow for petroleum investment in 1960 was only slightly above half the amount used for manufacturing plants. Seven years later these were almost equal.

But the most startling fact about American investment abroad is its rate of increase and durability. In 1946, only 230 million dollars went for direct foreign investments. Ten years later this figure was 1.9 billion. In 1965, 1966, and 1967 it topped 3 billion dollars annually. Finally, in 1968, direct investments began to taper off but still amounted to the not inconsiderable sum of 2.7 billion dollars. Taking the entire period from 1946 to 1968, a total of 35.6 billion dollars was invested abroad.

All of these investments abroad may mean additional profits for U.S. business, but they also represent a considerable drain on the dollar. Vast sums are shipped abroad to be invested in foreign economies and hence are destined to fall into the hands of foreigners and eventually of their governments. Once again they become a potential threat to the dollar, because they may be turned in at any time for gold. This threat is, however, lessened by two factors—Europe's own need for dollars for investment and the return on American investment—that is, the profits which are shipped home to the United States, representing the payoff for the initial outflow.

No real European capital market exists.* This means that if a European firm needs to raise capital by floating a bond issue, it must normally choose a single national market and label its issue in the currency of that country. The resources available in any one country are limited, not only because of its size but also because of the ingrained investment habits which make many Europeans distrustful of placing their savings in corporate bonds rather than in more tangible forms like real estate. The influx of dollars, readily acceptable in all countries, helped ease this burden by providing

* See "Euro-Dollars and Euro-Bonds," pp. 43-45.

an entirely new source of funds for local investment. The dollars that were shipped to Europe and were never repatriated because they were used to supplement European savings available for investment have come to be known as Euro-dollars. They are simply expatriate dollars, with no immediate plans to come home. Corporate-bond issues which seek to draw on these funds by being labeled in dollars are called Euro-bonds, though these issues are being increasingly used to tap European supplies of Deutschemarks and other "hard" currencies.

If some dollars never came home, but caused no threat to the American gold supply, others came home to the American firms that have invested abroad. They represented the return on their investment. Though not all of these dollars were physically returned to the United States, they represented profits of American firms and appear on the plus side of the official balance-of-payments ledger. The income of U.S. direct investment abroad in the 1946–1968 period has always been substantial, totaling 54.1 billion dollars. This tops the amount that has been invested abroad in the same period. Naturally, there is a considerable time lag, and the return results from investments made many years earlier.

Another net inflow of capital which helps offset the drain of American direct investment abroad is foreign direct investment in the United States. It is, however, quite small in comparison with the amount of money sent abroad by U.S. firms. The value of foreign direct investment in the United States at the end of 1968 totaled only 10.8 billion dollars. And foreign investors also collect a return on their investment—some 2.1 billion dollars in 1968.

We have been discussing here "direct investment," or investment used for plant and equipment. In addition, Americans buy stock in foreign corporations and bonds issued by foreign governments. Non-Americans do the same in the United States. But the direct investments have by far the greatest impact on the American balance of payments.

American investment abroad has raised tempers from Paris to Ottawa, with many stops in between. Governments get peeved when they see important sectors of the national economy fall under foreign control. They are reluctant to admit that these sectors often would not have developed at all, for lack of domestic

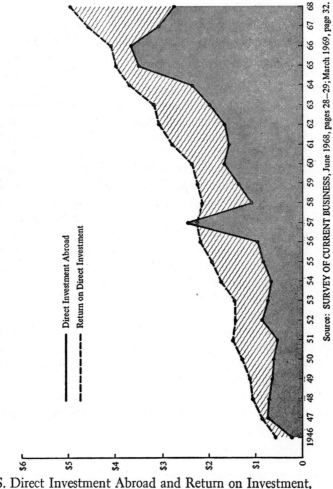

U.S. DIRECT INVESTMENT AND
RETURN ON INVESTMENT, 1946–1968

Direct Investment Abroad
Return on Direct Investment

Source: SURVEY OF CURRENT BUSINESS, June 1968, pages 28–29; March 1969, page 32.

U.S. Direct Investment Abroad and Return on Investment,
1946–1968 (in billions)

investment, were it not for the American capital that was pumped in. They only grudgingly recognize that the new investment leads to new and better-paying jobs for their citizens. On the other hand, they feel cheated when they do not get all the expected research-and-development spin-off within their borders.

Protests against American investment flow like the tide. For long periods, all is quiet. Then, suddenly, left-wing students and nationalist politicians protest violently against American domination of their country's economy and society. Very often a single small investment in a pet national plant will raise a greater storm of controversy than the take-over of most of the automobile sector. Some Americans have protested that it is grossly unfair to attack U.S. investments as a new form of imperialism only when the American balance-of-payments deficit is growing. They say that foreign investment should be judged on its own merits. But this is simply a vain hope, because, whatever the reasons for supporting or opposing it, U.S. investment will go where it can and when it can without much regard for the fate of the dollar. Even if they don't like this dollar invasion, foreign governments usually bark far worse than they bite. Nonetheless, as we shall see later, the American government has become increasingly sensitive to the effect of business investment on the dollar and to the increasing hostility to American investment abroad on political and monetary grounds.

American investment abroad has undoubtedly become the touchiest issue relating to the international role of the dollar. The dollar has become international money, serving international ends and making American firms into international enterprises. But somebody has to pay for all this. The investments may make money for business; they may cost the U.S. government gold.

### TRADE AS AID

The one bright spot in the American balance-of-payments picture has been trade. Despite the constant outflow of dollars for military programs, foreign aid, and investment, the United States has for more than one-hundred years made a handsome profit on its international trade transactions. In simple terms, the United States sells abroad goods worth more than the value of the products it purchases from foreign countries. This means a big plus in U.S. trade accounts with foreign nations.

The favorable American trade balance has often seemed to be a natural phenomenon. The United States, richly endowed with a wide variety of natural resources, depends only to a limited extent on imports. But it produces many goods not available anywhere else in the world and pioneers in the development of the most advanced products for agricultural production, manufacturing, and the consumer. Moves to lower American protection against foreign-made products, which have been matched by similar gestures aimed at aiding U.S. exports, have apparently helped the United States and other nations to reach higher plateaus of prosperity.

Soon after he came to office in 1961, President John F. Kennedy became preoccupied with the alarming outflow of gold which was already well under way. He believed that many programs which led to a dollar and gold outflow were essential and that it would be unwise to affront American business by slowing investment abroad. He decided instead to promote a program designed to increase American exports and thus to earn more dollars back through straight commercial means.

Kennedy recognized that in order to obtain concessions from other nations which would allow for more American sales abroad, the United States would have to ease access for foreign-made products. He pledged that his policy was designed to help all nations, but he persisted in believing that, whatever happened elsewhere, the increase in U.S. exports would help the balance of payments. In 1962 the major legislative effort of the Kennedy administration was the campaign to pass the Trade Expansion Act, an imaginative enlargement of the liberal trading policies begun in 1934. In fact, Kennedy attached so much importance to this law that he probably expended far more political capital than was necessary in assuring its passage.

The 1962 Trade Expansion Act paved the way for the Kennedy Round of trade negotiations among the major trading nations of the non-Communist world. The Kennedy Round was based on the American assumption that Britain and other European nations would be admitted to the European Common Market, and that in order to assure continued American access to this expanded market with its single tariff wall against foreign imports, the United States would have to offer to cut its own protection in order to induce the Europeans to do the same. The French veto of British membership in 1963, reducing the expected political and economic significance of the Common Market, was a severe setback for the Kennedy Round, but it remained an important economic exercise. The tariff cuts, agreed upon in 1967 and to be gradually made until 1972, amounted to an average of thirty-five to thirty-seven percent of the tariff levels of the participating nations, the largest trade liberalization package ever negotiated.

Despite the international move toward freer trade and the promise of a substantial increase in world trade, the hoped-for improvement in the American trade balance did not materialize. World trade did increase substantially, and American exports followed suit. But U.S. imports climbed at an even faster rate. From 1964, when the American trade balance showed a surplus of some 6.6 billion dollars, the black ink in the trade ledger dwindled to about one billion dollars in 1968, with no signs of real improvement.

Growth of American sales abroad has been slower in the last half of the sixties than in the first half. This performance, though far from sluggish, has been due to relatively poor judgment about the kinds of products other nations want and to relatively bad choices of markets in which to push American exports. In other words, the United States did not sell enough machinery and transportation equipment abroad and did not fully exploit the opportunity of the European Common Market. Yet, on the whole, the United States did reasonably well in holding its own in international trade, though it was totally unable to increase exports in line with President Kennedy's original plans.

The failure to improve the trade balance was mainly due to the rapid increase in American imports, which in turn was largely a reflection of a major domestic economic problem—inflation. In recent years the rate of increase in imports has been twice as high as the growth rate for U.S. exports. A booming economy, with more wealth for most people, will stimulate both the desire and the ability to pay for foreign goods. But inflation also puts more dollars in the hands of purchasers, while it makes domestic goods relatively expensive because demand outstrips supply. Other factors, including the failure of American automobile manufacturers to offer the consumer a true compact car, also led to an increase in imports.

Though it was easy to analyze why the hitherto healthy American trade balance was melting rapidly, the problem of finding a solution remains unsettled. In the long run, most politicians and economists believe the American economy will cool off and American consumers will be encouraged to buy in their own market, where they will be able to obtain products at reasonable prices and in greater quantity. But, according to the well-worn phrase of Keynes: "In the long run we are all dead." Many congressmen believe they will be politically dead if they don't produce some results in the short run. They are attracted by the idea of raising trade barriers against foreign goods, as a way of reducing imports, but they overlook the inevitable reaction of other nations, who would retaliate by slapping on their own restrictions against American exports. In these swirling mists of protectionism, which threaten the liberal trend of the past thirty-five years and which could lead to lower exports for everybody, with resulting recession or depression, the United States officially remains in a quandary about trade policy. The net result, once again, is bad news for the dollar. Kennedy may well have been incorrect in his belief that the United States would benefit more than other nations if world trade were made freer; it is not at all certain that the United States would suffer less than any other nation if world trade became less free.

## FROM "DOLLAR GAP" TO "MIRROR IMAGE"

In the early postwar years, it may be recalled, the threat appeared of a permanent "dollar gap," which meant that Europe would constantly be borrowing dollars from the United States, to be used to purchase American goods. But the Marshall Plan represented a monumental effort to get Europe back on its feet economically, making it less dependent on the United States and capable of producing goods that it could sell profitably in America. In addition, the Europeans, demoralized by two world wars, buckled down to business and left the problems of peace and war to the Americans and Soviets. The tide began to turn.

Nothing indicates the change in the economic relations between the two sides of the Atlantic better than the holdings of gold and dollars by the United States and the European nations. In 1959 the United States held 19.5 billion dollars' worth of gold out of a world total of 37.9 billion. Ten years later the American share had decreased to 10.8 billion dollars out of a total of 38.9 billion. In the same period, the gold holdings of the industrial nations of Europe (excluding Britain) rose from 10.5 billion to 18.3 billion dollars. Dollars held abroad which could be turned in for gold amounted to 10.1 billion in 1959 and 17.5 just ten years later. This means that the United States could have paid off all the short-term claims against the American Treasury in 1959, but could not have done so, if it had been asked to, in 1969.

The astute reader will note that the total amount of gold hardly increased over the ten years. Admittedly, South Africa did add newly mined gold to the world's supply, in addition to the periodic Soviet sales to finance purchases of wheat in the West. But industrial needs for gold, the demands of dentists and jewelers, and the penchant of hoarders cut deeply into these new supplies. At the same time, world trade more than doubled. Internationally acceptable money had to be found to finance this trade—to give nations the wherewithal to pay for trade transactions. Most of this money took the form of American dollars, which, as we have seen, were flowing freely into the monetary channels of the world. The United States claimed that had there not been a persistent American (and British) balance-of-payments deficit, there would not have been enough internationally acceptable money available, and the world would have faced a "liquidity crisis," an overall shortage of funds.

If the Europeans were unhappy with the chronic American deficit, they should help do something about it, according to the U.S. government. The growing European surplus, evidenced by its increasing gold stocks, was, after all, the "mirror image" of the American deficit. Europe should find a way of pumping more money into international channels, perhaps by encouraging hoarders to take some of their savings out from under the bedsprings and place them in developing money markets. In addition, the Americans urged that both sides agree on new forms of internationally acceptable money which would be used to finance growing world trade.

Undoubtedly the United States has gotten itself into serious debt and serious trouble. The welfare of its currency is at least partly in the hands of foreigners. The U.S. government can bank on their need for dollars to finance trade and investment as some guarantee that they will not suddenly make a run on the Treasury. But this belief is based on economic rather than political considerations. What if a nation were ready to take the economic risks inherent in an attack on the dollar because it wanted to "punish" the United States for taking "unfair advantage" of the international monetary system that permits the Americans to be constantly in debt to their neighbors? Perhaps no single nation would be able to undermine confidence in this monetary system, but this was a gamble for the Americans, at least until it was proved that such an effort was doomed to failure.

In any case, the United States could not count on anybody's help. The Europeans grudgingly accepted the idea of the "mirror image." They were even willing to make a feeble attempt to keep their interest rates down in order to encourage available savings to seek investments in the American market rather than in Europe. But even on this score they were unwilling to be overly generous. In effect, the supposedly automatic functioning of the monetary system began to show serious defects as nations demonstrated that they had retained considerable discretion in their policies. Short of a fundamental change in the relationship of gold and the dollar, the United States had less freedom of action than anybody else. Either in terms of the American economy, where serious belt-tightening was called for, or of the international monetary system, where the prestige of the United States and its dollar was at stake, some sacrifices would have to be made.

## EURO-DOLLARS AND EURO-BONDS

Some dollars go abroad and then find their way home again as payment for American exports or for American gold, or as investment by foreign governments or private individuals. But other dollars seem to like life abroad and take up foreign residence. They may be used to finance international transactions in which the United States is not involved or they may be used by American firms operating overseas. They may make occasional trips back home, as when a foreign branch of an American bank lends them to its parent in the United States, but, in this case, they will eventually be paid back and move out of the country again.

These dollars look just like any other, but money managers call them Euro-dollars.

Euro-dollars have the great advantage of almost instant acceptability in almost all countries. With holders of Euro-dollars apparent in all European countries, they have become a European currency, perhaps more than the money of any single European country. If a European or an American in Europe wants to obtain Euro-dollars he will almost certainly buy them in the London money market. He will pay a premium for them, partly because they are relatively scarce (at least in terms of need) and partly because they are so widely acceptable and thus so useful. He can use the Euro-dollars he obtains for investment in plant and equipment, for speculation, for paying his bills, or perhaps for buying gold.

The use of Euro-dollars has expanded markedly since early 1968, when the Johnson administration slapped controls on further dollar outflows for investment in Europe. And interest rates for borrowing Euro-dollars have climbed sharply as demand for them increased, especially when, in 1968–1969, interest rates for domestic dollars hit record highs and American banks began to try to find dollars anywhere they could, but especially in Europe. The accompanying chart shows just how popular Euro-dollars have become in recent years. The figures are estimates, because there is no way to measure them accurately—which is one of their advantages.

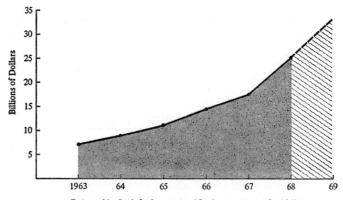

Estimated by Bank for International Settlements, except for 1969

Other Euro-currencies have now appeared, although the Euro-dollar is still by far the most popular. The Deutschemark has gained in strength and popularity, for example, and it too is widely accepted for a variety of purposes in many countries.

Because of the narrowness of European money markets—for example, there may well not be enough French francs available for all investment needs in France—a Euro-bond market has grown up. Initially Euro-bonds were almost always issued in Euro-dollars. This meant that any investor in any European country who had Euro-dollars could purchase the issue. Thus, Euro-bonds opened a far broader investment pool than had been possible in the past. Now that some European currencies have established their strength and acceptability, Euro-bonds are also issued in these currencies. The share of Euro-bonds actually denominated in dollars has declined over the years.

If, one day, the Europeans should create a common currency, making it possible for savings to be transferred as easily from Italy to the Netherlands as they are from New York to California, the role of the Euro-dollar and the Euro-bond as we know them today might be ended. In the meantime, they seem to have achieved a lasting and key place in the monetary system.

During the 1950's, extended spells of lethargy in official Washington were occasionally interrupted by a few economists who spread the alarming word that the dollar was in trouble. In general, officialdom persisted in believing that the monetary crisis would go away as mysteriously as it had appeared and that, in any case, the United States held all the pieces in the monetary game and could not possibly lose.

Eventually Washington was to be aroused to the threat to the dollar. In the 1960's an impressive array of plans, ploys, and plots was tried in order to stem the dollar outflow. But most of them —except the most drastic—had little or no effect. Some of the measures used by the U.S. government were highly ingenious. But they could not work, as we shall see, because they did not change anything; they merely papered over the problems.

When Dwight Eisenhower left office, he bequeathed to his successor a persistent deficit in the American balance of payments and a sluggish if not completely stagnant domestic economy. The Republican administration had gradually become aware of the threat to the dollar and had in fact presided over a considerable depletion of the national gold

CHAPTER **3**

# The Defense of the Dollar

stock. Eisenhower and his advisers did not seem unduly alarmed by this state of affairs, partly because they were preoccupied with other problems.

Dwight Eisenhower also bequeathed to John Kennedy a Republican who was to achieve greater eminence under the Democrats than he had under his own party. Douglas Dillon, a New Jersey socialite and a Wall Street investment banker, impressed Kennedy as a hardheaded monetary expert who had sufficient knowledge to understand what was needed and sufficient administrative ability to know how to do what was needed. Dillon also had an acute appreciation of the situation in Europe, for he remained close to his French origins and operated one of the most renowned vineyards in France. He had served as American ambassador to de Gaulle's France, Undersecretary of State for Economic Affairs, and, finally, Secretary of the Treasury. In this position, the Republican banker, with his clipped and cultured speech, which was, together with his name, his calling card in the world of high finance, became the chief fireman in the U.S. effort to snuff out the flames of monetary crisis each time they broke out.

The second man in the team that was to be in charge of the defense of the dollar in the early sixties was Robert Roosa, who became Undersecretary of the Treasury for Monetary Affairs after having served for more than a decade at the Federal Reserve Bank of New York. Roosa was, above all, an economist, having headed the Fed's New York research staff. But far from being a theoretician, he was a working economist with a highly creative mind. He seemed to savor the challenge of monetary problems, and he became the single source of most of the ideas for stopgap monetary reforms that averted a serious breakdown of the system.

Despite their drive and imagination, Dillon and Roosa had an essentially conservative job; they were to defend the status quo, to keep in operation the Bretton Woods monetary system which had served the United States so well. The Kennedy administration and indeed the American public were unwilling to promote a fundamental change in the monetary system for the simple reason that the United States and the dollar had nowhere to go but down. Any reform—and as we shall see later, there was no lack of plans—meant that the privileged international role of the dollar would be placed in jeopardy. Kennedy, particularly after the Bay of Pigs fiasco, was opposed to any policies, in any sector, which might even seem to be weakening the American position in the world.

Dillon and Roosa were good firemen. They had or devised a complete arsenal of countermeasures which could be used to buttress the dollar and to calm the persistent and increasing doubts of the Europeans about its ability to serve as an international reserve asset alongside gold.

## TINKERING WITH THE SYSTEM

American Treasury officials, left to their own devices by a President who simply wished that they use whatever means were necessary to prevent the dollar from being consumed in a world-wide monetary conflagration, laid out two lines of defense. In the first instance, as the leaders of the monetary establishment, they sought to preserve the Bretton Woods system by the introduction of a few modifications that would enable it to meet needs that had not been foreseen in 1944. The second approach might be called fire-fighting tactics, because it consisted of a variety of imaginative, often hastily conceived (and applied) schemes for preserving the American gold stock against a run on the Treasury by foreign nations holding excess dollars.

In the first phase, more funds were pumped into the international monetary system by increasing the IMF's working capital through quota increases, IMF sales of gold to central banks, and the creation of an inner directorate of monetary powers, known as the Group of Ten, which created new borrowing arrangements among its members. Here is how these measures, designed to make the Bretton Woods system work better, were devised.

The most obvious way to improve the International Monetary Fund was to increase the amount of money deposited with it, which would, of course, even further increase the amount of money that could be drawn out of it by nations, including the United States, that found themselves persistently in debt internationally.

The original capital planned for the IMF was 8.8 billion dollars, but the Bretton Woods accord, recognizing that international trade might grow and require additional financing, provided that once every five years the quotas of IMF members could be increased. In 1960, for example, most national quotas were raised by fifty percent, and some members even accepted a greater boost in their contributions and, of course, also in their drawings and voting rights.

In 1965 an American request for another major increase in quotas ran into stiff opposition, especially from France, as we shall see later. The Europeans were not enthusiastic about contributing more of their currencies, already in great demand, into the IMF currency pool. The Americans didn't mind shipping more dollars off to the IMF, though they were somewhat more grudging in their willingness to pay up the gold portion that is part of any quota increase. Finally, Europeans acquiesced, even agreeing, through a process known as "mitigation," not to turn in their surplus dollars to the United States in order to obtain gold for their own increased quota contribution.

What the Europeans sought out of the quota increase was an increased say in future IMF decisions through the quota increase. Though the general increase was twenty-five percent, the quotas, and hence the voting power, of sixteen nations, led by West Germany, were further increased to take into account their growing economic importance. As a result, total IMF assets rose from sixteen to twenty-one billion dollars.

The IMF's rules continued to require the assent of the United States and Britain, as reserve-currency nations, to any major decisions, but the Americans had to pay a price for their 1965 quota increase. The Europeans made it clear that they fully intended to assert their right for a greater say in monetary affairs. In 1970, quotas were increased thirty-five percent to 28.9 billion dollars. The Europeans, except the British, again improved their relative position.

The five-year quota review conducted by the IMF represents an element of considerable flexibility in the monetary system. Additional international reserves could be built up through this process, while, at the same time, the changing economic and political importance of nations could be reflected in their quotas and voting power. Any country that had a good case for being given a bigger role in the IMF had only to increase its contribution to obtain it. This kind of flexibility in altering the contribution and voting power of sovereign states is virtually unheard of in other organizations.

The European reaction to American requests for more international credit (though, it will be noticed, the Americans modestly refrained from asking for it for themselves alone) came as something of a surprise to Washington. To some, especially in Congress, Europe may have seemed like Frankenstein's monster, which, having acquired strength and a will of its own, turns against its master. "Rank ingratitude," some grumbled. Other American leaders claimed that European monetary independence, increasingly asserted during the sixties and notable in the talks on increasing the IMF quotas, was a result of a successful American policy which had put Europe back on its feet. After all, they would say, the United States is not looking for international yes-men. In any case, the Americans did not have to worry about having them.

In addition to quota increases, the IMF added to its available currency supply by selling gold. Additional currency supplies could be obtained by purchasing them from their country of origin for part of the IMF's gold stock. Then, these currencies could be pumped into the monetary circuit. At first the IMF bought dollars in this way, but by the sixties it was using gold to purchase other currencies which had become relatively more scarce than the dollar.

As early as the Eisenhower administration, a plan was developed, designed to help increase the IMF's resources, but more importantly to ease the strain on the dollar by giving the United States, at least temporarily, a larger gold stock. The IMF purchased some eight hundred million dollars' worth of U.S. government securities, which were repayable with interest. Thus the IMF assumed part of the American debt and as a reward it was assured of a profit on its investment. In order to purchase these securities, the IMF used part of its gold stock. Thus the gold flowed into the U.S. Treasury in payment for the bonds. This was one of the few instances in which gold itself, held as a reserve, could be used to earn interest. When each U.S. government security reaches maturity, America repays to the IMF all of the gold used to purchase it in the first place, plus interest. The United

States got short-term help in boosting its gold stock (which could thus serve as "window dressing" in making the American monetary position seem stronger than it actually was), and the IMF made a profit on the arrangement, which left it with more currency for financing international trade—though the currency was the dollar.

But the major reform of the IMF system—probably even more important than the quota increases—was the creation of the Group of Ten.* While the Group sounds to many outsiders like some murderous band that challenged Sherlock Holmes, it is in fact the inner directorate of the IMF and is composed of the chief monetary powers of the world. Membership in the Group of Ten is based mainly on a nation's gold and dollar holdings, and it includes all the countries whose participation in any new arrangements is essential.

The Group of Ten was formed out of fear. In 1960, persistent drains of dollars and sterling led to widespread concern that confidence in these reserve currencies would completely disappear and a major upheaval take place. The speculators were investing heavily in Deutschemarks in the belief that a revaluation of the German currency was likely. Large sums of money were shifted out of dollars and pounds. The IMF had the responsibility of making additional reserves available to nations whose currencies were under such pressure—just as the American government insures bank deposits in order to discourage a run on the banks. But the IMF directors were fearful that their organization did not have enough money available to shore up the faltering currencies if the speculators continued to pour cash into their bets on the Deutschemark. The efforts to increase the IMF quotas and the IMF purchases of dollars and pounds in return for gold had not been sufficient to stem the tide of speculation.

Instead of attempting to expand the IMF further, a lengthy and difficult legal procedure, the major world monetary powers entered into immediate negotiations in Paris in an effort to preserve the system. On January 5, 1962, well after the 1960 speculation but well in advance of other and far more serious runs on the pound and the dollar, the Paris Club—the Group of Ten—agreed to a new system for making international loans, limited to

* See "The Group of Ten," pp. 71-72.

those countries participating in the agreement. The accord was known as the General Arrangements to Borrow, or, less elegantly, the GAB. A total of six billion dollars was made available to supplement the IMF's resources, though if Britain and the United States were to use all the credit available to them, the maximum amount of credit actually available was only three billion.

The IMF is merely the middleman in the GAB operations. When one of the Ten asks the IMF for a loan of foreign currencies, the IMF managers check their inventory to determine if they can meet the demand. Thus, for example, Britain might ask the IMF for Deutschemarks with which to buy pounds in Germany. This will lessen the pressure on the British Treasury from these outstanding pounds, which could, at any time, be turned into gold. The British would hope that the mere knowledge that they had sizable reserves of foreign currency with which to counteract the build-up in foreign holdings of the pound would discourage others from speculating against the pound. If the IMF finds that it does not have a sufficient supply of the desired currencies, it may request the other members of the Group to make available some of their currencies. This money is, in theory, lent to the IMF, though only as part of a broader operation designed to support a currency in trouble. The money is lent for a limited period—three to five years—and the borrowing nation must pay the symbolic interest rate of two percent (one quarter of which is the IMF's commission).

The GAB has provided an important boost to the abilities of the IMF to meet the needs of Britain for foreign exchange and has in general strengthened confidence in the ability of currencies to withstand pressure of speculation. More than 1.7 billion dollars has been made available under the GAB, and in extreme cases the Group of Ten has put up about forty percent of the total loan package put together by the IMF.

## EVEN SHORTER SHORT-TERM MEASURES

Bigger IMF quotas, gold sales, the Group of Ten and the GAB all seemed, in Washington at least, to help in taking some of the heat off the monetary system in general, the dollar in particular. But these were cumbersome measures, negotiated in full public view and slow in taking effect. As a result, the U.S. Treasury and Federal Reserve, in a second stage of their operations to defend the dollar, initiated a series of more urgent steps. Reduced U.S. foreign aid, foreign purchases of military hardware in the United States and sales of dollar bonds to foreign governments all were aimed at stemming the dollar outflow. In addition, central banks set up new loan arrangements, which they hoped could be used in relative secrecy, as well as deals for short-term swaps of currencies. They also moved to ensure that the price of gold would remain stable, thus discouraging speculation in favor of gold and against the dollar or pound. The sum total of these measures was a dazzling display of monetary inventiveness, though the desired effects were a good deal more disappointing.

In order to increase the ploys available to stave off monetary crises, the Americans and their colleagues of the Group of Ten developed other measures which yield short-term but major aid to a currency in trouble. Behind the American sponsorship of this approach was the belief that the United States, while it might be in serious trouble, was not in permanent trouble. If the war in Vietnam could be brought to an end and if net capital outflows could be cut, U.S. leaders believed that the American balance of payments would begin, once again, to be written in black ink.

Foreign aid gradually became less of a drain on the dollar, partly because the overall program was reduced and also as a result of the increased use of the practice of tying of American aid. This meant that any nation that receives financial assistance from the United States is required to spend most, if not all, of the money in the United States. Thus American foreign aid amounts in most cases to a subsidy to American producers. No matter that the same product can be obtained elsewhere at a better price, making it possible to stretch the aid dollar further; that dollar must be spent in the United States to ensure that the net outflow of U.S. currency is kept to a minimum. Although some nations complain loudly about this tied aid (in fact, the Nixon administration has decided to give in to Latin American demands and untie aid to those nations), they take what they can get.

American military aid presents different problems. Often it takes the form of U.S. troops stationed in a foreign land, and it is impossible to force the nation that receives the dollars scattered by these servicemen to spend them in the United States. Naturally, the American government may threaten to withdraw some or all of the troops if the dollars are not repatriated, but this approach cannot be pursued with full vigor because it is in contradiction to the claim that the troops are stationed abroad as much in the American interest as in the defense needs of the host country. Yet succeeding administrations in Washington have found means of bringing the dollars back home or at least of ensuring that they are not turned in for gold. One method is to convince the host nation to purchase its armaments in America. Often the U.S.-produced weapons are of higher quality or better design, and there is thus little doubt that arms purchases would have been made from American suppliers in any case. But host countries are asked to make "offset" purchases for the military-aid dollars spent there regardless of the attractiveness of American weaponry. As a result, each year sees protracted negotiations between the United States and these nations (mainly West Germany) to ensure that a high percentage of the military-aid dollars are spent in the United States.

Another method that has been promoted by the United States is the sale of so-called Roosa bonds. A nation with a surplus of dollars, often acquired through a military-aid program on its territory, is asked to purchase U.S. Treasury bonds which yield them no interest but which promise repayment at a guaranteed exchange rate. Thus those who buy bonds are protected against any devaluation of the dollar. The deal is a straight quid pro quo: U.S. troops stationed abroad will not be cut back, provided a nation buys its share of Roosa bonds. The Germans, who apparently see American troops stationed in their country as hostages guaranteeing the use of American nuclear weapons in their defense (that is, of both the troops and the Germans), buy the Roosa bonds without much complaint, though they can hardly believe they have made a good financial deal. But, in any case, the dollars are only frozen; they are not actually repatriated.

In 1961, while the plans for the GAB were being worked out, the so-called Basel agreements were concluded among the leading members of the little-known Bank for International Settlements. Once each month, central bank officials from the major BIS member countries—virtually the same as the Group of Ten—meet in an unimpressive building in Basel for a weekend of informal talks, with just a perfunctory official session with other BIS officials. The BIS is a bank for hire, willing to perform a great variety of banking functions for governments. Originally, as a channel for war reparations, it collected what it could from the Germans and transferred the proceeds to the treasuries of nations entitled to damages for the ravages of World War I. Subsequently it has been assigned other functions, including service as a clearinghouse for foreign-currency operations between European countries.

But the BIS has proved to be a handy instrument for tackling the weightier problems of international finance. As a result, at the informal weekend meetings which take place in the Euler or Schweitzerhof hotel, the better restaurants of the neighborhood, or at the BIS itself, talk centers far more on the current state of monetary affairs than on the more formal business of the bank.

No "political" officials attend the Basel meetings, only representatives of central banks and occasionally of national treasuries. Politicians would, in any case, be lost in the technical world of permissible fluctuations on exchange rates, credits, and the like. The Basel group is essentially a team of maintenance men, trying to keep the mechanism of the international monetary system humming smoothly, by making just enough changes in the status quo to ensure that all the members maintain at least a minimum of monetary stability—in other words, being able to avoid devaluation or, if it can't be avoided, minimizing the harmful effects on other nations.

The BIS's Basel agreements avoid all the formality of the GAB and the IMF; they simply allow for direct three-month loans by members to one of their partners that finds itself short of foreign currencies. The BIS itself may sometimes put up part of the loan money. These multilateral loans are made to meet short-term monetary problems; they do not have the kind of economic strings attached, characteristic of IMF credits.

Loans made under the Basel agreements can be decided upon rapidly and can be kept secret, unlike IMF quota increases or GAB loans. Mainly because of the need to keep the exact extent of loans confidential, newsmen have found the BIS bankers just about the most difficult news source. Because the world is likely to know the amount of IMF-GAB help, thus allowing speculators to push a weak currency to the limit of the international reserves made available to support it, the bankers of the BIS wisely calculate that the only way to outfox the speculators is not to let them know these limits. Because the Basel loans can be granted rapidly, newsmen must, however, watch every monthly session carefully in hopes of breaking the big story of major international help to a faltering currency. Thus far, they have usually been foiled. Eventually they can uncover the total amount of a BIS credit line, but they cannot discover how much of the credit has been drawn. This is meant to help a battling central bank fight off speculators, though it may even add to the market's distrust of a country's monetary strength.

Britain has been the primary beneficiary of a series of BIS loans designed to help shore up the pound. But these loans have all been short-term, and it has often been necessary to make a new loan simply to pay off an outstanding one.

Still another ploy used to preserve the stability of the monetary system in the face of the British and American deficits is the so-called "swap" arrangement. Roosa and the officials of the Federal Reserve Bank of New York worked out with other central banks a scheme for swapping currencies as they were needed by one of the Group of Ten plus Switzerland and Austria. Two countries participating in the arrangement agree to exchange their national currencies (in limited quantity, of course) for three months. Repayment at the end of the period is guaranteed at the same exchange rate as at the time of the swap—a devaluation guarantee. The swap is actually "one-sided," because the central bank initiating the exchange almost certainly is in critical need of the foreign currency, while the other nation is not. The swaps give the "purchasing" country, often the United States, the foreign currency to fight speculation. The amount of currency the central banks are willing to put into the swapping pool has been gradually increased, until accords involving the United States now amount to 10.68 billion dollars. Though other countries are reticent about giving details of swap arrangements, the U.S. swap agreements are not kept secret—some fifteen have been made. The central bankers can activate the swaps on a few hours' notice, which helps undercut speculation against any currency almost as soon as it gets under way. Swaps alone would not be sufficient to save a currency, but together with the changes in the IMF system and the other tricks in the bag, most Group of Ten nations regard it as a useful deterrent—and one from which they all stand to benefit at some time.

The swap system was buttressed by the appearance of the Federal Reserve Bank of New York in the world's money markets. The United States is committed under the Bretton Woods rules only to buy and sell gold at thirty-five dollars an ounce, but it is not obliged to buy and sell other currencies at any price at all. That is the duty of the other IMF members, who have to stabilize their own currencies by buying and selling dollars. But when the foreign-exchange markets got agitated in the early 1960's, the Fed decided to take a more active role. Acting through Charles Coombs, its chief foreign-exchange expert, the Fed began buying and selling foreign currency in an effort to maintain the value of the dollar relative to other currencies. But the Fed accepted part of the responsibility for taking this kind of action when the other major currencies started toward the ceiling—in other words, when the dollar started toward the floor. It has also acted in this way to support the pound. This active intervention in the foreign-exchange market by the Fed is quite rare, not having been done since the early 1930's.

Still another move to maintain the parity of the dollar was the creation of the "Gold Pool" in 1961. A year earlier, the United States and Britain had begun buying and selling gold in the open market in an effort to keep the free market price of gold at or close to the official price. Then, six other countries joined them, thus practically ending the free market fluctuations above the thirty-five-dollar mark. When the price appeared ready to fall below this level, the eight countries bought gold; when it began to climb, they sold gold and brought the price back down. The Gold Pool lasted until the climactic days of 1968, by which time the eight found they were consistently selling gold. We shall examine the breakup of the Gold Pool more fully later. But during much of its relatively brief life the pool served as an effective deterrent against speculation.

## LBJ TRIES TO SAVE THE DOLLAR

Roosa, with Dillon's backing, proved to be an excellent fireman. Presidents Kennedy and Johnson knew they were equipped with the best in technical help to defend the dollar. But the efforts of both Roosa and other countries to preserve the Bretton Woods system were based on the belief that the United States would be able once again to get into the black, thus putting a halt to the outflow of dollars and the persistent threat to the American gold stock.

Despite their efforts, the dollars kept flowing out. The disastrous drain of American gold, which was seen in Washington as a drain on American prestige, became increasingly a political embarrassment to the administration. Kennedy had become aware that more than technical policies designed to put out the brushfires of the international monetary crisis were necessary. But Lyndon Johnson found himself saddled with the burden of making political decisions that would cut the dollar drain. With great reluctance, he made them.

Johnson had no pretensions to being an economic or financial expert. Throughout his long career in Congress he had never been known for his ability to fathom the intricacies of economic policy. He was essentially a populist—a man who believed that money should not become so expensive that the poor people would be unable to pay their mortgages and other debts. But this approach was of relatively little help in the international sphere. Indeed, it prompted Johnson to support policies which led to increasing inflation, itself one of the major causes of the dollar outflow. Finally Johnson lost the expertise of Dillon and Roosa, who were replaced by men more familiar with Johnson's freewheeling methods of operation.

Although no economic eagle, Lyndon Johnson was almost without peers in his understanding of Washington politics. The monetary crisis was essentially a foreign-policy matter—an area where the President had limited experience—but the decisions that would have to be made would affect the domestic economy and would have to be made palatable to the major business and banking interests, which had strong advocates in Congress. Although he did not always please Wall Street and Main Street, Johnson made the decisions which were virtually forced on him.

One way to reduce American military expenditures abroad was to pull back some troops. With the exception of the hawkish congressional leaders who were willing to follow slavishly the demands of the Pentagon, there was no widespread opposition to a gradual reduction in American troop strength abroad. In fact, as the sixties wore on, sentiment grew, undoubtedly because of Vietnam, that the United States should retire from its role as the world's policeman. But the nations in which troops were stationed saw things differently. The United States had abandoned the policy of massive retaliation in favor of the flexible response which required the commitment of conventional ground forces, and now Johnson was planning to withdraw some of these very troops. In addition, if they left, the host nations might lose some of their leverage on American foreign policy, because the troops they had treated as hostages would no longer be available to them. Worst of all, they might have to place more men under arms themselves. As a result they carried their bitter protests to Washington; and Johnson, caught between conflicting objectives of American policy, retreated. He did manage to gain agreement for relatively minor withdrawals, often with the commitment to keep the troops ready for return to their foreign bases on a moment's notice, but in general, troop reductions never reached levels that would provide much help for the dollar.

Another step, in the trade sector, was more successful, though it, too, aroused the strong opposition of other nations, especially while the Kennedy Round was under way. Under the so-called Buy American Act, executive departments were ordered to cut their purchases of foreign products except when foreign prices were well below American levels. In some instances, purchases could be made if the foreign products were selling at six percent less than comparable American items, but more often the saving had to be fifty percent. On the more positive side, the federal government undertook more vigorous efforts to promote American products abroad, especially through efforts of the commercial staffs of U.S. embassies. American pavilions were seen at more international trade fairs than ever before. But none of this did anything to make American goods cheaper and thus did not bring a sizable increase in U.S. exports.

Still another positive effort was the creation of the U.S. Travel Service, which was given the task of trying to attract more foreign tourists to America. The 1967 Montreal Expo, far more than this program, did bring more foreigners into the United States. Congress grew restive about appropriating money to attract tourists, and the Visit the U.S.A. program was cut back. Once again, high domestic prices were the chief deterrent to foreign tourists, and nothing was done by Congress to reduce them. Airlines and bus companies did offer special rates to foreigners, but the total cost of a North American holiday remained uncompetitive with what Europe had to offer.

The Johnson administration also made a move to increase international confidence in the willingness and ability of the United States to pay out gold in return for dollars: it removed the partial gold backing of the dollar. American law required that the Treasury would hold on deposit an amount of gold equal in value to one-fourth of the face value of American currency. The historical origin of this requirement was the desire to prevent the government from printing greenbacks at will, thus making money unduly cheap. But by the mid-twentieth century, the danger that the country would be flooded with printing-press money had passed. As a result, Congress was willing to authorize, in effect, the government to say to the world that the entire U.S. gold supply could be mobilized to defend the dollar internationally, and it agreed to remove the gold "cover." But the move made a relatively minor impression on speculators, who knew that, in any case, there were more short-term claims, in the form of dollars held by foreigners, than there was gold at Fort Knox.

Not having succeeded through government action in stemming the dollar outflow, the administration began, somewhat gingerly, to force American citizens to do their part. American tourists had been permitted to bring into the country as much as five hundred dollars' worth of goods duty-free and to send to their friends ten dollars' worth of gifts daily, also free of duty. The biggest boon to returning tourists was the duty-free allowance for one gallon of liquor. These somewhat generous rules, which encouraged wild shopping binges by tourists (or their wives), were drastically reduced. The overall allowance was slashed to one hundred dollars, with daily gifts to be valued at no more than one dollar, and the liquor allowance was set at one-fifth gallon. Undoubtedly these new rules were of some help, and there was relatively little grumbling by Americans who had plenty of cash to pay the duties if necessary (the overseas liquor business hardly faltered).

Far more touchy was the effort to stem American direct and indirect investment abroad. Johnson proceeded carefully, because he was moving toward action that would strike at the very essence of the free-enterprise system. Despite its reputation as the party of labor and not capital, the Democratic party and Johnson had carefully nurtured a close relationship with business. They recognized that the days when Franklin Roosevelt could put together a coalition of the downtrodden and come up with an election victory were quickly fading as the American people became richer. Johnson took obvious delight in having the magnates of industry call at the White House. Yet now he felt forced to move against them and against many investors.

To reduce indirect investment abroad—the purchase of foreign securities—the Kennedy administration had asked Congress to adopt the interest-equalization tax. The philosophy behind the tax was simple: Americans could get a better return for the same amount of capital invested in foreign stocks than they could from U.S. issues and thus should be taxed on their purchases of those non-American securities in order to make the rate of return comparable. Obviously, if such a tax were applied, Americans would choose domestic issues and thus reduce the dollar outflow. Congress originally adopted the tax for a limited period, because many congressmen were reluctant to restrict the freedom of choice of the American investor. But the tax, set at a 1.5-percent rate, was continued from year to year at Johnson's request and is now more than five years old—virtually an American tradition. Wall Street and the investing community dislike the tax, but they have found ways of getting around it. Though not strictly legal, assets held abroad can be used to purchase foreign securities, and the U.S. Treasury can do little about it. And American stocks had been doing so well that the urge to purchase foreign issues might have been reduced anyway. As a counterbalance, the administration attempted to make American issues more attractive to foreigners through tax benefits. The program had some impact.

But the most important and controversial of Johnson's programs to improve the international position of the dollar was the effort to slow direct investment abroad. The granting of credits to foreigners and to American subsidiaries abroad was to be cut through a voluntary program under which U.S. firms would limit their transfers of dollars overseas. Johnson proposed a voluntary program because he feared the violent reaction of the business community to any government effort to slap on investment controls. Business could not help but understand that if a voluntary program did not work, mandatory controls would not be far behind. Many firms issued internal guidelines designed to implement the voluntary limitation on investments abroad. Some American firms, who still wanted to invest abroad, responded to the voluntary restraints by raising the needed capital abroad, that is to say, they borrowed the funds in the Euro-dollar and other foreign-money markets. But many businesses, while giving the appearance of cooperation with the Department of Commerce, which had been put in charge of administrating the voluntary program, did not, in fact, make a concentrated effort to alter their foreign investment policies. Profits from foreign subsidiaries were good, and many felt they would lose their competitive advantage if they adopted the voluntary restraints, while others did not. Profits earned abroad were not repatriated, but were used to provide additional investment capital. As a result of all these pressures, the voluntary program had relatively little effect, although investment abroad might have been even greater had the program not been instituted.

By 1968, a presidential election year, Johnson knew that he must take more stringent action. On January 1 he announced the toughest set of rules for economic and monetary discipline since World War II. He promised to put "all the muscle this administration has behind the dollar and to keep our financial house in order." Obviously the dollar's plight had reached disaster proportions.

The program of mandatory limits on foreign investment contained five points. All American direct investment in Continental Europe was banned. The developed nations, including members of the Group of Ten, which were not dependent on U.S. capital for their economic growth, were to receive no more of this capital. These were the very countries which held enough dollars to put the dollar in danger, should they cash in their holdings for gold. At the same time, a set proportion of earnings from overseas investment would have to be brought back home and the balances of short-term assets held abroad by American firms would have to be reduced. The second point required American banks to reduce their loans made abroad. Many of these loans had gone to American firms. Johnson also sought to reduce tourist expenditures. He appealed to Americans not to travel outside the Americas for two years. Later the administration submitted to Congress a plan severely limiting the amount tourists might spend abroad. But this proposal ran counter to the accepted right to freedom of travel, and congressmen, who could not afford to offend the great number of their constituents who planned trips abroad, did not adopt it. Undoubtedly, as the bill was being debated, some people were already planning to ask the courts to declare any such law unconstitutional. They were saved the need to bring their cases. In his final two points, Johnson ordered a cut in U.S. official spending in the amount of five hundred million dollars and pledged that necessary steps would be taken to boost the U.S. trade surplus by a similar amount.

Protests from the business community were immediate, violent, and prolonged, but the program was quickly put into effect. When the Nixon administration, supposedly more sympathetic to the needs of business, came to office, there was no attempt to end the program, although some vague promises of the sort were made. The mandatory measures did have their desired impact, and together with some adroit juggling of funds in December, 1968, by both the government and the business sector, the United States managed to show a small surplus in its international payments for the first time in a decade. At last a method had been found to slow the dollar outflow, but the political price was high. Business opposition to the Johnson measures undoubtedly contributed to the Nixon victory at the polls in November, 1968.

The net impact of the various government programs was supposed to be a reduction of some three billion dollars in the U.S. balance-of-payments deficit. Yet, with the exception of the mandatory program, the other measures failed almost completely to bring the desired result. Some said that the government had not applied them vigorously enough. But, to take only one example, the interest-equalization tax did have the effect of devaluing the investment dollar by about thirty percent, because it made American securities relatively cheaper and foreign issues more expensive. Nor could the failure of the official measures be attributed to what an accountant might call "extraneous and unrelated circumstances." The most obvious and simple reason for their failure was that European countries, despite their avowed desire to see the dollar strengthened, had no desire to see these specific measures work. If the United States cut its dollar flow to other nations, these countries were free to apply similar measures to stop cash flows to the United States. Thus everybody would keep the same relative position, and only the total of international financial transactions would be reduced. This was decidedly not the intention of Washington's economic planners.

The improvement in the American balance-of-payments picture —an increase in receipts and a decrease in expenditures—must be accomplished at the expense of those nations with sizable surpluses. Few countries in such a position are willing, especially before their own electorate, to pursue actively measures designed to run up a bigger debt in international transactions. Thus the best the United States could hope for was limited cooperation from surplus nations like Germany and the marginal benefits from a reduction in the total amount of capital flows. Yet no nation wants to reduce trade and investment because of a lack of internationally acceptable currency in circulation, and almost all admit, willingly or not, that the dollar is that international currency par excellence.

Johnson recognized his need for aid from Europe. Hence administration officials spoke repeatedly of the "mirror image" which existed between the American deficit and the surpluses of some European nations.

This kind of talk has been far less prevalent in the Nixon administration. High American interest rates, used to combat domestic inflation, have pushed up interest rates abroad. The Europeans have turned in gold at the U.S. Treasury for dollars they could lend. As a result, American gold stocks have grown, breeding complacency. But all this could change if interest rates fell. In any case, more dollars are flowing out than are coming in. A few officials realize that the balance of payments problem is as bad as ever, though some believe that the end of inflation might cure it.

## EUROPE LOOKS AT AMERICA

On July 4, 1962, President Kennedy, speaking at Independence Hall in Philadelphia, called for a declaration of interdependence which would recognize the partnership that was being created between the nations on both sides of the Atlantic. He did not speak so much of an Atlantic community, which had come to mean for some a prolonged American rule in this vast area. Instead, he looked forward to the day when a stronger and more united Europe could take its place as an equal partner of the United States.

Kennedy was no doubt sincere in his desire for an Atlantic partnership, though the actual desire of Washington officials to share someday the chief decision-making role in the West was, to say the least, questionable. And even Kennedy recognized that Europe was going to have to pass through an agonizing war against traditional nationalism before it could claim to be the united political entity that he required as a full and equal partner. Thus, the declaration of interdependence entered into the Valhalla of long-range American goals, almost all worthy of a great nation, toward which successive generations might strive without any clear idea of when they would be achieved.

The French veto of British membership in the European Common Market in 1963, just six months after Kennedy spoke, seemed to delay further the day when equal partnership could be a reality. But despite such setbacks, monetary affairs offered Europe the chance to play the partnership role far earlier than had been expected. Europe's development as an equal partner was not the result of conscious political decision to merge the economies of the Six, but instead Europe simply acquired more gold than the United States while amassing dollar claims against the American Treasury which could wipe out all that remained of the Fort Knox gold stock. The United States would be forced to come to terms with the Europeans, simply because they actually were equal in monetary power.

Most Europeans, both the elect and the electors, took quiet satisfaction from the drastically changed American fortunes which forced Washington to ask favors from Europe. For those resentful of the alleged "occupation" by American troops—even if the presence of these troops was at their express request—there was delight that the mighty had been humbled. Although most Americans were completely unaware of their government's efforts to attract European support for the dollar, many Europeans believed that America was gradually coming to recognize the extent of dependence on its transatlantic allies.

More enlightened European officials, usually central bankers and treasury men, recognizing that the continued American deficit could bring the downfall of the dollar and the international monetary system, agreed that cooperative efforts should be undertaken to slow the dollar outflow, or at least to ensure that foreign-held dollars were not turned in for gold. They were unwilling to consider any drastic change in the monetary system, except for an increased role for themselves in it, mainly because it had worked so well and because, like official Washington, they believed that the U.S. debt to other nations could be wiped off the slate in a short period if the Americans took the necessary steps. Thus, they too regarded the American deficit as a transitional stage, not a permanent state of affairs.

Because America could remedy the situation itself, many Europeans believed that it should. Why should Europe make sacrifices for the United States, which had been the cause of its own problems? Why should Europe, still far behind the United States technologically, sacrifice its own rate of growth simply to aid the United States? They believed that even if the dollar should be supported in order that their own currencies would not be threatened, the Americans themselves would not let the monetary situation get out of hand. But even more serious was the European desire to isolate Europe from the virus of monetary difficulties. "I'm all right, Jack," expressed this attitude with sarcastic finality.

Just as the Kennedy and Johnson administrations relied on fire-fighting techniques to stem any attack on the dollar, the Europeans appeared to prefer ad hoc solutions to any single formula for remedying the ills of the monetary system. This, too, was partly an example of the "beggar-my-neighbor" attitudes, because though the Europeans had created many organizations to foster economic cooperation, they acted as if none existed. There might be French plans, Belgian attitudes, German desires, and British concerns, but there never was a European policy. As a result, the strength that could have made Europe an Atlantic partner was frittered away. Washington might not have found a coherent European front to its liking, but, after all, it was less important to please the administration in power than to save the world's monetary system. In any case, the Johnson administration came to see the Europeans more as a swarm of pesky and persistent gnats than as a true partner in the role of arbiter of the West's affairs.

The only opinion the European nations held in common was that it was up to the United States to solve the dollar's problems —and at no cost to Europe. Their constant refrain was that the administration should bring American inflation under control, and the constant reply was that that was exactly what was being done. It was a bit like the chorus in the *Pirates of Penzance*, when the soldiers claim they are marching off to battle and the ladies politely but persistently sing: "Yes, but you don't go." Perhaps European leaders believed that the only way to get their citizens to accept the consequences for themselves of any degree of American austerity was to have Washington force it on them, for the Europeans seemed blissfully unaware that leaving the choice of measures strictly to Washington would mean that Europe would have to pay part of the price, like it or not, and that Europe would not be able to choose which sacrifice it would make.

Johnson's decision to stop direct investment in Europe stung, and within days cries of pain were heard in capitals all over the Continent, even in Paris. But by then American officials were in no mood to make many concessions, though they spent many words on calming the worst fears of the Europeans. Then, when American interest rates were raised to near-record levels as a means of cutting inflation, the Europeans again felt the pinch. U.S. firms abroad, who could no longer finance their overseas expansion by exporting funds from the United States, simply began acquiring Euro-dollars, thus driving the interest rates for these and other European currencies up toward or even beyond American levels. The Europeans, of course, had to pay the same high interest rates and found that they had to pay much the same price as the Americans to halt inflation in the United States.

With Lyndon Johnson concerned more with Vietnam and failing to grasp the nature and the importance of the problem confronting the dollar, with administration officials lacking in the boldness and imagination to devise a reform of the Bretton Woods system and the U.S. deficit, the Europeans had their first real opportunity in the postwar era to take over the leadership of the West on an issue of considerable importance. Atlantic partnership, at least in the conscious political sense intended by Kennedy, remained a dead letter. But despite the missed opportunities, the interrelationship that actually did exist among the nations of the Atlantic basin was not ruptured, and its reality was brought home as much to the Lyons businessman who found that the costs of loans to expand his operations were rising sharply in 1969 as to the New York home buyer who found that mortgage rates that year hit what once were considered usurious levels.

## THE AMERICAN QUANDARY

The decline of the dollar did not stop itself, nobody in Europe seemed to have any helpful ideas, and Lyndon Johnson was content to live from one day to the next so that he could concentrate on Vietnam, which hurt the dollar, and on his domestic Great Society program, which might help it in the long run. At the end of the sixties, just as at the beginning, American policy was the absence of policy plus the makeshift arrangements of the moment. Failure to come to grips with the monetary crisis was distinctly bipartisan.

Actually, to hold the line as well as possible seemed far more preferable than the other alternatives for the dollar that kept popping up in unofficial discussions among more free-thinking officials and bankers. For if something drastic were to be done about the dollar, this could only mean devaluation or the end of the fixed and special relationship between the dollar and gold.

One possibility was a small devaluation of the dollar in terms of gold. But this measure would work only if other countries maintained the parity of their currencies to gold and thus increased their parity in terms of dollars. In this way the United States

would enjoy the same freedom to devalue (or revalue) to a limited extent when necessary. But, in practice, it would be virtually
impossible to ensure that other countries would not also cut the
value of their currencies in relation to gold to the same extent as
the Americans. This would, of course, nullify the effects of devaluation. The more the United States would devalue, the more other
nations would feel forced to do the same, because of the world-
wide importance of the American economy. If the U.S. Treasury
kept the reduction small enough to discourage devaluation by others, the cut in the exchange rate between the dollar and the other
moneys might not be sufficient to make U.S. goods significantly
cheaper or foreign articles much more expensive in the United
States. And, in any case, some nations might well take advantage
of any American devaluation to cut the exchange rates of their
currencies even more than did the United States. Finally, given
the magnitude and duration of the American deficit, it is unlikely
that a small devaluation would do the trick. It might only serve to
further undermine confidence in the dollar and the Bretton
Woods system and to encourage speculators to bet against the
dollar again since they could now see that, like any other currency, it was no longer sacrosanct.

A second alternative would be a major devaluation of the dollar in terms of gold, which would inevitably entail similar large
devaluations by most other countries. In other words, the price of
gold would be increased, just as Jacques Rueff, the French economist who had General de Gaulle's ear, had been suggesting. This
proposal was in some ways tempting, because with the stroke of a
pen, America's debts to the rest of the world could be done away
with. But there are good economic arguments against such a
sweeping change. Inflation could be expected to run rampant in
many countries, especially those that already have a surplus in
their international payments and hold sizable stocks of gold and
dollars. How soon and to what extent such inflation could be
brought under control is a big question, for if it continued
unabated, most of the effects of the major devaluation could be
wiped away. If, for example, gold was sold at seventy dollars an
ounce instead of thirty-five, and then the price of a pair of shoes
or an automobile doubled, the effect of the devaluation would
disappear. Another economic argument is that even after devalua-

tion the monetary system would be based on gold, a commodity not in sufficient supply to meet the needs of international commerce and finance. The dollar or some other internationally acceptable medium of exchange would be needed. If it were the dollar, the world might be back where it started.

The Johnson and other American administrations were, however, probably less swayed by the economic arguments than the political ones. At a time when the United States was trying to convince its allies and potential allies that it does not welsh on its commitments (whether to the domestic electorate or to foreign countries), it would be in fact breaking its long-standing obligation to sell and buy gold at thirty-five dollars an ounce—even though it much rather not be called on to sell any more gold. South Africa and the Soviet Union, both prime sources of gold, and the speculators and hoarders who had bet on devaluation would be rewarded. Even more important would be the implicit victory for de Gaulle. And most important would be the smashing blow to American prestige were the United States forced to admit that its currency was no longer the unexcelled standard of the world, to say nothing about the effect of such a move on confidence in the world's monetary system.

No American administration would be happy about paying any of these political costs. And any administration would have to ask Congress for authorization to devalue the dollar, a step it would deem as catastrophic as a major monetary crisis. (Congressman Henry Reuss of Wisconsin has promised to bring impeachment proceedings against any President who devalues the dollar without the consent of Congress.) In addition, it should be noted that a formal request for congressional action would tip the hand of American policy-makers and would thus allow speculators sufficient time to discount in advance many of the desired effects of devaluation.

The final alternative would simply be to refuse to exchange gold for dollars, or the reverse. This is called the demonetization of gold. Unless the United States then stepped into the international money market to maintain the parity of the dollar to other currencies, it would be violating its Bretton Woods commitments. Nonetheless, a policy of allowing other nations to drain off all the gold they wanted, and then, in effect, for the

United States to go off the gold standard for international trans-actions, appeals to those with a vindictive streak. This policy could reinforce the leading international role of the dollar, or it could seriously undermine it, and no one can be sure which result would be the more likely. In any case, it might lead to wholesale chaos and the end of a single international monetary system, be-cause currency blocs built around several key moneys or gold could be created. And nations which found themselves with large stocks of now "worthless" gold might conceivably retaliate against the United States by nationalizing some or all of American invest-ments on their territories. The breakdown of the Bretton Woods system would open the door wide to a return to "beggar-my-neighbor" policies. The United States would be branded an inter-national scoundrel.

None of these alternatives for unilateral action to change the dollar's international role is particularly appetizing. Admittedly only the most drastic of the short-term measures makes a dent in the U.S. balance-of-payments deficit. But the disadvantages of the unilateral measures make it all too evident that the only way out for the United States is to bring the American debt to other coun-tries under control or to improve the world's monetary system—or both.

Solving monetary woes cannot always be done free from politi-cal constraints. We have already seen the kind of pulling and hauling required even to get short-term measures into operation. These political potshots occasionally tossed back and forth across the Atlantic are piddling compared with salvos launched in Paris and aimed at Washington.

## THE GROUP OF TEN

Formally created in 1962, the Group of Ten includes the world's chief monetary powers—the United States, Britain, West Germany, France, Italy, Japan, the Netherlands, Canada, Belgium, and Sweden. The members chose themselves partly on the basis of their reserve holdings and partly because they already were part of a monetary "old boys' network." Switzerland, which, in its pas-sion for neutrality, is not an IMF member, is an unofficial, but regular, participant in the Group's lending operations.

Originally formed to supply GAB loans, the Group of Ten soon grew into a far more important organization, a kind of holding company for the international monetary system. It is a highly political group, in contrast with the Bank for International Settlements, being composed of top Treasury or Finance Ministry officials. Speaking on behalf of their governments, these men often make decisions on the functioning and future of the monetary system.

By participating in the Group of Ten, its members signify their willingness to support the Bretton Woods system. But, unlike formal international organizations, the Group has no real structure or staff. Every time the Group is asked by one of its members to discuss an interim patch-up or a full-scale reform of the system, each must decide if it wants to participate in the exercise. Generally, they do agree to cooperate, because they recognize the need to maintain confidence in the currencies of all members as a way of ensuring that the monetary system itself will survive its periodic crises.

The Group of Ten makes decisions on major proposals, like the creation of "paper gold." Such decisions would be extremely difficult if not impossible in the IMF, where ten times as many nations are represented. Formally, the small countries have never been asked to sacrifice their sovereignty and their voting rights by handing over decision-making powers to the ten richest countries. In practice, however, these ten countries are so important that they are almost certain to be able to push through anything they can agree upon. Thus, if they meet in the relative informality of the Paris Club, as the Group is also known, they can come to terms and then present their agreement to the full IMF for what amounts to ratification.

Not all Group members are always cooperative. In the case of some loans to Britain, for example, the French have surprised their partners by their refusal to participate in providing the needed credits. Their representatives have claimed that Britain has not taken stringent enough measures designed to cut domestic purchasing power, and thus was not worthy of international help. Other officials who may have agreed with the morality of the French policy have recognized that its effects could be disastrous. While they have tried to impose rigid conditions on the granting of aid to Britain, they have been unwilling to risk a serious monetary crisis just to prove a point.

One morning in the mid-1960's, Michel Debré, then the French Minister of Finance and the Economy, seated himself at his desk in his plushly furnished office on Paris' swank Rue de Rivoli. A note, left by a bright young aide, caught his eye. "Last night I read something very much in line with what you have been saying for years," the young man had written. Quoting the writings of Cosmas, an early Alexandrian Christian, the note continued: "The true sign of the power of the Romans was that their money was accepted everywhere in the civilized world."

Debré could not help but smile. The young man was certainly trying to make points with his chief, but, after all, he was right. The single phrase from antiquity did sum up the way in which the French Finance Ministry, headed by the most loyal of Gaullists, viewed the international monetary scene.

CHAPTER 4

# De Gaulle Attacks the Dollar

Yes, the Americans were the Romans, dominating the Western world with their economic and military might, but France, at least in the eyes of the Gaullists, was Greece, the cradle of civilization, and Greece was going to make a surprising comeback.

Ever since the humiliating defeat of France in 1940, Charles de

Gaulle's overriding ambition was to restore France to the position of greatness in world affairs that was her due. The only obstacle that de Gaulle and faithful followers such as Debré could see to France's ambitions were the "Anglo-Saxons" (another one of the code words of our times which carry a derisory and semiracist meaning). The Americans and British had, it seems, committed the unpardonable sin of having rescued France from the Germans twice in thirty years and then taken outrageous advantage of their victories to dominate the postwar world. As an illustration of the kind of monetary support the United States gave France, former U.S. Secretary of State Dean Acheson cites the remark of a European official who suggested that since the United States placed the words "In God We Trust" on its currency, it should inscribe on French liberation money the words "I know that my Redeemer liveth."

## IN QUEST OF GREATNESS

When de Gaulle returned to power in France in 1958, after more than a decade in the political wilderness, he set out immediately to restore greatness to France and, incidentally, to himself. With a mixture of conceit and realism, he judged that he alone had any chance of pulling off the coup and that only a limited number of years remained to him to do it.

At the outset, the only resource de Gaulle had was himself. France was engaged in a bloody and costly war with the Algerians, who were not interested in France's quest for *grandeur* and wanted to go their own way. The French economy was only a patched-up version of the wreck left by World War II. Weakness at home dictated sweet reasonableness abroad. De Gaulle's strategy called for an announcement of his intentions and a simple, open request to the "Anglo-Saxons" to share their leadership with him. He did not expect that they would accede to his request. Indeed, there was no reason on earth why they should. But his request would serve as a warning. Then, after France had gathered her strength, de Gaulle would recruit other European nations to his cause and together they would end the domination of the Americans and British. And if this tactic did not work because the other Europeans were too servile or stupid to recognize that independence from the United States and its British vassel was in their own best interests, France would go it alone.

On September 17, 1958, less than six months after a desperate French Parliament had called him back to Paris from his country retreat at Colombey-les-deux-Eglises, de Gaulle made his first move. In a letter to President Eisenhower he stressed one of the themes that was to be part of the litany of French foreign policy for the next decade: Europe must be given a greater role in the decisions relating to Western defense. He proposed that a political directorate, composed of the United States, Britain, and France, be created to adopt any political decisions to determine the policy of the Atlantic Alliance.

The force of French logic was undeniable—at least to the French. Three of the four "great powers" of the world were members of NATO. These nations, with global rather than merely regional "vocations," should be in a position to determine the fortunes of the Alliance. The United States, as the leading nuclear power, would speak for North America, Great Britain for the Commonwealth and other European areas in its sphere of influence, and France for its empire and the other nations of Western Europe, including Germany. It was all very neat and very logical, de Gaulle implied: let us divide the Western world into good, old-fashioned spheres of influence, and France might be willing to behave herself.

When the letter was transmitted to Washington, it did not raise much of a stir. The State Department saw it as a gesture by the General, intended to evoke a kind of French *grandeur* which existed only in his mind's eye. It was also an oversimplified view of the real distribution of power in the Alliance. The NATO defense policy was based on the concept of "massive retaliation," of which John Foster Dulles had been the chief proponent. If the Soviet Union or its satellites attacked Western Europe, the United States was committed to an immediate counterattack on the Soviets, using the nuclear armaments in its arsenal. Because of clear American nuclear superiority, it was reasoned, the Soviets would be deterred from such an attack.

The strategy of "massive retaliation" meant that decision-making about the deployment of NATO had to be concentrated in the hands of those who already held the retaliatory force—the

Americans. The U.S. government was thus reluctant to share this decision-making power with countries who were not in a position to make a significant contribution to Western defense. In addition, the French proposal would mean that the European nation which was making the most significant military contribution— West Germany—would not have a place in the political directorate. At this stage, the Germans, pleased with the tough line Dulles had adopted in the defense of Berlin, were content to leave ultimate decision-making in the hands of the Americans, to whom they had good and direct access. Finally, President Eisenhower and his advisers were frankly concerned about the effect that the creation of any inner circle would have on the willingness of smaller European nations to participate in the Alliance. Though their military contribution was small, their participation gave the United States the legal excuse to intervene in case of a Soviet invasion and provide the necessary forward bases to create a "trip wire" which would signal such aggression and allow the United States sufficient time to launch a nuclear response.

When President Eisenhower sent his polite but firm rejection to de Gaulle on October 20, the French leader was not in the least surprised. In fact, the only thing that would have surprised him would have been a wholehearted acceptance, for General de Gaulle understood the Americans and British well.

General de Gaulle has a long memory, especially for the slights and insults inflicted by other countries on France—or on himself, the legitimate "incarnation" of France. The word that rankled most in the dictionary of insults and the one most often cited as the symbol of the hated hegemony of the "Anglo-Saxons" was Yalta. It was in this Soviet Black Sea resort city that Stalin, Roosevelt, and Churchill met to carve up the postwar world in March, 1945, when Hitler's defeat was a virtual certainty. Stalin, Roosevelt, and Churchill were there, it may be noticed, but not Charles de Gaulle. He noticed, all right, and resented it ever after. (Churchill was unperturbed by de Gaulle's absence; he had once remarked: "The heaviest cross I have to bear is the Cross of Lorraine.")

By sending his 1958 letter to Eisenhower, one of the few Americans for whom he had a warm personal attachment, the General believed he was giving his allies another chance to treat France as an equal. Though he kept his reaction to himself, he was obviously hurt by what he knew would be their inevitable rejection. The Americans and, by implication, the British had refused to undo the wrongs of Yalta, and de Gaulle became even more determined to upset the not-too-tidy arrangements made there as soon as he was able. But in the meantime, other more immediate tasks were at hand, and as he tackled these de Gaulle knew he could count on American and British support. In fact, Washington and London were far more conscious of de Gaulle's willingness to accept their help than of his underlying rancor toward them.

De Gaulle faced two major problems when he took office in 1958 that would have, and in fact had, daunted lesser men. The French economy seemed simply to be limping from one crisis to the next, and France was clearly the twentieth-century version of the sick man of Europe. Probably in part because de Gaulle knew little about economics, he believed that this problem could be solved quickly. But he knew quite a bit about politics and the military and thus he knew his second problem, bringing an end to the war in Algeria, would take some time.

The Gaullist policy of restoring France to its former greatness depended on giving the French a renewed sense of self-confidence. Instead of letting Frenchmen feel that their country must forever live on the dole from the "Anglo-Saxons," he wanted to provide France with a new weapon, almost never before available in modern French history—economic power. Even if he did not fully recognize just how difficult this would prove to be, he was a master at exploiting the public psychology, and psychology, as any good stockbroker knows, matters more than any other single factor in a policy designed to make the economy grow.

The traditional way to bring order out of economic and financial chaos is devaluation, and de Gaulle did not flinch from the need to cut the value of the franc. France had devalued the franc by 20 percent in 1957, but it had continued to decline in value on the money markets, where nameless men make and lose millions by trading one currency for another. On December 28, 1958, de Gaulle devalued the franc by 17.5 percent, slapped on drastic domestic measures designed to stop inflation, and, as the first sign that France was getting ready to play in the same league with other, healthier nations, made it easier to convert French francs to other currencies. By these moves de Gaulle hoped to prepare Paris for the day when it would be a major financial center on a par with New York and London.

In an effort to take the sting out of the psychological setback inherent in any devaluation, de Gaulle pulled a master stroke by simply moving a decimal point. Had he simply devalued, the resulting parity would have been 492 francs to the dollar. How ignominious for France, or at least for the France of de Gaulle, to have such an exchange rate when there were only about four Deutschemarks to the dollar. By the simple device of sliding the decimal point two places, de Gaulle created the "new franc," pegged at 4.92 to the dollar. Even the faces of the old bills and the aluminum coinage, which had felt like play money, were gradually replaced by bright new and rather heavy francs.

Though these economic measures were initiated by a simple stroke of the master's pen, the solution of the so-called "Algerian episode" took more time. Brought to power by a military cabal which wanted Algeria to remain French, de Gaulle carefully led the nation toward the ultimate acceptance, in 1962, of an Algerian Algeria. This maneuver, which stopped short a tremendous drain on the nation's resources and manpower, was accomplished only after several attempts on de Gaulle's life and at least one known attempt at a coup d'état. In 1958 de Gaulle had told the generals who brought him to power: "I understand you." They thought he meant that Algeria would remain French. Four years later, firmly settled in some of the nation's best prisons, they knew better.

The United States and Britain were the victims of a similar calculated misunderstanding. Once the unpleasant exchange of letters was out of the way in 1958, the "Anglo-Saxons," whose postwar policies had been devoted to the reconstruction of Europe, encouraged de Gaulle in his efforts to strengthen the economy and to end the war in Algeria. They thought that de Gaulle was content to let them carry on as before in NATO in return for their support. They did not recognize that de Gaulle was simply buying time.

But just as soon as the Algerian "episode" was "liquidated"

(the French language can make the worst of things seem best), de Gaulle was ready for his next move. It all had to do with a project called Skybolt.

Skybolt was supposed to be a missile carried by aircraft and launched in the air against airborne targets. The only problems with Skybolt were that it was enormously costly (for that time, at least—it was estimated to involve a total development expenditure of 3.3 billion dollars) and that it was far from certain that such a missile could be successfully built. Britain had been counting on the Skybolt for its own defense and had cut back on domestic missile development in anticipation of being able to buy Skybolt from the United States. In late 1962 the Skybolt program was canceled. Then, in December, 1962, under the azure skies of the Bahamas, President Kennedy told Prime Minister Macmillan that, instead of Skybolt, the United States would make Polaris missiles available to be used on submarines that would form part of a NATO "multinational force." Though this was less than the British might have hoped for, they at least did not leave the conference empty-handed. But the shadow of General de Gaulle, who once again was absent from the councils of the great, seemed to hover over the discussions at Nassau.

At the time of the Nassau talks, other negotiations, on British entry into the European Common Market, were taking place in Brussels. Macmillan knew that he needed the General's support or at least his acquiescence if the Brussels negotiations were to end successfully. He had been warned by de Gaulle, as late as November, 1962, that the "special relationship" which had bound the United States and Britain during World War II could turn France against Britain on the grounds that it was not sufficiently "European." Thus Kennedy decided to extend the offer of Polaris missiles to France as well as to Britain. This was a reversal of American policy, for it would help strengthen the development of the independent French nuclear force that had been begun even before de Gaulle came to power. But Kennedy thought of the offer as an indication that the United States was willing to share the leadership role in NATO with an integrated Europe. He believed that by extending the offer to France, de Gaulle would not be ruffled by having been excluded from the three-day Nassau meeting and would be encouraged to extend his cooperation with Britain, specifically by taking favorable action on the British application for Common Market membership.

The Nassau offer was doomed to failure, mainly because de Gaulle intended to make good on the implicit threat in his 1958 letter to Eisenhower—to declare France's "independence" of the United States. Kennedy was somewhat unaware that de Gaulle was now in a position to follow through on that warning. Kennedy was a victim of wishful thinking. In his reply to the General, Eisenhower had held out the possibility of talks on making NATO "more useful in the face of changing conditions," which meant that some accommodation would be possible, not among the big three of the Alliance, but between the United States and an integrated Europe. The fact that de Gaulle had made no move to take him up on the offer had been considered both inevitable, coming from the General, and insignificant, coming from France.

## UNLEASHING THE ULTIMATE WEAPON

The Nassau offer gave de Gaulle the first opportunity to show off his new-found strength and freedom of action resulting from the domestic economic reforms and the end of the Algerian conflict. In January, 1963, the General made his move: he turned down the Nassau offer and he instructed his negotiators in Brussels to break off further talks with Britain on entry into the Common Market. Without France, Britain could not enter the Common Market. Without French acceptance of the Nassau offer, Britain could not shed its "special relationship" with the United States. De Gaulle had found one powerful weapon that could make the Americans and British pay for their previous attitude toward France. That weapon was the word "no."

The General had declared war on the "Anglo-Saxons." Britain was his not altogether innocent victim. (France, too, was a victim, as shall be seen later.) But the United States was the real target. De Gaulle repeatedly told Frenchmen who crowded town squares from Strasbourg to Biarritz that France must be free from the dual "hegemony" of the United States and the Soviet Union. But despite the strong French Communist party, the Soviet Union was no political threat to France. The Americans, on the other hand, had troops stationed on French soil and a sizable stake in the French economy. De Gaulle's repeated blasts against "hegemony" in general were clearly understood to be directed against the United States in particular. When, on January 14, 1963, the General, sitting on his raised dais at the Elysée Palace, announced the French veto of British membership in the Common Market, his most venomous words were reserved for the United States. He claimed that if Britain were admitted, "in the end there would appear a colossal Atlantic Community under American dependence (sic) and leadership which would soon completely swallow up the European Community." Then, as a bitter afterthought, he cast serious doubt on American willingness to defend Europe in case of a Soviet invasion. De Gaulle's double veto marked the beginning of the end of French cooperation with NATO.

As a substitute for the plan suggested at Nassau, the United States began peddling a plan in European capitals which was aimed to tighten the ranks of the faithful and perhaps to make de Gaulle rue the day he said "no" to Uncle Sam. The plan was known as MLF, the multilateral force that would enable Europe to participate more directly in the Alliance's nuclear defenses. The United States would make nuclear warheads available to a fleet (originally to be composed of submarines, but later shifted, under what the British called the Atlantic Nuclear Force, to surface vessels) manned by mixed crews from NATO-member countries. In this way the supposedly burning German passion to lay a finger on the nuclear trigger could be kept within bounds. In the history of military alliances, the MLF was undoubtedly one of the most blatant gimmicks ever proposed, and despite lukewarm German acceptance and a massive display of American salesmanship, the plan died aborning.

De Gaulle went on, while abruptly rejecting all offers of cooperation in NATO which would provide a measure of real nuclear deterrence to France, to pursue his own plan for a French *force de frappe*, or striking force whose main purpose seemed not to be deterrence of the Russians but annoyance of the Americans. By 1967 the idea of American oil running through American pipelines on French soil and the very sight of the Stars and Stripes floating over anything but war cemeteries in France was more than the General could bear. Once again ascending the dais at the

Elysée, de Gaulle delivered another blast at the Americans and sent U.S. and Canadian troops packing. At the same time, he withdrew all French troops and armaments from NATO control. Then, despite repeated calls for reform of the Alliance, he never came up with any concrete suggestions. Finally the NATO political headquarters was hastily yanked out of Paris in 1968 in a combination of a fit of pique and the supposed desire to keep political and military headquarters (which had been moved from France to Belgium) within shouting distance of each other.

The NATO episode proved to de Gaulle, if any proof were needed, that he could not break American "hegemony" simply by asking. Of course, he recognized well before the end of 1962 that the Americans could be obliged to modify their policies only in response to a display of force. As early as 1959 he had begun trying to construct an anti-American alliance with other governments. He was to spend a decade in this fruitless effort.

### COMMON MARKET—COMMON CRUSADE?

The European Common Market, which groups France, West Germany, Italy, and the Benelux nations, provided an obvious framework in which the French could attempt to build support for an assault on the Americans. Certain areas, like defense, though no doubt tempting for de Gaulle, were excluded from the Common Market. The one area where de Gaulle had the greatest reason to hope for the creation of a "European" (that is, French) policy toward the United States was the economic sector, the heart of the Common Market operation.

France under de Gaulle was not the most enthusiastic member of the Common Market. Indeed, it is safe to assume that had de Gaulle been President of France in March, 1957, his government would never have signed the agreement to create the Common Market in the first place. But de Gaulle did not come to power until May of the following year, and the best he could then do was to attempt to bring the Common Market into line with his national objectives. (He completely rejected the underlying idea of European economic integration—that national policies were to be brought into line with a "European" policy.) De Gaulle offered his partners a choice between taking what they could get, even if less than they wanted, or getting nothing at all. The Common Market was less than four years old when the French made it clear that they would accept no political integration (in such fields as foreign and defense policies) and that they would prevent further economic integration unless the Common Market adopted an agricultural policy that suited de Gaulle. The other five members acquiesced, but the French approach had left them with a bitter taste that made further cooperation with de Gaulle or any of his initiatives for Common Market action most unappetizing.

The crowning blow to the high hopes for true economic and political integration, and, incidentally, to de Gaulle's hopes for leading his partners into a policy of economic defiance of the United States, was the French veto of British membership in the Common Market. While Americans saw the rejection as a brutal exercise in power politics and a successful attempt of one man to defy the will of many governments, the Europeans were stung more by the form than the substance of the rejection. Representatives of the Common Market and British delegations were grouped around television sets in Brussels on January 14, 1963, when de Gaulle issued his veto at a Paris press conference. The first news that any present in Brussels had of the French decision came from the televised reply to a press conference question. They all knew that it was against Common Market rules for one nation, acting alone, to end the negotiations. They all knew that any decision to end the talks would have to be made by the six members, though they must remain unanimous if the talks were to continue. They all knew that de Gaulle had some valid objections to the lengthy and often frustrating negotiations, but had not expected him to move so quickly and high-handedly to end the talks. But de Gaulle did the illegal, the unexpected, the unprecedented: he alone vetoed Britain.

Despite this affront to the sovereignty of other nations in the name of the sovereignty of his own, de Gaulle expected that his Common Market partners could be rallied to his anti-American policy. Once again it was a triumph of French logic over cold reality. He reasoned that they might well be unwilling to follow French leadership, but that the economic situation placed them in the same boat as France and would lead them to draw the same conclusions as the French. And because de Gaulle was the first to recognize that a new European economic policy toward the United States was necessary, France would be the logical leader of a new European economic bloc.

Trade negotiations, taking place in Geneva, were to be the test case. The so-called Kennedy Round of trade negotiations had started out as a grand exercise in Atlantic partnership, a harbinger of the kind of man-to-man relationship Europe and the United States might have after some further progress toward European integration. Instead, just as the talks got under way, de Gaulle vetoed the British. In defiance of the General, his five partners insisted on plunging ahead in the most ambitious tariff-cutting exercise in history. At the same time, de Gaulle knew that the United States wanted a successful Kennedy Round because American leaders thought that freer trade would mean bigger U.S. sales abroad and hence would help strengthen the international reputation of the dollar. In addition, despite brave talk about France being able to hold its own with the best, the French feared that their industry could not stand up to the full blast of international competition that would result from freer trade. As a result, French representatives tried every kind of foot-dragging and diplomatic blackmail before they were hauled by their Common Market partners to the bargaining table in Geneva. Along the way, they managed to obtain some additional concessions on Common Market rules affecting their agricultural production, but they were unable to prevent a largely successful result to the Kennedy talks.

Unfortunately, France's partners took their victory as a sign of French capitulation to their vision of a united Europe. They pushed a plan to turn the Common Market into a well-financed agency, independent of national controls. Though de Gaulle had not been able to say no to the Kennedy Round once he had given his initial approval, he wasn't buying integration in 1965 any more than he had in 1963. Not only did he say no to the new Common Market proposals, he simply walked out, in the accepted Soviet manner, and said he would not come back until the others were willing to play the game by some new rules of his devising, the net effect of which would have been to turn the Common Market into another one of the colorless international debating societies, with few real powers. The final arbiters of the contest were the French voters, who in December, 1965, let the General know that even they would not swallow all his high-handed international maneuvers. De Gaulle suffered a shock by being forced into a run-off election for the French presidency when a sizable bloc of moderate voters turned against him on the Common Market issue. In January, 1966, de Gaulle returned to the fold, and a tacit agreement was made that he would not try to change the Common Market if the Common Market would not try to change him. Both sides lost the encounter—de Gaulle because his bluff had been called and the Common Market because it caught a serious case of stage fright from which it has just begun to recover.

Not only was the European club unenthusiastic about making him its chief, but de Gaulle met similar reactions in his courtship of other possible partners for a marriage hardly made in heaven but at least founded on the solid foundation of anti-Americanism. Adenauer's Germany was docile enough, but as it got richer it also got more careful of how it spent its money. The Germans weren't about to pay a higher price to buy French nuclear protection when they were already satisfied users of "Uncle Sam" brand. Adenauer thought it would be all right to teach French in German schools, but the Germans said no thanks to anything that cost cold, hard Deutschemarks and might also alienate Washington. Under Kiesinger the Germans even began to question why they, the most powerful nation in Western Europe, had to pay their penance for their prior transgressions in the form of blind obedience to France.

China, good for a brief flirtation, proved to be too far removed and too inscrutable, even for the General. The Soviet Union looked like a natural ally against the United States, but somehow France did not seem that important to the Kremlin. The Soviets thought it would be all right to buy color television from the French, but when Czechoslovakia had to be invaded, they politely ignored de Gaulle's murmurings about no hegemony from the East. Finally, in 1969, de Gaulle had a brief "affair" with Britain. The British thought it would be all right to pinch the exchequer dry to build a supersonic aircraft with the French (though they had frequent second thoughts), but they preferred not to place their foreign policy in the General's hands.

De Gaulle had thus failed to convince his European neighbors that the Americans were public menace number-one and that their military and trade supremacy was an evil that only he knew how to handle. But the General still had what he thought was his best card to play, the weakness of the dollar and growing discontentment (for example, Servan-Schreiber's *The American Challenge*) with U.S. economic domination. His bet was that the common interest in reforming the world's monetary system would virtually force other nations to support his anti-American policy. If he were successful, France would at last be given its rightful place.

"GAULLEFINGER"

Of course, de Gaulle's desire to topple the dollar and the pound sterling had historical roots that other nations couldn't be expected to share. These two currencies are the national currencies of the United States and the United Kingdom. And de Gaulle smarted at the fact, brought home to him daily, that the national currencies of the chief "Anglo-Saxon" nations were the monetary standard, on a footing of absolute equality with gold, of the Western world.

Whenever de Gaulle talked about the Bretton Woods system he spoke with distaste of the "gold exchange standard." Though a perfectly valid French translation exists for these words, he always used the term in a heavily accented English, as if to show his disdain for an alien monetary system to which he had not been a party. And, in fact, de Gaulle, busy with the liberation of France, had not paid much attention to the Bretton Woods conference, and the United States and Britain had paid little attention to him. Thus, as with NATO and the European Common Market, he accepted existing arrangements when he came to power, but with the caveat that he had the right to alter them, or at least the French role in them, if he could.

The fact that the Bretton Woods monetary system had functioned relatively smoothly over the years since 1944 and that the world had been nowhere near the brink of international economic catastrophe characteristic of the period before World War II was of little importance to de Gaulle. What he saw was that the monetary rules seemed to give the United States and Britain a privileged position, and this he would not tolerate. It was all right for the Americans to use their postwar dollar surplus to aid in the reconstruction of France, but when that surplus turned to deficit, Uncle Sam had to be punished for his indiscretions.

American dollars had been flooding into France, as into other European countries, as U.S. business rapidly expanded its operations abroad. France was particularly attractive because wage rates were relatively low and labor was abundant, thanks to the influx of French Algerians, or *pieds noirs*, who streamed into the "Metropole" as the ultimate victory of Algeria's National Liberation Front became increasingly inevitable. In addition, France was a keystone of the European Common Market, which was gradually erecting a tariff wall that would keep out some American goods. What simpler way was there to leap that wall than to produce those very goods within the Common Market?

The same American dollars, which poured into France and provided de Gaulle with a lever which could be used against the United States, helped France in the meantime. De Gaulle made ineffectual and mostly symbolic moves to halt the influx of dollars. They paid for factories which provided jobs, especially outside of Paris in the less-developed regions of the nation. They paid for some local research-and-development projects which helped prevent France from falling too far behind the United States and such economically powerful neighbors as Germany in the technological race. They helped bring the most modern equipment and business and production techniques into France.

The French were in a quandary about American investment. To see such wretched imperialist names as Libby's canned peaches or Coca-Cola plastered liberally on factories across the nation stung as much as the American flags flapping over Army bases. (On some occasions, however, like the removal of a Remington plant, the French charged that the Americans were being just as cavalier as when they built a new plant.) In 1964 de Gaulle almost reached breaking point. General Electric purchased a controlling interest in Machines Bull, the leading French computer manufacturer, and with a stroke of a pen, virtually the entire French data-processing industry fell under American control. Enraged by this fresh affront to his sovereign rule, de Gaulle vowed he would crack down on American investment in France. Yet, within two years, he had abruptly changed course. He cordially invited Henry Ford II, the epitome of American capitalism, to the Elysée to plead with him to build an automobile plant in France. France had found that it could not do without U.S. investment, particularly when its European neighbors and competitors continued to welcome it with open arms. And, in any case, more investment meant more dollars for the French, who could use them as pawns in their effort to topple the "Anglo-Saxon" domination of the monetary system.

All six Common Market nations had benefited from massive inflows of dollars as U.S. direct private investment mounted precipitously each year. U.S. military expenditures in Europe remained at a high level. As a result, the dollar reserves of all Common Market members were increasing in direct proportion to declining American gold reserves. Indeed, there was a cause-and-effect relationship, because whether a country was basically hostile toward the United States (like France) or basically friendly (like Belgium), it preferred to hold a high proportion of gold in its national reserves rather than in dollars in excess of its needs. These dollars represented valid claims on the U.S. Treasury that had to be met on demand with gold. Thus one truckload after another pulled out of Fort Knox, where the American gold reserve was stocked, to make bullion deliveries to the subterranean vaults of the Federal Reserve Bank of New York, where the gold holdings of most Western nations were kept. The General, or "Gaullefinger," as some called him, ever mistrustful of the United States, was even discontent with the procedure and dispatched several special Air France planes to carry cargoes of the precious yellow metal back to Paris for safekeeping. It was as if the government was following the well-known custom of those it represented, many of whom had seen too many devaluations and now kept their personal gold hoards stuffed in mattresses or buried under the roots of trees.

The franc zone, a small club of newly independent African states who did their banking in Paris and kept their reserves of francs there to settle their debts with the mother country, also provided dollars for de Gaulle. When these states succeeded in collecting dollars, often through American foreign-aid programs, they shipped them to Paris to bolster their reserve accounts with the Banque de France. The French simply bought the dollars for francs and shipped the greenbacks to the Federal Reserve.

De Gaulle blithely pursued the most obvious tactic to weaken the pound and the dollar: he cashed in every pound note and dollar bill he could for gold, thus reducing the backing of these international currencies. With Britain in severe economic difficulties and heavily dependent on international loans to keep the pound afloat, no nation would consent to hold any sizable part of its reserves in sterling. France actually participated in several major loans to Britain sponsored by the IMF. The French contribution to these loans in the 1964–1967 period totaled more than 635 million dollars out of a total of 3.8 billion dollars. At the same time, France made francs available to the Bank of England on a short-term basis; in 1966, for example, it lent the British ninety million dollars' worth of francs. De Gaulle was thus helping to preserve the pound sterling from a devaluation which might cause repercussions throughout Europe and require some parallel devaluation of the French franc. Later, as we shall see, he reversed this policy.

If the weakness of the British economy led to an end of the international reserve role assigned to the pound sterling in fact if not in law, the situation of the dollar was different. The American economy was strong and was in the midst of the longest period of sustained growth in history. Though the dollar was legally backed by gold reserves, which could be wiped out if all foreign-held dollars were presented for redemption at the U.S. Treasury, a basically sound economy, though one in which inflation was increasing alarmingly, provided a sounder underpinning. Unfortunately for the United States, gold counted most heavily in the official reckoning, and as we have seen de Gaulle saw to it that as much gold as possible was shifted from the vaults of Fort Knox to the Banque de France. In 1965, he announced an official policy aimed at getting rid of all excess dollars—estimated at 300 million dollars at the time. At the same time, de Gaulle tried to prevail upon other European nations to pursue a similar policy of massive redemption of dollars for gold. Because they did not share his hostility toward the United States, they demurred—officially at least. But central bankers could not afford to see the dollar weakened while they went on holding significant amounts of dollars, and quietly they began increasing the proportion of gold in their total reserves by cashing in excess dollars. There was, of course, a natural limit on the amount of dollars that could be turned in, because some were needed to pay for purchases made abroad. If dollars were not available to make such payments, actual transfers of gold had to be made, and this defeated the purposes of the operation. But France and other nations did gradually build up their gold holdings by reducing their holdings of dollars.

All of this was legal, and de Gaulle made it even seem morally justified. Before stepping up French dollar redemptions, de Gaulle made advance payments on his country's remaining 660 million dollar World War II debt to the United States. These payments ate up surplus dollars and freed him from the charge of rank ingratitude. While some American congressmen claimed that France should also pay off its World War I debts, suspended over thirty years earlier, few took this complaint seriously, for it was generally believed that those debts had in fact been written off.

## THE EXOTIC "CRU" AND THE GOLDEN RULE

The Americans were happy with the monetary system they had built at Bretton Woods. The most obvious way to surmount the problems of the moment was simply to make that system work more, if not better. The Americans thus proposed that the quotas, both in terms of what members must contribute to the IMF and what they might get out of it, should be increased by fifty percent above the sixteen-billion-dollar level. The chief beneficiaries would be the United States and Britain, who had the largest shares in the IMF and would thus get the greatest part of the new rights to draw funds from it.

The French, through Finance Minister Valéry Giscard d'Estaing, said no once again. Giscard claimed that the increased quotas would simply help the "Anglo-Saxons" get off the hook by providing them with new sources of internationally acceptable funds. They would be relieved of any requirement to slow the outflow of their own currencies. Throughout 1963 and 1964 a quiet tug of war took place between France and the United States, with other nations shuttling back and forth seeking compromises. Giscard was ultimately in a weak position because the Americans had enough votes to swing some increase in funds for the monetary system. But the French did succeed in cutting the amount of the increase to twenty-five percent and in boosting the amount of gold that the United States and Britain would have to pay into the IMF for the privilege of getting currency out of it. At the Tokyo meeting of the IMF in the warm autumn of 1964, the new quotas were adopted.

Giscard, the leading opponent of the increased quotas, appeared with some embarrassment before the French National Assembly. Angry Gaullists threw his own anti-quota arguments against him. To counter them, Giscard promised that the increased quota was only a small concession which would have to be repaid when plans for a broader reform of the international monetary system came to fruition.

Throughout 1964 Giscard was busy promoting the "cru," which sounded more like some exotic South Seas bird than the imaginative monetary reform plan that it was. The "cru" (or composite reserve unit) was to be created, not in the framework of the IMF, but among a select group of nations—those holding the largest amounts of gold. "Crus" would be distributed to each participating nation in proportion to its gold reserves and would take their place beside gold and dollars as an internationally accepted medium of exchange. The idea of a new reserve was acceptable to all nations (indeed, the Americans were especially enthusiastic, because the "cru" had originally been the idea of an American); the idea of linking it directly to gold was acceptable to none besides France. The "cru" plan was instantly recognized as a disguised increase in the price of gold, and since it was tied to gold and limited to the major monetary powers, it would only help the rich get richer.

De Gaulle saw two weaknesses in the "cru" plan: first, the Americans were showing signs of interest in it; and second, he had never been fully consulted about it. When he did stop to think about it, what bothered him was that even if the "cru" was linked directly to gold, it wasn't gold.

Once again ascending his favorite rostrum, in the Elysée's ballroom, de Gaulle dropped another of his famous bombshells at his press conference of February 4, 1965. The well-known rhetoric about the need to change the international monetary system dominated by the money of a single country surprised no one. But what, he asked rhetorically, should be the basis of the new system?

Actually, it is difficult to envision in this regard any other criterion, any other standard than gold [he said]. Yes, gold, which does not change in nature, which can be made either into bars, ingots, or coins, which has no nationality, which is considered, in all places and at all times, the immutable and fiduciary value par excellence. Furthermore, despite all that it was possible to imagine, say, write, or do in the midst of major events [an allusion to Bretton Woods], it is a fact that even today no currency has any value except by direct or indirect relation to gold, real or supposed.

Gone in the space of these three sentences was the "cru." Indeed, nothing else would do but what de Gaulle, in an unashamed pun, called the "golden rule." Giscard was hurriedly called out to translate the sibylline pronouncement into everyday language and, incidentally, to reconcile his "cru" plan with de Gaulle's pronouncement. Not without new embarrassment, Giscard explained that, just as France was already doing to a great extent, all cash transactions between nations should be in gold. Reserves should be in gold alone, not dollars. All major currencies, not just the pound and the dollar, should be convertible to gold. If all of this was accomplished, the General might allow Giscard to hope for the modest creation of a few "crus."

## RASPUTIN AND THE GOLD STANDARD

Obviously, gold was something de Gaulle could understand. As he spoke at the Elysée, one could almost feel that he, too, had golden sovereigns stuffed into his regal mattress. But his proposal of the gold standard and nothing less was not his own idea; it came from a man who had easy access to the General, though he occupied no official position.

Jacques Rueff is a mild-mannered, scholarly economist who occupies one of the forty privileged seats in the prestigious Académie Française. His election to membership in the Académie was all the more noteworthy because he represents the "dismal science," not the more traditional fields (for the Académie, at least) of arts, letters, politics, and the military. Rueff thinks like an economist, talks like an economist, consorts with economists. But he came to be regarded as a French Rasputin, an exceedingly clever man who could dominate the thinking—in the economic sector, at least—of *mon Général*. But Rueff is not Rasputin. He could not have influenced his "master" unless de Gaulle already shared many of his values. In addition, he earned his place in de Gaulle's esteem and in the Académie through his efforts on behalf of the Republic. The French monetary reform of 1958 was chiefly his work—or at least his idea.

Rueff had been expounding his gold policy in one form or another almost since the gold standard was abandoned in the 1920's. He believed that the breakdown of the international monetary system between the two world wars was not the fault of the gold standard, which prescribed that all international debts were to be settled in gold, the only acceptable international reserve, but of the abandonment of the gold standard in favor of the gold exchange standard, which placed the pound sterling and the dollar on a footing of equality with gold.

The use of gold as the only medium of international exchange prevents any tampering with the basic law of supply and demand, according to Rueff. New international money can only be created to the extent that new gold is mined and placed in circulation. This is not likely to happen rapidly, but this potential shortage of international exchange will be an effective way to ensure that nations adopt policies of strict monetary discipline (in other words, living within their means in their dealings with other nations) in order to conserve enough of the precious metal for their most important needs.

The ultimate economic woe, as far as Rueff is concerned, is inflation. And inflation is caused by too much domestic purchasing power: when the people of one nation have more money than there are goods available domestically, they will tend to buy more from abroad and have less available to sell. But a damper can be placed on this kind of exported inflation by ensuring that purchases can be made from abroad only if they can and are paid for with gold, not the excess national currency. Since gold must actually change hands, the system will not allow for credit arrangements, which tend to delay the establishment of a balance in the international payments system (when the amount spent abroad is exactly equal to the amount received from abroad). In other words, Rueff sees the gold standard as the perfect solution to the problem of international monetary transactions, since it would ensure that each country would have its accounts in balance with every other country. If this placed an undue strain on some (for example, the new, poor nations of the world), it would nonetheless be an accurate reflection of their real economic strength.

But let Rueff speak eloquently for himself (in *The Age of Inflation*):

> The gold standard, therefore, governs all the components of our international transactions with faultless effectiveness. Like the price mechanism, of which it is only a specific aspect, it is a forceful but unobtrusive master, who governs unseen and yet is never disobeyed. Nevertheless, it is too wise to oppose the inclinations of men. It never, for example, prohibits the purchase of foreign securities; taking all their actions into account, it guides the conduct of men in order to prevent the upsetting of the balance it is supposed to maintain. We should also point out that while guiding men's actions it respects their freedom of choice. They are always at liberty to buy according to their preferences, but the monetary mechanism, in its omnipotence, will raise the price of those items whose purchase is contrary to the general interest, until such time as consumers decide of their own free will to stop buying them. The gold standard thus resembles an absolute but enlightened monarch; he does not destroy the man's freedom, but employs it for his own ends.

(The description of the gold standard, some say, sounds remarkably like one of General de Gaulle himself.)

If only the world had let itself be governed by this benevolent despot, the monetary tribulations of the interwar period which allowed for the spiraling inflation in Germany and in turn paved the way for Hitler could have been avoided. But people seemed to prefer complete freedom, even to the extent of casting off their "enlightened monarch." Rueff blames this move on the private sector in Britain and other countries. They wanted to be free to buy and sell abroad without respecting the strict accounting of the balance of payments. And so, governments began to accept dollars and sterling along with gold. This allowed for a relatively rapid expansion of reserves and the use of credit arrangements, which permitted deficits to extend over many years. Rueff believes that governments were wrong to give way before the demands of their constituents in the private sector. "The truth is that the public interest is not, as is widely believed, the sum of private interests, but is opposite," he says.

Rueff recognizes that it would be impossible simply to revert to the gold standard. If only gold actually held by each country were tomorrow to be reckoned as constituting their reserves, they would fall far short of their need for international funds to finance world trade (in other words, the need for a generally accepted medium of exchange which could be used to pay for purchases from abroad). In addition, a reversion pure and simple to the gold standard would quickly bankrupt the United States despite its powerful economy and its leadership role in the world. The dollars now held abroad represent short-term obligations of the U.S. Treasury, and the U.S. government must stand ready to pay out gold from Fort Knox for each foreign-held dollar that is turned in for redemption. In practice, these dollars are at present not all turned in, because, under the gold exchange standard, they can be used to finance international transactions just as if they were gold. In order to allow for their redemption once a gold standard was in effect, Rueff proposes a devaluation of the dollar in relation to gold. Gold is now officially valued at thirty-five dollars an ounce; he suggests that it might be increased to seventy dollars an ounce (thus making each dollar worth half as much as gold previously). After such a devaluation, the United States could pay out gold in return for virtually all outstanding dollars, though it would have little gold left after doing so and would thus be forced to submit without further struggle to the imperious rule of the gold standard. For countries like France, whose gold holdings represent a high proportion of their reserves (thanks to calculated policies of getting rid of dollars and sterling as quickly as possible), their reserves would be doubled by such a devaluation of the dollar.

Thus Rueff's gold policy consists of a return to the gold standard as it supposedly existed until the 1920's and a devaluation of the dollar by a significant amount. This is not Rasputin's mysticism; it is one economist's view of how to solve the international monetary crises resulting from a "permanent" deficit in the balance of payments of the United States and Britain. Rueff would certainly say that his policy is not directed against the "Anglo-Saxons," but that they, unfortunately, have the foot that fits the shoe.

Much of the reasoning underlying Rueff's gold-standard argument is grounded in the history of the interwar period and is based in particular on the "incompetence" of British and French policy and also the machinations of Hjalmar Schacht, Hitler's finance minister, who resorted to draconian measures to pull the German currency out of one of the wildest inflationary spirals ever known. De Gaulle knew this period equally well, and much of his policy, particularly with regard to Germany, was based on his frustrating experiences as an ambitious officer who was highly critical of what he thought were the blunders of his own and other governments and the diabolical moves of the Germans. Rueff offered de Gaulle the opportunity to rewrite the history of the interwar period and thus to show the ghosts of his mentors and tormentors that had they followed his advice (though he actually never gave any on monetary matters), France could have been spared the horrors of the Nazi occupation.

A final element of Rueff's proposals which appealed to de Gaulle was, of course, the attack on Britain and the United States for having tossed aside the discipline of the gold standard in favor of the gold exchange standard, which they, as leaders of the Allies, were able to force upon France and other nations. By pursuing Rueff's gold policy, de Gaulle saw not only a way of improving the international monetary system by capitalizing on a momentarily huge French gold cache, but a way of putting Britain and the United States in their proper place—equal with but not superior to France.

Though other Europeans did not share de Gaulle's passion for gold, they did appreciate his concern with the unending deficit the United States was running in its financial dealings with Europe. They had accepted a number of American stopgap measures, designed to ease pressure on the dollar, but they agreed with the French that a more basic reform was necessary. This was a clear French victory. The one vital ingredient for the successful operation of the monetary system is confidence, especially of the key governments, and de Gaulle, by his verbal barrage against the dollar and his calculated redemption policy, had been able to undermine the faith in the Bretton Woods system that the United States had tried to nurture.

Other European nations did not, however, want to go as far as de Gaulle, for a number of reasons. Probably most important was the fact that central bankers are a conservative breed; they did not want to adopt the most drastic of plans—reversion to the gold standard and devaluation of the dollar—when they thought that some less sweeping measures would provide sufficient reform. And de Gaulle was completely unable to force them to his will because they could merely cite his own dictum that "doubtless no one would think of dictating to any country how to manage its domestic affairs." They, like de Gaulle, believed, however erroneously, that monetary policy was clearly in the field of domestic affairs. In addition, many of the other European nations had their own ideas about monetary cooperation. In 1964, for example, when Italy ran into a serious monetary crisis which threatened to drain her reserves, she turned for help not to her European partners, but to the United States, which after all was the single country with the largest reserves. The Dutch, on the other hand, made a great show of supporting European unity, but they balked when it came to joining in a common monetary policy. They distrusted the French and de Gaulle's underlying hostility to the Common Market, and their centuries-long tradition of internationalism outweighed their commitment to Europe.

The Europeans, struggling to come up with an acceptable alternative, were doomed to failure because they sought to find an accommodation between the Americans and the General. All European nations are much more dependent on international trade than is the United States. While only four percent of the American gross national product—the sum of all the goods and services produced by the economy—goes abroad as exports, this figure is far higher in Europe, reaching more than forty percent in the Netherlands. If a breakdown in the monetary system meant that there were to be fewer monetary transactions and hence less trade, the United States could obviously survive the pinch far better than the Europeans. Gradually the Dutch, Germans, and Italians came to realize that France, through her membership in the Common Market, had placed herself in a position similar to theirs. In 1968, 13.6 percent of the French GNP took the form of exports, compared with 8.8 percent ten years earlier. They knew that de Gaulle was strong enough to destroy confidence and thus could spur the reform of the monetary system, but that he was in no position to get the kind of new system he wanted.

### "MICKEY MOUSE" AND MONEY

And so once again we return to Michel Debré at the Rue de Rivoli. In 1966 de Gaulle replaced Giscard, who had a superior monetary sense but who had gone too far afield in his quest of the exotic "cru," with Debré, a clever operator but, above all, a passionate Gaullist. Under Debré, French monetary policy became more aggressive but less effective. "Mickey Mouse," as he was called with something less than complete affection, knew that he had no chance of selling the gold standard, but he considered it his sacred mission to save the world from the Americans. The Europeans gradually began to give up any hope of an arrangement including the French as Debré set out to harass the Americans and hamstring negotiations aimed at a new stopgap to provide increased money to the international circuit. Perhaps the best-known instrument employed by Debré was the most highly respected newspaper in France, Le Monde. Unlike the national radio and television network and the overtly Gaullist press, Le Monde prided itself on its reputation for independent and in-depth reporting. The financial editor of the paper was a bright young journalist, Paul Fabra, whose name was as yet unknown in international monetary circles and totally unheard of in the United States. But Debré, through careful cultivation of Fabra, was to make his name famous (or infamous) among central bankers.

The game of international finance is played in the tightest secrecy (and with more success, it seems, than defense ministries have). If planned monetary moves become known before they are employed, they can be discounted in stock markets and money markets around the world and thus have little impact once they are announced. As a result, central bankers and finance ministers have developed tried-and-true techniques of avoiding being seen by newsmen or, if they are cornered, of smiling politely and saying nothing. This Mona Lisa approach only succeeds in infuriating journalists, who are under orders from their editors to get "hard facts" into their articles. And it means that their readers, the people directly affected, can't find out what is happening. Debré changed all this for Fabra, who became, almost overnight, virtually the only journalist in the world to get detailed briefings directly from one of the participants in monetary negotiations.

Fabra was not a Gaullist, though he may have appeared to be a Gaullist dupe. He saw himself simply as a newsman who was getting a story. How could he know whether what Debré told him was true or, if it were true, that it was going to remain so? Often on the eve of important monetary sessions, Le Monde would carry detailed explanations of the French position, which usually came as a jolt to other participants. Once in the session, Debré's position would appear different. Perhaps what he had told Fabra had been correct, but after his views were published they altered the situation and required Debré to change his approach. Or perhaps he had never intended to do what he had told Fabra. In some cases there could be no doubt that the Finance Ministry was using the pages of Le Monde to try to influence the course of events.

At the opening of the March, 1968, meeting of the Group of Ten at the Foresta Hotel in Stockholm, an edition of Le Monde with particularly startling news was distributed to all participants. In it, Fabra wrote that the U.S. balance-of-payments deficit in 1968 would be eight billion dollars, based on figures for the first quarter of the year. Even before that quarter was over, Fabra had found, from completely unidentified sources, that the three-month deficit would be two billion dollars and had simply multiplied this figure by four. When the official statistics were published, after the quarter had closed, the actual deficit was six hundred million dollars, and it proved unwise to multiply even this figure by four, because there had been strike-induced imports of copper and steel which ran far ahead of the normal U.S. import rate in the first quarter. But none of this was immediately evident to the participants in the Stockholm meeting. Nonetheless, Fabra's article was recognized as an attempt to undermine further

confidence in the dollar and thus weaken the American position in the debate over the creation of a new international mechanism designed both to increase the amount of money available to finance trade and to ease American balance-of-payments difficulties.

The Stockholm meeting represented the last fling of the French attempt to destroy confidence in the dollar. This meeting was to put a stamp of approval on the creation of "paper gold," a reserve that would take its place beside gold and the dollar without being based on them. France fought this decision every step of the way and eventually threatened simply not to take part in the "paper gold" system unless important changes were made in it. The other participants refused, and France made good its threat.

Early in April, *Le Monde* had given up much of its harassment of the dollar, and France seemed to have given up the gold standard. "The weakness of the [French] position," *Le Monde* (not Fabra this time) said, "stemmed from the absence of complete counterproposals to the lax but coherent system of the Americans and their European allies." The paper reported Debré as saying that not only the dollar, but all major currencies, should be made redeemable in gold and accepted as reserves on an equal footing with gold and the dollar. Exchange rates among the currencies or between individual ones and gold would be set by a general agreement among the major monetary powers. This amounted to giving up the attack on the dollar by seeking to give the franc an equally privileged position. As such it was even a retreat from Giscard's 1965 proposals. After duly reporting this change of course, *Le Monde* proceeded to punch holes in the Debré proposals.

The defection of *Le Monde* signaled the end of the French attack on the dollar. The effort had contributed to the economic exhaustion of France, for which she would eventually have to pay a high price. In the end, de Gaulle was forced to ease off his anti-Americanism and then to descend his elysian throne. But for a general well beyond the retirement age and knowing nothing about international finance, he had almost single-handedly brought the world to the brink of international monetary reform —and for all the wrong reasons.

CHAPTER **5**

# The Pound Falls–Or Was It Pushed?

**E**ver since World War II, Britain had been the sick man of Europe. The balance of payments had been in deficit more often than not, and the pound regularly had to be supported in the foreign-exchange markets. At certain moments, other countries (France, for example) faced serious crises, but over a period of twenty-five years the pound had been the weakest major currency in the West. In 1967 it had to be devalued, and General de Gaulle can claim much of the credit for the circumstances in which devaluation was carried out.

The most superficial explanations of Britain's chronic economic sickness tend to focus on things that happen inside the country. The union structure is old-fashioned, and damaging strikes are notoriously frequent. The British don't invest as much as other people in modern plants and equipment, and sometimes appear more interested in having a good time than in competing with the Germans and the Japanese. Income tax is sometimes said (by the British) to be too high, so that there is little incentive to get ahead.

But the overriding factors in Britain's economic weakness are external. The British thought they had won the war, but the

victory left them severely weakened, saddled with debts to the
United States and to the members of the Commonwealth, and
faced with the long, drawn-out task of dismantling the Empire
which had once made them great.

Even after the Empire had been dismantled and turned into a
loose Commonwealth of independent countries, many of the bur-
dens associated with the Empire remained. A quarter of a century
after the war ended, Britain still had military garrisons in many
parts of the world fulfilling an international peace-keeping role,
and though they also helped to protect Britain's vast overseas investments in such areas as the Far East, their chief rationale was
political. London had defense-treaty obligations to a host of developing countries, as a relic of the imperial past, and successive
British governments continued to believe that these obligations
could not lightly be denounced. They were strongly supported in
this belief by the United States, which had no wish to bear sole
responsibility for keeping the peace, and during the 1950's Washington's arguments reinforced the inclinations of the Tories, who
still hankered to preserve the trappings of the imperial heritage.
Gradually it became clear that the economic cost of overseas military spending was too great for the country to bear, though it was
not until the Tories had been replaced by a Labor administration
that the decision to withdraw from east of Suez was finally taken.

The other major factor which helped to drag Britain down was
the pound's role as a reserve currency, even though its reserve
function was very much more limited than that of the U.S. dollar.
None of the major industrialized countries now holds any sterling
in its reserves, apart from minimal amounts as day-to-day operating balances. Some of them did before the war, but the central
banks of France, Belgium, and Holland in particular have never
forgotten (or forgiven) the severe losses they suffered when the
pound was devalued (and with it the value of their sterling reserves) in 1931. So great was the loss by the Netherlands central
bank, indeed, that a cruel little ditty became current shortly
afterward: "In matters of sterling the fault of the Dutch/ is caring
too little and trusting too much." And in France the long-
standing memory of the potential weakness of a reserve currency
like the pound was, no doubt, an additional reason for distrusting

the reserve-currency system, quite apart from General de Gaulle's more crudely political motives.

By contrast, a large number of Commonwealth countries are members of the so-called sterling area, and they have continued to hold reserves in London, together with Egypt and other Middle Eastern states which were in the past under more or less direct British control. These sterling balances are a perpetual burden on Britain's reserves. If a sterling-area country wants to take its money out of London, for fear that the pound will be devalued, it only needs to sell it for dollars or some other asset. In practice, the total volume of the sterling balances in London has not shown any long-term downward trend since the war. It has fluctuated from time to time, and while some like India and Pakistan have tended to reduce their sterling investments, others like Kuwait and Hong Kong have increased theirs. On the other hand, the overseas sterling-area countries as a group have shown their distrust of the pound by putting any additional reserves into other forms of assets.

Even to maintain this degree of stability in the sterling balances, Britain has had to pay a heavy price. Unlike the United States, it is not powerful enough politically or economically to be able to force other countries to hang on to their sterling assets for very long, though successive British governments have undoubtedly exerted a certain amount of moral pressure on their Commonwealth associates. But the only way during most of the postwar period that Britain has been able to prevent sterling-area countries from moving their assets out of London has been to pay a high rate of interest, and this is something that the United States has never had to do.

The trouble with giving high rates of interest on British government stocks is that it is not a permanent solution, and actually increases the vulnerability of sterling. When times are good—that is to say, when the British balance of payments is in surplus and the pound looks strong—private individuals are attracted by the high return to invest their money in London, and this produces an increase in the gold and foreign-exchange reserves at the Bank of England. But when the times are bad—and they have more often been bad than good—these private balances move out of London just as fast as they came in, and the reserves go down. The only possible course to slow down the flight of this so-called "hot money" is to raise interest rates still further. The consequence is that since the war Britain has almost always had a higher level of interest rates than most other rich countries.

Sometimes the sterling area has helped cushion the impact of Britain's own balance-of-payments difficulties. For if sterling-area countries earn surpluses at a time when Britain is in deficit, and if they deposit their increased reserves in London, they can offset the British loss. In practice their deficits are just as likely to coincide with a British deficit as not, and in recent years they have shown little inclination in general to increase their London-based reserves.

These drawbacks might not matter so much if Britain were as large and as powerful as the United States. While the United States is far the largest and most dynamic industrial country in the world, the least dependent on foreign trade, and the most important export market for the majority of industrialized countries, Britain has a faltering economy, a heavy dependence on foreign trade, and a comparatively small market for foreign exports. And while in both countries gold reserves are lower than the foreign liabilities, in Britain the gold reserves are low also in relation to imports.

This means that Britain cannot stand a deficit for very long without running out of reserves. Time and time again since the war the country has been set on an expansionary course, consumers have spent part of their bigger wage packets on imports, the trade deficit has soared, and the whole economy has had to be brought to a shuddering halt once more. This "stop-go" cycle has prevented Britain from having as high an average growth rate as most of its foreign competitors and has made it more difficult to modernize and streamline the economy.

Countries are very reluctant to run their reserves down if they can possibly avoid it, and when they run into deficit they would much rather borrow abroad than spend their precious hoard of gold and foreign exchange. In Britain's case, borrowing has not merely been a preference of the government; it has been inevitable if ruin were to be avoided, for without it the reserves would have disappeared long ago. Over the years British borrowings, both in short-term credits from foreign central banks and in medium-term drawings from the IMF, have spiraled almost out of control, and it is difficult to see just when, or even how, they will be paid off.

Indeed, for the layman it has now become virtually impossible to work out, even roughly, just how deeply Britain is in debt. The IMF drawings are published; but they have accelerated to the point where the one-billion-dollar standby negotiated in June, 1969, has had to be used partly to help pay off previous IMF drawings. Moreover, the total size of the outstanding debt to the Fund is almost certainly dwarfed by the volume of short-term debts to other central banks. The details of these central-bank swaps (which can normally be terminated with only three months' notice, at least in theory) are never published, except in the form of unconfirmed rumors from Basel or in carefully planted leaks in Le Monde in Paris; but it is probable that at the end of 1968 they amounted to at least 4.8 billion dollars, and the total was almost inevitably increased substantially in the wake of the speculative rush for Deutschemarks in the spring of 1969. If it is recalled that at the end of 1968 Britain's foreign-exchange reserves amounted to just over 2.4 billion dollars, while the potentially volatile sterling balances, including the liabilities both to governments and to private institutions, totaled 8.9 billion dollars, with sterling-area central banks alone accounting for 3.9 billion dollars, then it is easy to understand the profound weakness of the pound as a reserve currency.

## DE GAULLE TURNS ON THE POUND

As far as General de Gaulle was concerned, however, the pound enjoyed special (and undeserved) privileges because it was a reserve currency, and as such it symbolized the economic domination of the "Anglo-Saxons." It did not matter that the privileges were illusory (apart from Britain's disproportionately large quota and voting strength in the IMF), while the disadvantages were only too real. It did not matter that the French franc was itself, in a small way, a reserve currency, in the sense that it was employed in France's former colonies in Africa. It did not even matter that the French, like the other European countries, refused to allow their currency to be used as a reserve by major trading nations, because they could see all the disadvantages. None of this counted for de Gaulle in comparison with the symbolic privileges enjoyed by Britain, and when his 1965 campaign in favor of a return to the gold standard failed to bring the dollar crashing down, he switched his attentions to the pound.

Anything which undermined the pound was liable to put additional pressure on the dollar, not least because the United States was so heavily committed through swaps and other credits to keeping the pound afloat. But de Gaulle's long-standing hostility to Britain was not based solely on the aims of his international monetary policy. He regarded Britain as little more than the vassal of the United States, meekly following Washington's orders and anxiously extracting as many compensating benefits as possible. During the 1961–1963 negotiations on British membership of the European Community, it was a classic gibe of French propaganda that Britain was only America's Trojan horse, whose assigned aim was to destroy the Community from within. The United States shared far more of its military secrets with Britain than with any other member of NATO and had done its best to prevent France from building up its independent nuclear *force de frappe*. After the Polaris agreement at Nassau between Macmillan and Kennedy, de Gaulle's hostility to the negotiations in Brussels hardened into absolute veto.

How far this assessment of the Anglo-American relationship was fair, or indeed how far it really reflected de Gaulle's attitude, is neither here nor there. It was certainly given color by statements and behavior of both London and Washington. On the other hand, he may well have feared that Britain would prove too powerful inside the Common Market, not merely through her links with the United States, but in her own right, and would prove to be a serious rival to France for the leadership of Europe. But whatever the mixture of de Gaulle's motives, the incontrovertible fact is that French policy was consistently directed against Britain, both in monetary and in other political fields.

For three years after the French veto of January, 1963, relations between Paris and London were strained but comparatively calm. The situation got suddenly much worse in the early months of

1966, however. When General de Gaulle announced France's withdrawal from NATO, Britain took the lead in rallying the remaining members of the Alliance against France. Though France had decided to withdraw from the military organization, she remained a member of the Alliance and continued to attend meetings of the political council of NATO in Paris. But for a while at least Frenchmen at the Porte Dauphine headquarters near the Bois de Boulogne were regarded as pariahs by the other NATO members, and the responsibility for this atmosphere of hostile confrontation probably lay as much with the cheerleading efforts of the British as with the neutralist policies of the French.

General de Gaulle could not work on the pound in the same way as he had worked on the dollar, since the decision not to hold sterling in the French reserves had already been taken a quarter of a century earlier, and there were therefore virtually no pounds at the Banque de France to sell off. What he could do was to refuse to provide any French help when Britain got into economic difficulties and to conduct a full-scale propaganda campaign against the pound.

In some ways it is surprising that he waited so long before attacking sterling directly. The French seriously considered raising objections to the reserve role of the pound during the 1961–1963 negotiations for British membership of the Common Market, on the grounds that this would give Britain inequitable privileges against the other members of the Community. But finally they decided not to make an issue of it. The reasons for this decision are still not clear, but they must have been aware that a discussion of the sterling area would expose them to demands from the Five and from Britain that there should also be discussion of the franc zone. Like the sterling area, the franc zone was a monetary relic from the age of empire; the difference between them was that, while the sterling area was a historical accident which continued in operation because there was no easy way of getting rid of it, the franc zone was consistently employed by Paris as a means of maintaining its influence over its former dependencies in Africa. Perhaps British governments would not have been averse to making use of the sterling area in the same way as France used the franc zone if this had been possible; but while the franc-zone countries were small and economically weak in relation to France, Britain had become economically weak in relation to the sterling area.

It is also slightly surprising that France continued to participate in loans and credits to Britain, even after General de Gaulle launched his campaign against the reserve-currency system at the beginning of 1965. One possible explanation, as we have mentioned, is that while the French resented the privileged position of the reserve currencies, they were aware not only that the sterling area was a very mixed blessing for Britain but also that France's economic strength might not prove to be very permanent. Britain's balance-of-payments difficulties were magnified (though not created) by the existence of the sterling balances, and there were advantages for France in seeing things stay that way. At the same time, France had only recently started to remove its traditional barriers against imports in the harsher environment of the Common Market, and there were (and still are) many Frenchmen who feared that French industry might have great difficulty in facing up to international competition. Despite the apparent weaknesses of the British economy, the United Kingdom had a long history of industrial development and international trade, and might prove a much more dangerous competitor for France if it were forced to take really drastic steps to put its house in order. "Temporary" loans made it possible for the British to put off that evil day.

## THEORY AND PRACTICE:
## THE ART OF THE POSSIBLE

But one should beware of putting too much faith in simple explanations for the course of French diplomatic policy under de Gaulle. The broad political targets he was aiming at were generally pretty clear to all concerned, but he tended to leave the handling and choice of tactics to his ministers and experts. During the 1961–1963 negotiations they knew that he was not enthusiastic about the idea of British membership, but there was evidently a considerable degree of doubt over whether he attached more importance to keeping Britain out or to using the British negotiations as a bargaining tool for strengthening France's position in the Community. Michel Debré, who was not merely one of de Gaulle's most unconditional followers but also Prime Minister until the middle of 1962, encouraged the French negotiating delegation to make sure that the British negotiations were successful. There is no doubt that the French also used the British negotiations as a lever for extracting concessions from the Five on a common agricultural policy in the Community, and did their best to screw the highest possible price out of the British. But it was not clear, until just before the veto, that de Gaulle was not prepared to have Britain in at any price; indeed, Edward Heath, Britain's chief negotiator, received personal assurances from French ministers that there would be no political veto, only a matter of weeks before the political veto was actually pronounced. The British saw this as an example of characteristic French perfidy; in reality it was largely a demonstration of the fact that even the French government received its instructions from de Gaulle only one page at a time.

This element of ambiguity and confusion was a constant feature of French diplomacy under de Gaulle. The outside world, and France's antagonists in particular, could never be sure what the French would actually do next, and quite frequently it was apparent that the French ministers and diplomats were themselves uncertain how the were expected to act, or how they should translate the lofty generalizations delivered at the General's press conferences into detailed negotiating briefs.

But it was most apparent in the long, drawn-out monetary controversy. That de Gaulle was not himself an expert in international monetary affairs hardly needs repeating, and his quasi-idolatrous praise for the virtues of gold was clearly based more on emotional nostalgia than on reason. When it came to negotiating with other countries, therefore, the French technicians were in considerable difficulties, for they could never know just how literally they were to take de Gaulle's demand for a return to the (or rather "a") gold standard. According to the most extreme interpretation, gold would become the only form of international reserve asset. But since this would mean the elimination of dollars and pounds from reserves, there would be a massive reduction in total official monetary assets; therefore the logical way of ensuring that gold was sufficient to meet these liquidity needs would be to increase its price substantially, say, from thirty-five to seventy dollars an ounce, or even more.

As an end result, such a return to a gold-based system would have the merit of reducing the monetary predominance of the dollar, at least in theory. But it would also have major drawbacks. Recurrent devaluations and Continental wars have encouraged the habit of gold hoarding in France, and though no one has any real idea how much is now hidden in rural mattresses, it is probably on the order of six billion dollars, give or take a very wide margin of error. To double the price of gold would inevitably bring a substantial proportion of this gold hoard onto the market, and the resulting increase in domestic liquidity would give rise to a massive surge of inflation in France. The monetary stability which had been one of the primary objects of de Gaulle's economic policy would thus be swept away, and with it, no doubt, a large part of the gold and foreign-exchange reserves which had enabled France to play an independent role.

Most important of all, however, was the fact that there was absolutely no chance whatever of being able to secure an international agreement on a return to the gold standard. The French were free to behave as though the gold standard had been restored—that is to say, they were free to make all official payments and receipts in gold, and that is the policy they claimed to be following in 1965. But this solitary stand could not achieve the purpose of undermining the American position to any significant extent unless other surplus countries could be persuaded to follow the French example. It became clear, in the course of 1965, that de Gaulle's sensational gesture was not going to bring the dollar-pound system down in ruins, and the French had to resort once more to negotiations.

Now, that art of negotiating, like politics, is the art of the possible, and it makes little sense for a negotiating delegation to propose a course of action which has absolutely no appeal for the other delegations sitting around the table. Those French officials who actually had to deal with other governments, and who were charged with the task of achieving a result which would fit in with General de Gaulle's underlying political aims, were naturally placed in a most difficult position. They were careful never to say outright that they wanted an increase in the price of gold, but they encouraged widespread uncertainty over their real intentions by perpetually emphasizing the importance of gold in one way or another. For a long period, running into years, they made use of an apparently extreme position on the role of gold as a way of preventing any progress in the negotiations. Some of them may sincerely have believed France had a mission to save the world from itself. But once it became clear that they could not indefinitely prevent any progress from being made, and that unless they were prepared to be more flexible the rest of the world would reach an agreement without them, their tactic swung around from pure negativism to bargaining.

This switch of emphasis did not, of course, take place overnight. There were violent oscillations in the terms of public pronouncements by General de Gaulle and his ministers, and even in the final stages of the international negotiations there were moments when the French appeared to have reverted to their original posture of total negativism. But inside the negotiation room, the French did progressively move from stalling to bargaining, and the change took place during 1966.

## THE DEVALUATION OF THE POUND

It is no accident that 1966 was also the year in which the French started stepping up their pressure on the pound. The confrontation over the French withdrawal from NATO no doubt helped to precipitate a more actively hostile attitude toward Britain, but the real reason was the evolution of international monetary affairs. The French, having failed to bring down the dollar directly with their gold tactics, now found themselves forced to take seriously the danger that the other rich countries would reach an agreement on a reform of the monetary system without them. But they still hoped to be able to strengthen their negotiating position by shaking the pound.

The first shot in the French campaign against sterling came in the autumn of 1965. For several years France had contributed substantial sums to various international support operations for Britain, either in the form of short-term credits negotiated between central banks through the Bank for International Settlements at Basel or in the form of medium-term loans under the General Arrangements to Borrow through the International Monetary Fund. But when Britain ran into yet another foreign-exchange crisis in the autumn of 1965, France refused to help, and the central-bank credits which were set up on September 10 (for about one billion dollars) did not include any French participation.

The political significance of the French abstention was heightened by the nature of credits as a central-bank operation, and not as a political arrangement between governments. This distinction may seem unreal, since most central banks are nowadays directly controlled by their governments. Historically, however, central banks have enjoyed a considerable degree of autonomy from the political centers of power, and a few (like those of the United States, Germany, and Japan) are still extraordinarily independent. Even those which have effectively lost their independence still tend to talk and behave as though they had not. Leslie O'Brien, the governor of the Bank of England, does not in practice have anything like the same autonomy as his German counterpart, but he still feels free to make public speeches criticizing the government's economic policy. In international monetary negotiations it is quite usual for national delegations to have two top spokesmen—one from the Treasury or Finance Ministry, and one from the central bank—and it is not uncommon to find that they adopt perceptibly different lines; the banker will often speak with the authority of a semi-independent institution, but the Finance Ministry official will always be looking over his shoulder for instructions from his political masters.

Moreover, the central-banking world is one where international cooperation is always highly valued, and sometimes indispensable. The central banks have the task of stabilizing the foreign-exchange markets at the levels registered with the IMF, and though in theory each country has sole responsibility for making sure that its own exchange rate does not get out of line with its official parity, when speculative pressures really start building up it may well be necessary for a number of central banks to concert their buying and selling of foreign exchange. In the past ten years this habit of cooperation has been systematized in a massive network of regular swap standby arrangements, as explained earlier, and the regular monthly meetings in Basel have fostered an atmosphere of central-bankerly camaraderie which is not normally found at the less frequent encounters between Finance Ministry officials.

The abstention of the Banque de France from the September, 1965, package was taken as a shocking repudiation of this central-banking freemasonry, not only in Britain but also elsewhere. Now, the corollary of informal camaraderie and of coordinated operations in the foreign-exchange markets is secrecy, and central banks almost never publish their arrangements, let alone explain them. But the unofficial explanation which leaked out was that France considered the British balance of payments to have been in deficit for far too long already, and that a new international support package for the pound would merely encourage the British government to postpone any decisive improvement in its economic policies.

The following year, however, when yet another international loan package was set up for Britain, the Banque de France did extend a credit to the United Kingdom. This package set a major precedent, for it marked the beginning of the end of the pound as a reserve currency. Recognizing that Britain's reserve functions were an additional burden for an economy in difficulties, the central bankers specified that the one billion dollars in swaps they were offering was to be used to relieve pressure on the pound arising from fluctuations in the sterling balances, but not to finance Britain's own balance-of-payments deficit. In other words, the central-banking world was virtually endorsing the French view that Britain's payments deficits had gone on far too long.

The French did not participate in this joint arrangement, which was set up through the BIS in June, 1966, since participation would have implied not only an endorsement of the reserve-currency system as such, but also a readiness to take over some of the responsibility for keeping the system afloat. But the Banque de France did make available an entirely separate and parallel credit of one hundred million dollars, without any limitation on how it was to be used. The irony of this was that the price of making a gesture to repudiate sterling's reserve role was a credit which could be used to finance Britain's own deficit—a reversal of the position adopted nine months earlier. In reality it is not always easy to draw a hard and fast line between Britain's own payments balance and the impact of it on the sterling balances, and it may seem silly of the French to take so much trouble to make a political gesture. But these political gestures, with all their inconsistencies, are the very stuff of which international diplomacy is too often constructed.

The French continued to be inconsistent toward Britain during 1966. After the end of their boycott of the Common Market institutions in Brussels, they claimed to have won a major victory over their five partners, and senior officials at the French Foreign Ministry began predicting that Britain might be allowed to join the Community. These friendly noises were never publicly endorsed by the government, and may have been no more than unauthorized kite-flying. But when Georges Pompidou, the French Prime Minister, visited London during the summer of 1966, he put out discreet feelers in private talks with the British government for closer links between the two countries.

But he appeared to be playing a double game. For in public—perhaps primarily for the consumption of General de Gaulle back in Paris—he made a number of speeches which could only be read as recommending a devaluation of the pound. He did not put it quite so crudely, of course; French diplomacy is often brutal, but seldom crude. But his repeated comparisons between the present situation of the United Kingdom and that of France in 1958, when the franc was devalued, left no room for any other interpretation. At the same time, the French press was full of articles on the same theme. It was perfectly legitimate to believe that the pound's problems could be solved only by devaluation, and indeed, many reasonable people felt that it should have been devalued at the end of 1964, when the Labor government came to power. But it was peculiar, to say the least, for a foreign statesman to say so out loud while he was a guest of Britain, and the wave of articles in the French press suggested a carefully orchestrated campaign.

Now, France had no real interest in seeing the pound devalued. It would improve Britain's competitive position vis-à-vis other countries, France included, and it might solve Britain's economic difficulties and might thus remove one of the major strains on the international monetary system. But so long as London and Washington appeared determined to avert a sterling devaluation, the

French propaganda campaign against the pound would whip up speculation, undermine confidence in the monetary system, and cause major losses to the British reserves. Devaluation, when it finally came, would look like a bitter blow to British prestige and would feel like balm on the smarting resentments of General de Gaulle.

## PARIS VERSUS THE CITY

Loyal Gaullists had long resented the preeminence of London as a financial center, and their resentment was heightened by the fact that the City remained strong even though the British economy as a whole was weak. Paris, by contrast, remained only a second-line financial center, even though France was politically and economically strong. The weakness of Paris was partly the result of an old-fashioned banking system but even more the result of a deeply ingrained tradition of state supervision, control, and interference in all forms of economic activity, which made it difficult for a capital market to operate freely.

Michel Debré, who took over from Giscard d'Estaing as Finance Minister at the beginning of 1966, made no secret of his ambitions to turn Paris into Europe's leading financial center. To this end he removed a number of controls on the movement of gold and foreign exchange into and out of France at the end of January, 1967, despite the fact that the French gold and foreign-exchange reserves were at that moment declining. At the same time, he pressed France's partners in the Common Market for joint measures to promote the creation of a European capital market, in the clear belief that the Community would overtake London in finances, and that Paris would play the leading role in the Community. There was nothing foolish about Debré's proposals, which were based on the idea of harmonizing withholding taxes on dividends throughout the Community. But he spent too much energy in attacking the tiny grand duchy of Luxembourg for having adopted the status of a tax haven and for thus being in a position to attract large numbers of foreign, and particularly American, companies. Secondly, the liberalization measures adopted in France had not gone nearly far enough to make France an effective capital market, for while most types of gold and foreign-exchange movement had been freed, foreign borrowing and foreign investment in France were still strictly controlled, and the state had done nothing to relax its grip on domestic monetary affairs. And thirdly, any proposals coming from France were bound to be regarded with the greatest suspicion by her five partners in the aftermath of General de Gaulle's 1965 attempt to break the Rome Treaty, the Common Market's constitution. Michel Debré may have believed that he was adopting a plausible European posture, but his hostility to everything which placed the Community interest above that of France was too sincere, too passionate, and too familiar to be concealed by fair words. It was therefore inevitable that his proposals should fall on deaf ears. In any case, within little over a year France had been forced by the May Revolution to revert once more to strict exchange controls, and Debré's ambitions of making Paris into Europe's leading financial center had to be indefinitely postponed.

In the meantime, however, General de Gaulle had pressing reasons for stepping up the attack on sterling and its role in the international monetary system. By the beginning of 1967 Britain was clearly on the point of renewing its application for membership of the European Community. Prime Minister Harold Wilson and the current Foreign Secretary, George Brown, were embarked on a pilgrimage around the six capitals to sound out the reactions of the governments, to get some idea of the topics that would have to be negotiated, and above all to convince the Europeans that the Labor government really had been converted to the idea of European integration, which it had so opposed at the time of the Rome Treaty.

In retrospect, the British's government's European campaign can be seen to have been a hopeless enterprise, but this was not obvious at the time. No one doubted that General de Gaulle was still inexpressibly hostile to the admission of the British or that he had no sympathy for Harold Wilson and his left-wing government. But there were those in London (and, though to a lesser extent, on the Continent as well) who believed that there was a chance of success. General de Gaulle could be counted on to raise the maximum number of obstacles, but it seemed (according to this view) that the Five would not let him get away with a second outright veto; but in reality this assessment proved altogether too sanguine, and before the year was out General de Gaulle had imposed another veto without attracting any serious retaliatory action from the Five. But with hindsight, one can argue that the 1967 British bid, though apparently sterile in itself, had important and constructive long-term implications for the Community. The cumulative effect of the second French veto damaged irreparably General de Gaulle's claim to represent the interests of the Community, endowed the question of British membership with the significance of an absolutely fundamental principle for the Common Market, and may to some extent have contributed to General de Gaulle's defeat in the 1969 referendum in France.

This takes us ahead of the story, however. From the start, French opposition to British membership took the form of economic and monetary objections, and as 1967 wore on it was these objections which hardened into an absolute veto. When Wilson and Brown visited Paris in January, as part of their European pilgrimage, the French government made it clear that it had serious reservations about the compatibility of sterling's reserve role with British membership of the Community. In May, after Britain had formally renewed its application for membership negotiations, the French again raised their objections to sterling's reserve role and argued that the British government showed no signs of wanting to get rid of it. The 1966 Basel arrangements (for protecting Britain against fluctuations in the sterling balances) had been proposed by the Dutch, and only reluctantly accepted by the British Treasury. And at every three-monthly renewal date, the British continued to talk as though the arrangements were a temporary stopgap to tide the pound over a little local difficulty, and not the first step toward a long-term solution.

The dilemma for the British was that no long-term solution would be easy, and none could be undertaken by Britain alone. If the United Kingdom was to be relieved of the burden of the sterling balances, then it would have to be taken over by someone else—the IMF, for example, or a group of rich countries. It might be possible to negotiate with the sterling-area governments to have their sterling assets transferred elsewhere, but it would be a great deal more difficult to do the same for the foreign individuals who owned British government stock. Worst of all, a funding operation of this sort would actually mean that Britain would have to ask for a massive international long-term loan to replace the sterling balances. The rules of the IMF do not allow it to give loans for more than five years, and none of the rich countries was in any obvious hurry to participate in such a loan. And even if the balances could be transferred and a loan secured, Britain would be faced with the herculean task of paying off the loan. It seemed easier to leave the balances where they were and hope that the problem would go away.

Partly because of the difficulties of finding a solution, therefore, but partly also because some retarded British politicians quite unreasonably regarded the reserve role of sterling as a national status symbol, the standard British line had been that there was no need to tamper with the system. Once Britain got back into payments surplus, the argument went, confidence in the pound would be restored, and there would no longer be any need to fear a flight of the sterling balances from London.

The trouble with this argument was that the promised surplus was always around the next corner but three, and in the meantime the balance of payments was deteriorating. The pound was under heavy suspicion, and while it was unfriendly of the French to say so out loud, there was evidently a possibility that it might have to be devalued. Devaluation is always a loaded political issue, because it seems to imply that the government has frittered away the nation's wealth, but in Britain's case it was doubly political: having accepted the role of international banker, British governments felt inhibited from devaluing, since this would seem a betrayal of the trust placed in the pound by foreign countries. In fact the overseas sterling countries were more than compensated for the risk they ran by the high rate of interest they earned. But the Labor government, which should perhaps have devalued as soon as it came to power in 1964, kept on putting off the evil day, and only made the British situation worse by borrowing more heavily abroad from non-sterling countries. These extra foreign debts were not labeled in pounds, and their weight would automatically be increased the day that devaluation became unavoidable.

## STERLING AND THE COMMON MARKET

The French hammered away at the weakness of sterling, and once it became clear that Britain's Common Market application might stand or fall on this issue, the British Chancellor of the Exchequer, James Callaghan, was forced to adopt a slightly more realistic line. In May, 1967, he announced in the House of Commons that the government was ready to consider a change in the role of the pound, but he argued that any solution must take place on a broadly international basis, rather than in a Community context. In other words, while he was prepared to admit that sterling did pose a problem, he was not prepared to admit that the problem was of particular concern to Britain's future partners in the European Economic Community, or that it needed to be negotiated with them.

This was characteristically shortsighted. France was not the only member of the Community to raise doubts over the sterling issue, even if it was the only one to do so aggressively. The Italians, in particular, had long argued in favor of a funding operation which would relieve Britain of the sterling burden—and they had been rudely rebuffed by London on each occasion. The other members were uneasy at the prospect that Britain's economic difficulties would disrupt the Common Market, and they were clearly dissatisfied by bland British assurances that there was no problem.

As the months passed, it became obvious that Callaghan would have to go further, and at the annual meeting of the IMF in Rio de Janeiro in September, 1967, he started to fish for offers from the Community to help over the sterling problem. By that time it was too late, however, for the Common Market Commission soon gave the French a virtually cast-iron excuse to pronounce the veto.

As the executive arm of the Community, independent of the six member states, the Commission had been instructed to prepare a report on the British membership application. The Five had failed to persuade the French to agree to the opening of negotiations with the British, and they believed that the Commission's report would be bound to put additional pressure on the French. They believed the Commission had no option but to echo the Rome Treaty, which says that the Community shall be open to other European countries which wish to join. They believed the Commission would argue that the problems of British entry could be solved by negotiations. And they believed, therefore, that the Commission would inevitably recommend the opening of negotiations.

On all three points, the expectations of the Five proved correct. But they failed to take account of the fact that the commissioner in charge of economic and financial affairs was a Frenchman, Raymond Barre, who had only recently arrived from Paris. Legally, the Commission is an independent institution, and the body of fourteen commissioners who head it are bound by oath not to take instructions from any national government. There is no evidence that Raymond Barre actually received any explicit instructions from Paris; it is merely a curious coincidence that the chapter on the British economic and monetary situation which appeared in the Commission's report, and which was naturally prepared by Raymond Barre's department, bore an uncanny resemblance to the known views of the French government.

Barre's assessment of the British economy was the only harsh element in the report, but it served French interests ideally. It said that Britain could not be a member of the Community while sterling remained a reserve currency, and it came as near to recommending devaluation as it is possible to do without actually using the word.

When the report was submitted to the Council of Ministers of the Six in October, 1967, the French Foreign Minister, Maurice Couve de Murville, decided to bring matters to a head. At the first debate in Luxembourg on October 23, he told the other members of the Council of Ministers that France would not agree to negotiations with Britain until the British balance of payments had been restored to surplus and the reserve role of sterling had been abandoned. With an additional reference to the economic measures taken by France in 1958, he implied once more that the pound ought to be devalued.

The French government's open campaign against the pound was an unprecedented break with tradition, and for that reason its impact was the more powerful. On most topics outspokenness has now become familiar, and on some it is fashionable to tell and show all. On international monetary matters, however, privacy and hypocrisy are still normal practice. It may be obvious that a currency is due for devaluation, but to say so out loud is generally considered to be an act of deliberate hostility. No one, not even an economist, can foresee the future, and some are unable to explain the past; it is therefore conceivable that a currency's difficulties may prove to be temporary, without devaluation being necessary. But since these difficulties are very largely composed of the expectations of the market as to the future, a government which predicts or advocates a devaluation can only be making it more likely. Even in very private international meetings, Finance Ministry officials from one country seldom if ever tell their foreign colleagues anything like the whole truth; by contrast, nothing that is said in the Council of Ministers of the Six ever remains secret for very long, and on this occasion Couve de Murville personally retailed the French argument to journalists waiting outside.

Of course, customs change, and in monetary affairs conventional standards of conduct have been altered out of all recognition by the French propaganda technique. Up to and including 1967, it was almost unheard of for a British newspaper openly to discuss the pros and cons of a sterling devaluation. Since then, and to a large extent as a result of the French example, this sort of patriotic modesty has disappeared—no doubt a healthy development. But for a government to indulge in this sort of plain speaking is another matter, and the French have had their tactics turned against them: when Franz-Josef Strauss, German Finance Minister, predicted in November, 1968, that the French franc was likely to be devalued, he helped to accelerate the flight of money out of France.

The French pursued their campaign with enthusiasm. In October, 1967, *Le Monde* reported that Britain was unable to meet its debt repayments to the International Monetary Fund. On November 13, after Britain had secured 250 million dollars in credits through the Bank for International Settlements to meet these debt payments (having asked for one billion dollars), *Le Monde* reported that Britain's outstanding short-term-debt liabilities had risen to two billion dollars in the previous four months.

### THE FINAL STRUGGLE

By this stage devaluation of the pound had become virtually certain, though the British government still struggled to hold the line until the very last moment. Sterling had been under heavy pressure from speculators for several months, and there were massive losses from the reserves. Three days after securing the 250-million-dollar central-bank credits in Basel, Britain was reported from Paris (by the BBC this time, not *Le Monde*) to be negotiating with the Group of Ten for a very much larger medium-term advance from the IMF. The French no longer needed to keep up the pressure through the press, for James Callaghan, British Chancellor of the Exchequer, only made matters worse by refusing, when questioned in the House of Commons, either to deny or to confirm that negotiations were taking place. All that the French needed to do to maximize the difficulties of the pound was to slow down agreement on a loan—and to place obstacles in the path of a sterling devaluation. As it so happened, the Bank of England increased its own difficulties by its tactics in the foreign-exchange market. For it was not merely fulfilling its normal IMF obligations by supporting the pound in day-to-day transactions, but was also supporting it, quite unnecessarily, in the forward market—that is, it was undertaking to sell dollars against pounds at or near the $2.80 rate one, two, or three months ahead. This meant that it was still losing reserves after devaluation at the old exchange rate, when these contracts fell due. The amazing thing is that the Bank continued to make these forward contracts right up to the moment when it was glaringly obvious that the pound was about to be devalued. (Since November, 1967, however, the Bank of England has prudently stayed out of the forward market.)

For, in fact, the talks in Paris on a loan for Britain were about both issues. The British government, which was virtually obliged to agree to devalue in return for a loan, was anxious to ensure that no other major country would devalue at the same time and thus reduce the improvement in Britain's competitive position. The object of the exercise, therefore, was to set the amount of devaluation while at the same time securing an undertaking from the other members of the Group of Ten that they would keep their own currencies at the same level. Early in the proceedings eight of the other members gave such assurances on condition that the pound was not devalued by more than fifteen percent. But the French refused to make any such promise, demanded tough conditions for the loan, and spread rumors that the pound would be devalued by thirty percent.

To some extent the French were genuinely motivated by anxieties about their own competitive position. Their balance of payments was no longer as strong as it had been, and they feared that an improvement in Britain's balance of payments would be reflected in a deterioration in their own balance. When the Monetary Committee of the Common Market met on the Saturday afternoon, November 23, the French told their partners that they planned to devalue by five percent if Britain devalued by fifteen percent, and argued that all the Common Market countries should follow suit. The Five retorted that they had no need to devalue, and that a five-percent cut (either by France or all six Common Market countries) would be too small to make any useful difference.

But the real object of the French tactic was to delay a British devaluation, for every day that passed without a decision being announced produced a further drain on the British reserves. Such figures are never published, but it is quite possible that the three-day talks in Paris cost the Bank of England over five hundred million dollars in the foreign-exchange markets. On the Saturday night, however, the British government decided to act without securing an undertaking from Paris, since it was clear that no undertaking would be forthcoming, and announced the devaluation of the pound by just under fifteen percent, from $2.80 to $2.40. Within a few days a 1.4-billion-dollar standby credit with the IMF had been arranged—though the French continued to spread rumors that the credit was running into serious difficulties.

This was the first time ever that a currency devaluation had been internationally negotiated, and it was not a reassuring experience. In principle all countries are obliged to consult the Fund when they change their parities, and Common Market countries are obliged to consult each other. But on every previous occasion the consultations had been minimal, since governments

were concerned to maintain the greatest secrecy about any imminent change in their exchange rates, so as to forestall the speculators. It was hardly surprising that when the French came to devalue in 1969 they consulted neither the Fund nor their Common
Market partners; they had too much reason to know how damaging the process of consultation could be.

After the sterling devaluation, it began to look as though a large
number of sterling-area countries would put further pressure on
the pound by taking their reserve assets out of London, and some
of them hinted publicly that they were thinking of doing so. As
we have explained, the major foreign central banks had extended
a one-billion-dollar credit to Britain in the summer of 1966 precisely for the purpose of meeting any fluctuations in the sterling
balances. But this was far too small an amount to deal with a
wholesale exodus of reserves from London, and it was clear that
moral pressure by the British on the Commonwealth countries
would not be effective for very long. Some of those in the Far
East, in particular, strongly resented Britain's decision to bring its
troops home, thus depriving them of foreign exchange, employ-
ment, and a measure of military security.

Hong Kong was the jumpiest about the value of its London-
based reserves, and in the spring of 1967 the British government
negotiated a special agreement formally guaranteeing them
against another devaluation. But by midsummer a more embrac-
ing arrangement was being discussed to stabilize all the official
sterling balances in London. The major central banks replaced
their short-term one-billion-dollar 1966 credit with a two-billion-
dollar standby which would be available for three years and
which, if drawn upon, would not have to be repaid for ten years.
On its side, Britain concluded an agreement with all the overseas
sterling-area countries which guaranteed the dollar value of ninety
percent of their sterling reserves.

This agreement might be thought to make Britain's reserve-
currency role more permanent. In fact, it was recognized in London that the British economy was no longer strong enough to
bear the cost of any significant reduction in the sterling balances,
and that the Basel agreement was a first step toward some more
permanent arrangement which would transfer the responsibility
elsewhere. For the Commonwealth countries the Basel plan was

virtually ideal, for it gave them not only a guarantee of value but also the advantage of earning high British interest rates, and so long as the agreement remained in force they would have little reason to put their money any other place. But the agreement runs out in September, 1971, when it will either have to be renewed or else taken a step further.

Just what this step should be is not at all clear. There have been frequent suggestions that the sterling liabilities should be handed over to the IMF, and occasionally (by the British) that they should be transferred to the European Community as the first step toward the creation of a European reserve currency. The first suggestion has not been accepted widely enough for a fundamental revision of the Fund rules to be negotiated seriously, and the second has been received rather badly in Europe, where it is regarded as an offer to exchange Britain's debts for the assets of the Common Market countries.

There is little doubt, however, that some more permanent solution must be found to all of Britain's liabilities, if only to put them on a more realistic basis. At present Britain is saddled with enormous debts to foreign central banks, which are theoretically valid for only three months at a time. In practice the foreign central banks know that Britain cannot pay them back in the near future, so the credits are just rolled over every three months. Most central banks are not allowed to make loans which are explicitly long-term, but the convention that the loans to Britain are short-term is just a polite fiction. Everybody knows this, but nobody is prepared to face facts and convert them into long-term debts with a realistic repayment schedule. Yet it is also true that the problem has been substantially alleviated by the massive reversal in the British payments balance since mid-1969. It is probable that during 1969 Britain paid off something like 2.5 billion dollars of short-term debts to central banks.

The French did not rest content with their performance over the sterling devaluation. Early the following week *Le Monde* (presumably on the basis of information supplied by the government) revealed that France had backed out of its undertaking to help stabilize the free price of gold in the London market; two days later it reported that Britain's short-term debts had risen to four billion dollars. Throughout the week following the sterling announcement the French press generally was full of reports that Britain was meeting serious difficulties in setting up its 1.4-billion-dollar standby with the IMF, that the devaluation was doomed to failure, and that an increase in the price of gold was imminent.

It was almost inevitable that this barrage from the French press would trigger off a new wave of speculation. In the first place, the sterling devaluation had just taken place in circumstances of such tension and disorder that the foreign-exchange markets were on tenterhooks, and the British economy was obviously in such serious trouble that no one could believe that its difficulties would be easily or rapidly resolved by a change in the parity alone. Secondly, and more important, the defection of France from the

# CHAPTER 6

# The Gold Rush

Gold Pool appeared to make it very much more likely that the gold price would have to be increased above its official level of thirty-five dollars an ounce. As it was, the months immediately preceding the sterling devaluation had witnessed a substantial wave of gold buying as the speculators moved out of pounds, and the *Le Monde* story triggered off an even bigger wave. It was not entirely surprising that Henry Fowler, the U.S. Secretary of the Treasury, should have remarked a few days after the sterling devaluation that the dollar was "in the front line"—though it was nevertheless a very foolish thing to say out loud, for it could only add fuel to the flames.

After World War II the London gold market had been kept closed by the authorities because they judged that a free market price, resulting from the play of supply and demand, would be way above the official thirty-five-dollar level. But in 1954, when the price in other centers had dropped back to about thirty-five dollars, the London market was again opened, and for the next few years the price remained comparatively stable at around this level, without any help from the authorities.

But in the late 1950's, when the American balance of payments started to move into deficit, the operators on the gold market started to have doubts about the capacity of the United States to maintain the thirty-five-dollar price, and the free price started to move up in London. At this early stage, movements in the London price were very modest, but when it went up to forty dollars in October, 1960, the United States and Britain together decided to move in to stabilize the price. A year later they had persuaded six other countries—France, Germany, Italy, Switzerland, Holland, and Belgium—to join them; these eight countries together formed the so-called Gold Pool, which operated from the autumn of 1961 to the spring of 1968.

## THE GOLD POOL

The principle of the Gold Pool was that the Bank of England, as the agent for the other seven central banks, would buy when the price fell, and sell when it rose, and that the eight countries together would share in the profits or losses of the operation according to previously fixed proportions. The U.S. share was fifty percent, that of Britain, France, and Italy a bit more than nine percent each, that of Germany (as a symbol of its stronger reserve position) about eleven percent, and that of the three smaller countries about 3.5 percent each.

To begin with, the system worked smoothly, and the Gold Pool countries made a steady profit on the operation, in the sense that they were able to buy more gold at thirty-five dollars an ounce than they needed to sell. There was a steady supply of new gold coming onto the market of between 1.2 billion and 1.5 billion dollars a year, principally from South Africa, and at the same time the Soviet Union was also a regular seller of gold in amounts which varied between 200 million and 550 million dollars a year.

Private demand also remained pretty steady during most of the early 1960's, in the region of one billion to 1.1 billion dollars, and while there is no way of telling how much of this was bought for speculative purposes and how much for industrial and artistic requirements, such as jewelry, dentistry, and electronics, it is probable that until General de Gaulle launched his campaign in favor of the gold standard most of the demand was industrial and artistic.

As a result, the eight central banks were able to take what was left, which effectively meant that official gold holdings by the Western central banks went up every year in varying amounts, from 220 million to 840 million dollars. In 1965, however, private demand shot up to over 1.7 billion dollars as a result of de Gaulle's campaign, and very much less than usual was left for the governments to take. In 1966 the total volume of private demand eased off again to 1.5 billion dollars, but since the Soviet Union abruptly ceased to sell any gold on the London market, there was an actual fall in official monetary stocks of gold of forty-five million dollars. General de Gaulle had certainly done his best to get on friendly terms with the Soviet Union, and it is possible that Moscow's decision to suspend its gold sales was influenced either by the desire to support de Gaulle or by the belief that de Gaulle's campaign really would result in an increase in the official gold price. Evidently Moscow was not yet ready to subscribe to Lenin's dictum that the only "just and educational" use of gold would be as a material for building public lavatories.

General de Gaulle's attack on the dollar and his demand for an increase in the gold price was thus effectively operating through two quite separate channels. On the one hand, France was converting its dollars directly into gold at the Federal Reserve Bank in the United States, and to some extent provoking other countries to follow suit. But at the same time, France was stimulating speculative buying of gold by private individuals (and even by companies) on the London market; the mechanism of the Gold Pool meant that this private demand was causing an additional drain on the gold reserves of the eight participating countries, with the United States bearing half the loss. As a member of the Gold Pool, the Banque de France was also losing gold in 1966 and the first half of 1967. But when it ceased to contribute to the Gold Pool in June of that year, its share in the operation was taken over by the United States—thus further increasing the drain on the U.S. gold stock.

The Johnson administration repeatedly stated its determination to maintain gold's official price of thirty-five dollars an ounce, and in reality it could not be forced to change the price either by General de Gaulle or by the speculators. Washington could at any moment refuse to buy or sell any more gold, and from time to time veiled threats emerged from the administration that this course would be considered if the Europeans did not give up their gold raiding. Alternatively, it could decide to sell every last bar of gold in Fort Knox and simply go off the gold standard; at that point the rest of the world, including the French, would have to choose between taking dollars in payment from the United States or refusing to sell anything to the Americans, and there was no doubt at all which course they would take. Since the United States was, and is, the dominant force on the world scene, both industrially and commercially, no other country could afford to cut its economic links with America. If America remained in deficit, and could pay only in dollars, then the rest of the world would accept dollars.

The United States was reluctant to go to either extreme, however, for it would smack of virtually open monetary war against its European allies, who were still very attached to the convertibility of gold. There was also some danger that the exhaustion of the American gold stock, or the refusal of the United States to sell any more gold in exchange for dollars, would lead the Europeans to set up a new gold bloc which could, over a period of time, lead to greater protectionism against trade with America. Washington was also reluctant to do anything to control the private gold speculation, since this might be seen as an admission that the dollar was no longer "as good as gold." But at the same time, it was essential to do something to turn back the tide, for if the gold losses through the London market continued unchecked, the European central banks might be strongly tempted to join the rush themselves. Until now most of them (apart from France) had been prepared to accept a self-denying ordinance on gold conversion, but they might not be prepared to see what remained of their gold-conversion rights being filched under their noses by private speculators.

The first thing the Americans did in the week after the sterling devaluation was to restate the immutability of the thirty-five-dollar price, and they were backed up a few days later by a similar statement by the other seven members of the Gold Pool. But it is in the nature of speculators not to believe very much of what governments say, and in the last few weeks of 1967 they did not believe anything that governments said. As demand for gold on the London market reached dizzy heights, it was clear that mere words would not cut any ice with the speculators.

Moreover, the speculators had a strong inducement to buy gold, for the American administration was evidently running scared. On December 10, Frederick Deming, Robert Roosa's successor at the U.S. Treasury, attracted international attention by flying to attend a meeting of the Gold Pool countries in Basel. No statement was issued after the meeting—thus further heightening the tension in the bullion markets—but it was subsequently reported that Deming had tried to persuade his partners to step up their support for the Gold Pool by making prior deposits of gold with the Bank of England instead of waiting until the end of each accounting period before settling up. Naturally, Washington denied that it had asked for such gold deposits, for it had been turned down by Holland, Belgium, and Switzerland on the ground that they were obliged to hold gold as backing for their banknote issue. But the widespread impression that the United States no longer trusted its European partners to go on feeding the Gold Pool only served to whip up further speculative pressures. The Gold Pool countries did take some minor steps to hold down speculation, by banning private gold buying on credit, but it was far too late for such tinkering to have any serious impact.

Accordingly, President Johnson announced on January 1 a massive new program to improve the U.S. balance of payments, both on trade and capital accounts. But though this program created a profound impression and pushed American corporations into raising large amounts of capital in Europe, since they could no longer export investment funds from the United States, its impact on the gold market was short-lived.

Speculative demands soon gathered momentum again, and on March 10 the central bankers of the seven Gold Pool countries again met in Basel and issued yet another statement on the unalterability of the thirty-five-dollar price. Once more the bankers were offering only words, unsupported by an action which could make their policy seem both effective and durable in the face of the continuing drain of their reserves, and the speculative pressures swelled once more.

## THE END OF THE GOLD POOL

A week later, on March 16 and 17, the seven central bankers were again hastily convened, this time in Washington, and on this occasion they did announce decisive action. They closed the Gold Pool and shut off the supply of gold from official monetary stocks to private buyers. They claimed, as a totally new doctrine, that there was no need for any further additions to monetary gold held in countries' official reserves, and they announced not merely that they would no longer sell to or buy from the private market, but also that they would not supply gold to countries which did sell on the private market. In other words, their decision was intended to symbolize the fact that gold was no longer the indispensable element in the international monetary system.

At the start this seemed a very precarious game of bluff, and not merely because the Washington decision—which was taken without French participation, because the French were no longer members of the Gold Pool—was immediately denounced by General de Gaulle in Paris. The United States and its allies were effectively telling the gold speculators that they could speculate as they liked, but that they would only be speculating against each other and would no longer be able to drag gold out of the central-bank stocks. So long as the central banks stuck by the Washington agreement, and provided the other countries fell in line too, the speculators would be defeated. But the danger was that the price would rise so high on an unrestricted free market that the solidarity among the central banks would crumble. The primary safeguard against such an eventuality was that all central banks, by habit and instinct, prefer gold to any other form of asset, and though they might be able to make a nice profit by selling gold on the free market, they would probably prefer to hang on to their gold. But it was above all precarious because no one could foresee on March 18 how high the price would actually go on the free market.

Whatever the dangers, however, it had become absolutely imperative to stop the drain of gold from the major central banks. Between the sterling devaluation on November 18, 1967, and the closing of the Gold Pool on March 16, 1968, the seven members of the Gold Pool had lost over three billion dollars' worth of gold, and more than two billion dollars of that loss came in the first two and one-half months of 1968. The Group of Ten was at this time in the throes of the final stages of a negotiation of a wholly new form of reserve asset which would be entirely independent of gold, but none of the members could have afforded to lose more gold at the previous rate.

Yet it was difficult to believe that the Washington meeting had ruled out forever the question of an increase in the official price of gold. The London gold market was kept closed until the end of March, but in Zurich (where the market opened as usual on the Monday morning, March 18, 1968) the price reacted dramatically to the closing of the Gold Pool. It shot up immediately to forty dollars an ounce and then swung erratically between thirty-seven and forty dollars. During April and the first half of May it climbed steadily from about thirty-seven to thirty-nine dollars, and after the outbreak of the student riots and the strikes in France it shot up to nearly forty-three dollars an ounce.

Certainly the odds on a really massive increase in the price shortened considerably when South Africa announced that it would not sell any of its gold production on the free market.

Producer of three-quarters of the free world's gold, South Africa had long chorused the demands of Jacques Rueff for an increase in the official price. By staying out of the free market, the South Africans clearly hoped to be able to drive the price way up and thus crack the solid front of the central banks.

The South African tactic failed to produce the desired result. The gold price never rose even as high as forty-four dollars an ounce, despite the fact that 1968 was an unprecedentedly rich year for speculative panics, with the May Revolution in France and then the rush into Deutschemarks in October–November. (The price in Paris was regularly higher than in London or Zurich because the French market had been sealed off from the rest of the world by exchange controls.) The months passed, and gradually it came to be accepted that the gamble of the Americans and their partners might come off after all. What had started out as a desperate measure began to be reinterpreted as a wise and farsighted step toward the neutralization of gold in the international monetary system. Naturally, General de Gaulle, the South Africans, and the Swiss banks did not think it was a wise and farsighted move, but at this stage in the game they did not hold many of the cards. European central bankers were still strongly attached to the gold, but as we have seen, most of them were firmly opposed to any significant increase in the official price because of the inflationary consequences it could have. If they stuck by their agreement not to buy any more gold from the free market, and if they also carried through their plan to create a new form of reserve asset, the place of gold in the international monetary system would inevitably decline.

It was somewhat surprising that the South African tactic failed. Within eighteen months of the closing of the Gold Pool, the free price had fallen gradually but steadily, despite the fact that total supplies coming onto the market from all sources were less than half the normal level. One possible explanation was that the speculators had tied so much money up in the successive panics of 1968 that they had little spare cash to go on investing in gold; and that as hopes of a rapid increase in the official price evaporated, a great many of them, who had been paying storage costs on their gold purchases, but had of course not been receiving interest, decided to switch into other assets. In the second half of 1968 the

American credit squeeze started pushing interest rates up all over the world, and during the first half of 1969, international interest rates reached unprecedented heights. At one point it became possible to earn as much as thirteen percent a year on Euro-dollars.

Another factor which must also have played a part was that 1968 was a boom year on a large number of stock markets, including Wall Street, London, Tokyo, Sydney—and Johannesburg. A great many investors who might otherwise have been buying gold were doubtless diverted into buying industrial shares, and of course some of them hedged their bets by buying shares in gold-mining companies.

As a long-term investment, gold-mine stocks may be somewhat better than gold bullion, simply because they can produce a current return in the form of dividends. But in the end the attractiveness of gold shares will depend heavily on the price paid for gold on the free market. Until 1968 this price had remained pretty well unchanged at thirty-five dollars an ounce for some thirty years, whereas the costs of mining had of course risen considerably. The combined profits of the South African mines (which produce uranium and other minerals as well as gold) fell in 1966 and 1967, and although only about two percent of South African gold output is actually mined at a loss, the ten largest of the forty-four gold mines account for over two-thirds of the profits. Technological improvements in mining may reduce operating costs, but the long-term prospects for gold shares are bound to depend heavily on the free-market price for gold. If the major central banks do stick by their decision not to buy any more gold from the free market, demand for South African gold will be limited to industrial and artistic users on the one hand, and to speculators on the other. But if the speculators are convinced that the central banks are going to stand firm for a long time to come and that the official price of gold is not going to be increased, then they have very much less reason to speculate on gold. The professional operators in the market seem to have got this message quite early on: whenever the price started moving above forty-one or forty-two dollars in the first half of 1969, it produced a wave of selling orders. For someone who had bought at thirty-five dollars, this was a respectable twenty percent profit (less commission and less storage charges), even though it was not nearly as much as the speculators had originally hoped.

The South African government waged a long campaign first to undermine and then to circumvent the two-tier gold system (one official price and one free price), but all its attempts were systematically blocked by the United States. As far as Washington was concerned, it was essential to keep the free-market price as close as possible to the official price. Since the central banks had stopped supplying gold to the free market, it was essential that gold should be supplied by the only other large source—South Africa. For if the price rose too high, the two-tier system might break down, and the only way of keeping the price down was to keep gold coming into the market.

From the South African point of view, it was important to see the price go right up on the free market, partly because this meant bigger profits for the gold mines and bigger export earnings in the South African balance of payments, but partly because a really high free price might break the two-tier system.

During most of 1968 and 1969 the two governments were eyeball to eyeball in a vast game of bluff. The Americans calculated that the South Africans could not refuse to sell gold on the free market for very long, because this would mean the sacrifice of their principal export and source of foreign exchange. The South Africans calculated that the free price would rise to unheard-of heights and break the two-tier system.

As it turned out, the South Africans were able to put up with the loss of export earnings for most of 1968, because the boom on the South African stock market was pulling in investment funds and thus providing them with foreign exchange. But their refusal to sell on the free market became counterproductive in quite a different way. As the months passed, and the free-market price did not rise to astronomical heights, their unsold stocks of gold at home continued to pile up. It gradually became obvious that South Africa could not sell its accumulated production on the free market without driving the price down, and quite conceivably below thirty-five dollars an ounce, and Pretoria therefore started demanding the right to sell gold to official monetary institutions, such as the central banks and the IMF. Instead of being able to count on a massive increase in the price of gold, the South Africans were having to look for ways of avoiding a reduction in price: the only way of optimizing their position was to be able to sell equally to official and private buyers in whatever proportions would produce the best average return.

The United States rigorously opposed the South African demand, arguing that new gold production was not "monetary" gold, even if the South African government chose to put it into its own gold and foreign-exchange reserves, and could not under the terms of the Washington agreement be sold to central banks. By and large most of the major central banks fell in with Washington's wishes, though three small countries—Portugal, Algeria, and Congo (Kinshasa)—did make discreet purchases of relatively small amounts from South Africa. In other circumstances, no doubt, France would have bought gold, but she was now losing reserves and in no position to do so.

The IMF was a different case, however, for here the South Africans could argue that they had a legal right to sell gold to the Fund if they chose to. The articles of the IMF charter say that any member country can buy foreign currency from the Fund (i.e., sell gold to it) under certain circumstances. The South Africans claimed that their situation satisfied the conditions laid down, and on the whole most of the European countries were inclined to believe that the South Africans had a good case. The Americans argued, predictably enough, that they had no case at all. There is no need to go into the legal pros and cons, for the legal argument was merely the terrain for a political battle. The important point is that the Americans were able to prevent any official price and one free price), but all its attempts were sysdirect South African sales to the Fund between March, 1968, and the end of 1969.

One dodge tried by the South Africans to get around the U.S. veto was to draw on its quota in the Fund, thus securing foreign exchange, and to repay the drawing a few weeks later—in gold. But South Africa's automatic drawing rights were not large enough to solve its gold-stock problem, and though its lack of exports provided a good pretext for making a drawing on the Fund, repeated drawings for the simple purpose of exchanging gold for foreign exchange would certainly have been challenged as an unwarranted distortion of the Fund rules. However, under a subsequent amendment to the IMF rules, the right of member countries to draw on their gold tranche has been made absolute and unchallengeable.

Such back-door methods fall far short of what the South African government wanted, however, and on several occasions it attempted to negotiate a compromise with the United States. But Dr. Nicholaas Diederichs, the South African Finance Minister, made a name for himself as one of the world's worst prophets by repeatedly predicting that an agreement was around the next corner, for all that the Americans were prepared to offer was that South Africa would be allowed to sell its gold to official monetary institutions—whenever the free-market price dropped below thirty-five dollars. It was not until the end of 1969, when the free price of gold had slithered all the way down to thirty-five dollars, that the two countries finally reached agreement—on American terms.

## ZURICH VERSUS LONDON

Pretoria and Washington were not the only antagonists over the marketing of newly mined gold, however; there was also a major struggle between the bullion dealers in London and Zurich. Until the closing of the Gold Pool, London had been unquestionably the major market for wholesale dealings, partly because the Bank of England operated in London, partly because this was the traditional market for South African supplies. All the dealings are handled by five bullion traders (Rothschild's, Samuel Montagu, Mocatta and Goldsmid, Sharps Pixley, and Johnson Matthey), and they conduct the market with a good deal of old-fashioned solemnity. Twice a day the chief bullion dealers assemble in a room at Rothschild's and formally "fix" the price—though subsequent dealings after the fixing may well take place at quite a different price.

Zurich, by contrast, had long been primarily a retail gold center, especially for coins, but its volume had been much lower than London's. But when the Gold Pool was closed, and London lost its automatic monopoly of wholesale trading, the three big Zurich banks made a concerted attempt to capture a much larger share of the market. To some extent they may have succeeded, though since the volume on the London market is never published, it is impossible to tell how large the swing has been. What is clear is that the two markets are closely dependent on each other. The Zurich banks have sometimes claimed that they are the dominant force in bullion dealing and that theirs is the master price. But whenever they have tried to push the price significantly above the level operating in London, they have immediately drawn a wave of selling orders from the London dealers.

Now it is almost certain that South Africa, despite its declared policy of not supplying gold to the free market, did in fact make a number of secret sales. Neither in London nor in Zurich have the dealers admitted that such sales have taken place. But in May, 1969, the price remained virtually immobile at or near $41.50, and it seems probable that during this period the dealers were systematically stabilizing the price at this level (virtually taking over the role of the Gold Pool), partly no doubt by selling from speculators' hoards, but partly too by selling gold supplied for the purpose by South Africa. In any case the IMF calculated in its 1969 Annual Report that in the thirteen months following the closing of the Gold Pool, South Africa sold about eight million ounces on the free market, compared with a normal level of about thirteen million ounces annually.

The difficulty for the Swiss banks in 1968 and 1969 was that no one could be entirely sure any more what was the "normal" level of demand for gold and how much new gold could be sold on the market without driving the price down. Even though the three Zurich banks worked very closely together, they differed in their basic judgment on the supply-and-demand outlook. The Swiss Bank Corporation and the Union Bank of Switzerland tended to be more optimistic, and predicted that South Africa would be able to sell half its output without depressing the price significantly. But the third bank, the Swiss Credit Bank, took a much more cautious view, and calculated that even twenty percent of South Africa's output might be enough to drive the price down. The reason for this degree of difference is that a great many other markets were being distorted by the abnormal strains on the international monetary system, and the gold market might not return to its normal pattern of supply and demand until the crisis in the international monetary system was a good deal nearer a solution. But the fact that the gold price tended to decline gradually during much of 1969, when South Africa was apparently selling slightly less than a quarter of its production, suggests that the cautious assessment of the Swiss Credit Bank was closer to the mark—at least in terms of the prevailing circumstances. By the end of 1969, when the price dropped to thirty-five dollars, the three Zurich banks were bitterly regretting their substantial purchases from South Africa in the spring at well over forty dollars, and the Swiss Credit Bank was reported to be selling its holdings on the sly—to its two partners in the consortium. At the same time, it gradually became apparent that London had regained its former position as the dominant gold market, partly because its dealers could offer a more competitive price, and perhaps also because its judgment was less erratic.

The behavior of the free gold market since March, 1968, does suggest, however, that the arguments in favor of a doubling of the official price are a great deal weaker than Jacques Rueff would have had the world believe. For if the free price does not rise above forty-five dollars an ounce when left to its own devices, there is absolutely no good reason why the official price should be increased to seventy dollars, even if you leave aside the objections of the central bankers to such an inflationary step.

The final act in the South African–American drama came in the closing weeks of 1969, when the London gold price tumbled all the way down to thirty-five dollars and it became apparent that Dr. Diederichs had lost his gamble and could no longer afford to stay in the game. On New Year's Eve the International Monetary Fund announced that an agreement had been reached between the two governments which would allow South Africa to sell gold to the Fund (though not to other central banks) when the free market price fell below thirty-five dollars. This represented a total rejection of everything the South Africans had hoped for, but it did at least give them the negative satisfaction of knowing that they would never get less than the official price for gold (less a small handling and brokerage charge). And because South Africa produces three-quarters of the "free" world's gold, it also provides a comparatively elastic floor under the free market at around thirty-five dollars: if the price went below, South Africa would switch sales from London to the IMF and thus remove the downward pressure on the price. Unlike the Gold Pool, however, the agreement did not guarantee such a price to other sellers, and if the world's hoarders chose to unload their holdings at the same moment, so much the worse for them. The other significant implication of the agreement is that it would channel all new supplies of "monetary" gold to the IMF, which would thus become a monopoly source of official gold holdings. In other words, the IMF has reinforced the managing role which it received in the context of the SDR scheme. The swing of influence from the Fund to the central bankers' club in Basel, which occurred as a result of the multiplication of central-bank loans and swaps in the late 1960's, may be in the process of being reversed.

The deflation of South Africa's gold hopes was rammed home in the weeks following the agreement with Washington. For though the United States had effectively promised a flexible thirty-five-dollar floor for the free market, the speculators remained discouraged. During the first two months of 1970 the London price barely rose above thirty-five dollars by more than a few cents—most of the time it was either right on thirty-five dollars or slightly below—and the South Africans had to take up their option to make sales to the Fund. And this occurred despite the fact that one of the leading gold-mining groups published a long report purporting to *prove* that industrial consumption of gold was already larger than newly mined production, and that therefore the price was bound to rise. Seasoned London dealers have already started to talk of gold as "just another commodity" and though they may be leaping to conclusions somewhat prematurely, that certainly seems to be the way things are going.

The South Africans, and Jacques Rueff, argue that the price of every other product has more than doubled in the past thirty-five years, and that to keep the price of gold unchanged at the level it was given in 1933 is not only unreasonable but unfair. Political liberals would object to a doubling of the gold price on the grounds that it would provide an undeserved windfall to France and the Soviet Union, which have been unfriendly to the United States and its partners in the West, and to South Africa, which pursues an objectionable racist policy at home and exploits oppressed black labor to operate its gold mines. But the economic argument is more telling: if the central banks choose to pay no more than thirty-five dollars an ounce, they are perfectly within their rights to do so, and if the free-market price fails to rise to seventy dollars under its own steam, then there is little justification for pushing it that high artificially.

Gold still remains a valuable commodity. It is comparatively rare, it has a number of properties which make it useful for industry, and it is regarded as beautiful. For these reasons it is bound to go on being employed in certain circumstances as a measure and as a store of value, and it will no doubt continue for many years to play a part in the international monetary system as one of the constituent elements in countries' official reserves. But it also has a large number of drawbacks in any rational monetary system. The total quantity potentially available is limited, and it is laborious and costly to dig out of the ground. Moreover, in its original state it is distributed quite arbitrarily in different countries as a function of geology, without regard for how much is needed at any one time by whom.

# CHAPTER 7

# The Collapse of the Franc, the Rise of the Deutsche-mark

In 1968 the gnawing doubts about the international monetary system in general, and about the dollar in particular, crystallized into even graver fears. On top of the gold rush and sterling devaluation came the collapse of the franc and the rise of the Deutschemark, and most other European currencies were caught in the backwash of the biggest wave of speculative pressures for over twenty years. Countries on both sides of the Atlantic seemed to have lost control of the situation. Worse still, "responsible" governments of major nations appeared not merely incapable of taking the necessary steps to restore calm and order, but actually determined to make matters worse. It was no longer the monetary system which was in doubt, but the goodwill and intelligence of the governments who were meant to make the monetary system work.

The franc was brought low by a bolt from the blue—though it could also have been seen as a wry form of poetic justice. After almost precisely ten years of General de Gaulle's autocratic rule, the French people's penchant for anarchy reasserted itself. It is sometimes said that the French are incapable of either moderation or stability in their political affairs, and oscillate between the extremes of anarchy and one-man rule; the history of the past 150 years appears to confirm this judgment. In any case, in May, 1968, General de Gaulle, France's strongman, was all but swept from power in three ecstatic weeks of demonstrations, riots, bloodshed, arrests, and strikes.

He succeeded, when all seemed lost, in reasserting his authority, and in general elections which followed in June the Gaullists enormously increased their majority in the National Assembly. Yet his position was fatally undermined by the May Revolution, and in less than a year he was forced to withdraw from public life. "Les événements," as they were demurely described by the French, marked the beginning of the post-de Gaulle era.

The sequence of events in the revolution is widely known. A student demonstration at the Sorbonne on Friday, May 3, escalated into a serious clash with the police, followed by nearly six hundred arrests. The next week the situation deteriorated, and on the Night of the Barricades, Friday, May 10, some 367 people were wounded, 460 arrested. On Monday, May 13, about eight hundred thousand trade-unionists demonstrated in Paris in support of the students. The following day the first strike broke out spontaneously; within a week two million had downed tools, and within two weeks they had been joined by seven million more.

General de Gaulle, who had remained silent and apparently inactive in the face of the popular movement, left France at the height of the crisis on May 14 for a state visit to Romania and did not return until May 18. For six days he did nothing, and on Friday, May 24, he appeared on television to offer France a referendum on a group of legislative reforms: that night the street fighting reached a new peak, with fifteen hundred wounded, eight hundred arrested. The following day his Prime Minister, Georges Pompidou, started wage talks with the union leaders, and by dawn on Monday he had conceded increases ranging up to fifty-six percent for the worst-paid, and averaging about 13.5 percent.

Still the strike went on and demonstrations continued; the offer of a referendum was regarded with derision, and the wage agreement was rejected by the rank and file of the workers. The union bosses had as little control over their followers as the government over the students, and the political leaders of the

opposition parties were in total disarray. For all practical purposes the legally constituted government appeared to have disin-
tegrated, and in the confusion it seemed perfectly possible that
effective political power would pass into other hands.

At the last moment General de Gaulle reasserted his authority.
On the morning of Wednesday, May 29, his ministers arrived at
the Elysée Palace for the routine weekly cabinet meeting, only to
find that the President had abruptly left the capital. For several
hours his whereabouts remained secret, and Paris buzzed with rumors that he had resigned or was on the point of doing so. In fact,
he had flown to Baden-Baden to see General Jacques Massu, commander of the French troops in Germany and former commander
in Algeria, to assure himself of the loyalty of the army and to prepare for the use of military force to restore order and to prop up
the authority of the state. Two days later, as the tanks started to
move toward Paris, he gave his fighting speech on television,
which brought out a massive demonstration by Gaullist supporters, and the tide had turned. The first week in June saw a large-
scale return to work, and in the general elections held on June 23
and 30, the "backlash" against the strikes and the (wholly unreal)
danger of a Communist takeover brought the Gaullists a massive
victory.

By a curious coincidence, a few weeks later a number of French
generals who had been imprisoned for their part in the revolt
against the government at the time of the Algerian war were dis-
creetly released from jail. Evidently this was the other half of the
bargain made on May 29 at Baden-Baden.

One major question mark still hangs over the May Revolution:
why did the workers strike? The reasons for the student protest
were not very different from those of similar protests which had
been going on in a host of other Western countries: old-fashioned
and paternalistic universities which had entirely failed to adapt
either to the vast increase in the student population or to their
demands for a greater say in the running of affairs. But in no
other country did student demonstrations lead to massive strikes,
and whereas the opinions of Daniel Cohn-Bendit (Danny the Red,
as he was called, in a double reference to his left-wing politics and
his flaming red hair) became internationally celebrated, the nine
million strikers remained anonymous and leaderless. To this day,

no one has fully explained what made the spark jump from the Sorbonne to the factories, in defiance of the efforts of the official union leadership.

To begin with, there was certainly widespread popular support for the students, especially when the police resorted to counter-measures of remarkable brutality. But the strikes continued to spread long after general public sympathy for the students had waned, as the toll of violence and property destruction mounted, and they only reached their peak on May 22. Undoubtedly the student demonstrations triggered off the first strikes, but once the strike movement started, it acquired a momentum all its own. The nine million who stayed away from work were not striking on behalf of the students, and all the evidence suggests that they were not striking primarily in support of higher wages or shorter hours.

The wildfire spread of the strike, the incoherence of the strikers' demands, the initial rejection of the wage award, and above all the fact that many factories were not deserted by the workers, but were occupied by improvised soviets, who locked the executives in their offices, indicate clearly that their motivation was largely political. After ten years of undisputed rule by the aging General, the workers rebelled against his remote and authoritarian methods. It would be an exaggeration to describe France as a police state, but it was more of a police state than any other democratic country; since before the time of Louis XIV, French political authority and bureaucratic control have always been concentrated at the center, and the prolonged Algerian conflict left an additional legacy in the form of a proliferation of police and parapolice forces. General de Gaulle's own regime had a particularly strong flavor of illegality: his assumption of power in 1958, though it was inevitable, nevertheless took place in circumstances that almost smacked of a coup d'état, and there is no doubt that he subsequently bent the constitution which he himself had drafted. Even if one discounts these partial explanations as overdramatic, one fact stands out: de Gaulle set himself up as a remote and absolute ruler, concerned almost entirely with his diplomatic campaigns; no one could suppose that he was moved by either interest or sympathy for the doings of ordinary mortals.

There were, in addition, sound economic reasons for the strikes.

In the previous five years French wages had risen less than those in many neighboring countries—twenty-eight percent, compared with forty percent in Sweden, fifty percent in Holland, and thirty percent in Germany—and were lower than in most of the other Common Market countries. There was also a bigger gap in effective earnings between rich and poor: top French executives were better paid than those in Germany and Britain, while income tax was considerably lower and more easily avoided. At the same time, however, the proportion of the national product which went in taxes on consumer spending was considerably heavier and produced fifty-eight percent of total tax revenue, compared with only thirty-nine percent in Holland and twenty-four percent in Germany. This is a classic right-wing recipe for taxation, since it bears most heavily on the lower-income groups, and it is probably no accident that the two Western countries with the largest Communist voting strength—France and Italy—are also those with the most avoidable income taxes and the highest consumer taxes.

Dimly, no doubt, French workers must have realized that they were paying the biggest share of the costs of General de Gaulle's diplomatic wars. The true cost of developing the independent nuclear strike force has never been published, but it certainly constituted a heavy burden on the French economy, whose industry was not as large or as efficient as that of Britain or Germany. Equally punitive was General de Gaulle's relentless accumulation of gold and foreign-exchange reserves in the vaults of the Banque de France, as ammunition in his campaign against the U.S. dollar. When he came to power in 1958, the coffers were virtually empty and France was saddled by heavy debts; by 1968 French reserves of almost seven billion dollars were the third largest in the Western world after the United States and Germany, and the franc was one of the world's hardest currencies. A large part of this increase derived from the inflow of American investment dollars, but about half of it came from the export surplus of goods and services and represented a large volume of imports which the French economy had been denied. In other words, France could well have afforded a faster growth of prosperity at home if de Gaulle had not been obsessed by the need to amass an ever greater gold stock.

But for General de Gaulle the gold reserve was the symbol of his diplomatic strength, and he was reluctant to sacrifice any of it in the interests of faster economic growth. For several years, no doubt, the French electorate was won over by his policy of economic and military independence. But by 1968 they may well have wearied of the sacrifices it involved, sensing that it was not likely to bring home the promised bacon. General de Gaulle had succeeded in antagonizing most if not all of his Western allies; he had angered many Frenchmen in 1967 by his attack on the Israelis after the Six Day War; and he had rendered himself ridiculous by his support for the breakaway movement in French-speaking Canada. But he had failed to win recognition as the legitimate leader of Western Europe, to secure any fundamental change in NATO, or to destroy the power of the dollar, and there was little prospect that he would attain any of these objectives. Obscurely the French electorate must have felt that the jingoistic pleasures of a solitary diplomatic crusade were failing to compensate for the lack of the more material rewards of additional economic prosperity at home.

Whatever the causes of the May strikes, their consequences were glaringly obvious: a serious dislocation of the French economy, amounting to the loss of 750 million working hours, or some three percent of the country's annual production, a sharp increase in labor costs and consumer spending after the implementation of the wage increases, and an immediate loss of confidence in the value of the franc.

After the return to work, French production and exports rapidly recovered, but imports were bound to grow even faster as a result of the sudden growth in the workers' pay. To limit the trade deficit, the government introduced import quotas for a number of items, including cars, household appliances, and textiles, and handed out export subsidies to offset the higher wage costs. (Surprisingly, it also carried out on July 1, 1968, not only the cuts in import duties due under the Kennedy Round agreement of 1967 but also those which were scheduled to complete the customs union between the six Common Market countries.)

These measures may have done something to hold down the inevitable deterioration of the trade balance; they could not prevent it altogether, for French importers were strongly influenced by the widespread belief that the franc was likely to be devalued and that foreign goods would therefore become more expensive in terms of francs. In the second half of the year French exports were about nineteen percent higher than in the second half of 1967, but imports were up more than twenty-three percent, and over the year as a whole the trade balance deteriorated by two hundred million dollars.

## THE FLIGHT FROM THE FRANC
## AND INTO THE DEUTSCHEMARK

The expectation of a franc devaluation had much more serious consequences than this, however. With the outbreak of violence in May, ordinary Frenchmen reacted as they had always done in times of trouble and started taking their money out of the country; legally at first, and clandestinely in suitcases after the introduction of exchange controls on May 30. In June alone over one billion dollars left the country in various ways, the biggest single loss in recent history, and the French reserves fell to 5.5 billion dollars. Nor was this the full extent of the drain: rather than rely solely on his gold hoard, which had been painfully accumulated over ten years, General de Gaulle preferred to borrow abroad, and France drew 885 million dollars from the IMF in June, followed by a 1.3-billion-dollar line of credit from foreign central banks in July. (Britain, incidentally, did not contribute to the central-bank credit to France, just as France did not take part in the Basel arrangement being negotiated simultaneously to prop up the sterling balances. On economic grounds this mutual abstention was wholly reasonable, since both currencies were under pressure, but there was a certain element of tit-for-tat.)

It was not absolutely certain in the summer of 1968 that the franc was overvalued, even though it seemed likely that the lack of confidence in it on foreign-exchange markets would force a devaluation sooner or later: only a few years earlier Holland had undergone an even bigger wage explosion (though without a revolution or a massive strike), with a seventeen percent increase in wages in one twelve-month period, and had survived without being forced to alter its exchange rate. But the French have been through so many devaluations in the past fifty years that most of them automatically assumed the worst. In the real world (as opposed to tidy economic models), the present does not exist, or at least no one knows what it is until several weeks or months later; influenced by the past, people fear for the future, and today's expectations mold tomorrow's reality. In normal circumstances, no doubt, the French would have remembered that the Fifth Republic had abandoned the tradition of facile devaluations, and that pride alone would have prevented General de Gaulle from following the example of his predecessors. But even by French standards May and June of 1968 were abnormal.

In July and August the flight of capital from France slowed down, and the government decided to adopt a "forward strategy" for overcoming the effects of the strike and the wage increases. Tax increases had already been introduced to mop up some of the extra purchasing power in the hands of the consumers, but in September the administration tried to accelerate out of trouble and to restore confidence in the franc by lifting the exchange controls and introducing an expansionary budget. A similar dash-for-growth had been tried in Britain in 1964 by the Macmillan government, and it might have worked if it had not been cut short by the general elections, in which the Tories were defeated. It might have worked in France, too, given time and a stable international situation. The international situation was about as unstable as it could be, however. Time was not on France's side, and the experiment had to be abandoned within six weeks.

For in the autumn of 1968, after a temporary lull in the foreign-exchange markets, the world became convinced that the German currency (the Deutschemark) was about to be upvalued in relation to other currencies.* Everyone wanted to buy Deutschemarks, but the only way you can buy marks is by selling something else, and the biggest sellers were the holders of pounds and francs—pounds because the sterling devaluation of November, 1967, had not produced any significant improvement in Britain's overseas trading performance, and many people suspected a further devaluation; francs because the May Revolution and the strikes had seriously undermined confidence in the French currency, which also seemed to be ripe for devaluation sooner or later.

But the speculative money rushed to Frankfurt (the seat of the

* See "Speculation," pp. 174-177.

central bank and the German foreign-exchange market) from all over the world, for the primary idea of the speculators was not simply that the pound or the franc would be devalued, but that the Deutschemark would be revalued—that is, increased in value. Of course, by selling francs and pounds they were helping to weaken two currencies that were already weak enough, and were thus making their devaluation more likely.

They also thought—and how wrong they proved to be—that they were making a German revaluation more likely by buying marks. Where they were right was in thinking that the mark *ought* to be revalued, in the sense that its purchasing power was greater in terms of dollars than the official exchange rate (four marks per dollar) seemed to imply. There is no direct and simple way of comparing the purchasing power of two currencies, but the telltale sign of an undervalued currency is a balance of payments that remains in large and permanent surplus, while the symptom of an overvalued currency is a large and apparently incurable deficit. As we have explained, it is not always easy to know whether a country is "really" in surplus or "really" in deficit. But the yardstick most commonly used by the foreign-exchange markets—and the economists—is the trade balance.

By the trade yardstick it was evident that the Deutschemark was undervalued. In 1965, at the height of the inflationary boom, the German trade surplus had shrunk to 1.3 billion dollars, but in 1966, as the government started applying restrictive pressures on the growth of the economy, it swelled once more to 2.9 billion dollars, and in 1967, when deflation produced a real recession in Germany, the surplus virtually doubled to 5.25 billion dollars. In 1968 the economy began expanding again, but there was no reduction in the trade surplus: eighteen months of deflation had held German prices down while foreign prices were rising, and German exports were more competitive than ever.

By the summer of 1968 it was abundantly clear that Germany was headed for another export record—the surplus turned out to be nearly 5.75 billion dollars—and in the autumn foreign currency began pouring into Germany. The German government was later to protest that the trade balance told only a small and misleading part of the story: the outflow on the services account (insurance, transport, etc.) had reduced the current balance to 2.875 billion dollars, and this current surplus had been almost wiped out by an outflow of long-term capital of 2.825 billion dollars. How was it possible, it complained interminably, that the mark could be undervalued if the "basic balance" of payments was only just in surplus?

The protestations made no difference, either at the time or afterward. The world scrambled feverishly for marks, and the stream grew to such a torrent that in the first three weeks of November, 1968, the Bundesbank (the German central bank) took in nearly 2.5 billion dollars of foreign exchange, and at the most hectic moment, on November 15, it took in eight hundred million dollars in a single day.

By this time urgent international action was required to prevent the wholesale collapse of other currencies, for repeated statements by the Bonn government that the mark would not be revalued had made absolutely no impression on the foreign-exchange markets. On November 13 France had been forced to raise its official discount rate to six percent and to introduce credit restrictions, in the double hope of drawing back hot money to Paris and of persuading the foreign-exchange markets that the franc exchange rate would be maintained. But General de Gaulle only added fuel to the speculative flames when he remarked at a cabinet meeting that a franc devaluation would be the "worst possible absurdity," and made sure that the remark was leaked to the press. He intended to persuade the world that devaluation had been ruled out; all he showed was that devaluation had been considered, and that was enough to accelerate the flight from the franc.

The following weekend the governors of the biggest central banks held one of their regular monthly meetings in Basel, and when they dispersed without making any announcement, the rush into marks continued with fresh enthusiasm. The outside world has never been told exactly what went on in the conference rooms of the Bank for International Settlements, or in private confabulations in the rooms of the Hotel Euler and Hotel Schweitzerhof. But the shreds of evidence suggest that there was a fight between the French and the Germans, with Jacques Brunet of the Banque de France asking for German support for the franc, and Karl Blessing of the Bundesbank offering support—on brutally stiff

conditions, which the French refused to accept. In the echoing si-
lence that followed the Basel meeting, the French Prime
Minister, Maurice Couve de Murville, announced on Monday,
November 18, that all necessary support for the franc would be
available—but he did not say how or from whom, and he did not
succeed in restraining the one-way traffic of francs into Frankfurt.
The following day, the German government, while still refusing
to revalue, tacitly admitted that it ought to, by announcing a
four-percent tax on exports and a parallel tax remission on imports as a way of reducing the trade surplus, together with restrictions on foreign inflows of money. The French government
moved toward an economic program of greater austerity by
announcing a cut in public spending. But still the flood into
Frankfurt continued.

## THE BONN CRISIS

The German trade-tax announcement—equivalent to a half-
hearted backdoor revaluation—was a tantalizing gesture which
only inflamed the speculators; it also provoked sharp irritation in
foreign governments. Angry diplomatic messages flew around the
world; Prime Minister Harold Wilson took the unusual step of
summoning the German ambassador to an audience late at night,
to give him a piece of his mind. But the atmosphere really got
heated in Bonn on Wednesday, November 20, when the finance
ministers of the Group of Ten all flew in at short notice to see
the Germans.

The Bonn crisis meeting marked an all-time postwar low in international economic relations, and it was conducted in an
atmosphere of animosity and mistrust which has left durable
scars. The British, French, and Americans went determined to
pressure the Germans into revaluing the mark, and they did not
mince their words when they got there. The French were desperate for a German revaluation, because it seemed the only way of
stemming the hemorrhage on the French reserves. The British
were almost equally desperate, because in the absence of a German revaluation it seemed almost inevitable that the franc would
be devalued; this would not only bring further pressure on the
pound, but might even make a second sterling devaluation inevi-

table. Though Americans were not as close to the front line as either the French or the British, they knew that a forced devaluation of the franc and the pound would probably turn the speculators against the dollar.

This World War II triumvirate may have believed that their combined pressure could secure an appropriate compliance from Bonn, and on any previous occasion they would have been right. For twenty years and more after the war the German people had been second-class citizens in the West, and under the burden of the Nazi war guilt their governments had studiously avoided any overt political clash with the victors. But in November, 1968, for the first time, they openly asserted their sovereign rights, and stubbornly refused to revalue. They argued that the responsibility for the speculation lay not with Germany, whose economy was sound, but with the rest of the world, whose economies were sick; it was up to the others to take remedial measures. It was not common sense to argue that the whole of the rest of the world was out of step, but then the third week of November was not a time for common sense.

In any case, the meeting proved that neither market speculation nor political pressure could oblige the German government to revalue. A country which is fast losing reserves can be forced to its knees; a country which is gaining foreign exchange may be embarrassed but is not fundamentally threatened.

Naturally, the German government's real reasons for not revaluing were essentially political and electoral. First there were the industrialists to consider, who were major supporters of the Christian Democrat party (CDU), senior partners in the Grand Coalition, which ruled the Federal Republic. With exports of twenty-five billion dollars in 1968, they would not take at all kindly to an increase in the value of the mark, which would price them out of important foreign markets and reduce their profits at home. Then there were the farmers, another important buttress for the CDU, and even more essential to the Bavarian CSU wing of the party, led by Franz-Josef Strauss. Under the rules of the Common Market, uniform farm prices in the Six are fixed in terms of gold. If the mark were to be revalued in terms of dollars (and therefore also in terms of gold), the price actually received by the German farmer would fall. Finally, there was popular opinion to consider. With general elections scheduled for September 28, 1969, the German political parties were already limbering up for the campaign, and Strauss, an intelligent but ever-ready demagogue with his sights on the Chancellery, took the occasion to pose as the champion of the Deutschemark. There were some in Germany naïve enough to believe that a raising of the price of the mark would mean an increase of prices of other commodities in Germany; the reverse would in fact be true, since revaluation would lead to a slowing down of the export boom, increase competitive pressure from imports, and thus tend to stabilize domestic prices. By contrast, the maintenance of the exchange rate and the export boom could only lead to labor shortages, production bottlenecks, higher wages, higher prices—in short, to overheating and inflation. But Franz-Josef Strauss did not disillusion his followers, and he gained considerable popularity by standing as the heroic bastion against the pressure tactics of foreign governments and by representing himself (quite erroneously) as the prime guardian of monetary stability.

There were, however, intelligent voices in the German administration struggling to be heard. The Bundesbank was becoming convinced that a revaluation was essential, not because it would make life easier for the rest of the world by cutting down the export surplus, but because it was the only durable way of fighting the incipient inflation which had started making itself felt. The German Economics Ministry, too, had come to a similar view, and it prepared a paper suggesting a multilateral adjustment in the exchange rates of a number of currencies, including the mark. When the contents of its paper leaked to the press during the crisis meeting, the German politicians were somewhat embarrassed but not seriously incommoded in their defense of German independence.

Conscious of their impregnable position, the Germans were the only participants at the conference who were not glum, and as a result they were a great deal more talkative to the journalists assembled in the corridors outside. As an alternative to a mark revaluation, which they rejected, the Germans retaliated against France by openly advocating a devaluation of the franc, and they broke all the international conventions of traditional monetary diplomacy by their efforts to ensure that their proposal would be broadcast to the world: by itself the publication of the idea that a French devaluation was under consideration was bound to make it more likely. Even before the meeting opened, the chief German spokesman, Günther Diehl, told journalists that the outcome of the conference would "depend on a French decision whether to devalue or not," and the German delegation hammered away at the same theme throughout the meeting. By the time it ended, after telephone calls between Henry Fowler, U.S. Treasury Secretary, and President Lyndon Johnson in Washington, and between François-Xavier Ortoli, French Finance Minister, and Couve de Murville, his Prime Minister in Paris, the Group of Ten had agreed that France should receive a two-billion-dollar credit. They also thought it had been agreed that France would devalue, and Franz-Josef Strauss, the German Finance Minister, was gleeful enough to predict as much to the assembled newsmen. He was certainly not alone in his prediction: on the following day, Saturday, November 23, before any official statement had been made in Paris, the French press confidently announced devaluation and even gave the amount by which the franc would be lowered— 11.11 percent.

## CHARLES THE BOLD

They counted without de Gaulle. There is no doubt that a devaluation package had been prepared as a result of the Bonn negotiations and that it was submitted for General de Gaulle's approval at the cabinet meeting summoned on the Saturday. But the President rejected the plan, primarily because he felt it was beneath his dignity to be forced to lower the value of the franc at the behest of a politically inferior country. General de Gaulle was not accustomed to being bested by the Germans, and he did not propose to start in November, 1968. Instead he announced, on the next day, a complete reversal of the expansionary economic policy launched only six weeks earlier. The budget deficit would be cut by reductions in military spending and in subsidies to the nationalized industries, even more stringent exchange controls would be introduced than those which had just been removed, wages and prices would be frozen, and exporting industries would be subsidized by the abolition of the payroll tax and by an increase in the turnover tax on domestically consumed goods. General de Gaulle would not give way to the forces of "odious speculation."

Some people would think that it is at least as undignified for a government to be forced to switch its economic policy 180 degrees as to alter the exchange rate of its currency. But General de Gaulle's notions of national independence were partly satisfied by the knowledge that he was not doing what was widely expected. Symbolic questions of prestige have all too frequently frustrated rational decisions in international monetary politics. General de Gaulle may conceivably have persuaded himself that he could turn back the clock and by a forceful pronouncement on television restore confidence in the external value of the franc.

The world was disconcerted and impressed by the French President's decision, and Lyndon Johnson immediately cabled his congratulations: the United States had no cause to wish to see the franc devalued, since this could increase pressure on the dollar, and it was a rare opportunity to say something nice about the French. But it was to be General de Gaulle's last major dramatic gesture, and it was doomed to failure. There was room for argument over whether the franc was really overvalued in relation to the currencies of the rest of the world; it had certainly been undermined by the strikes, but it was conceivable that the extra wage costs could in time have been absorbed. There was no question, however, that the franc was overvalued in relation to the Deutschemark, and the close economic interdependence of these two leading members of the Common Market was bound to strain a realistic relationship between their currencies. If Bonn refused to revalue, it was almost inevitable that Paris sooner or later would have to devalue.

This was certainly the view of the foreign-exchange markets, which continued to maintain pressure against the franc (and, by extension, against the pound) and in favor of the Deutschemark, and by the end of the year French reserves had dropped to 4.2 billion dollars. Two events in the early months of 1969 were to swell the stream of funds out of France to another massive flood—a new round of wage talks in March between the unions and the government, and a political referendum in April in which de Gaulle was defeated.

The wage talks had long been awaited as an acid test of the government's firmness of purpose in enforcing its new austerity policy. The unions were determined to extract another large pay boost to compensate for the rise in prices which had followed their previous wage increase. The government was equally determined to offer only a very moderate increase, and indeed argued that the long-scheduled March meeting was not intended to award a cost-of-living offset, but merely to "review" the situation. When the talks ended in deadlock and the unions called a twenty-four-hour strike, the foreign-exchange markets concluded the worst, and the franc hit the floor.

The markets had judged the situation slightly wrong, however, for the unions had no serious intention of trying to re-create the massive strike pattern of 1968. It is doubtful if they could have done so, even had they wanted to; but in any case they did not want to, for they knew that industrial unrest was likely to play into the hands of General de Gaulle at the referendum due to take place six weeks later.

A year earlier, after the May outbreak, de Gaulle had been forced to abandon his referendum on greater popular "participation" in government and to hold general elections instead. From his point of view, however, the drawback of this change in tactic was that it substituted a poll which (as it turned out) restored the authority of his Prime Minister and the government, for one which might (or might not) have endorsed his own position as President. He was therefore determined, against all the advice of his cabinet, to hold a referendum and to turn it into a vote of popular confidence in his personal rule.

Formally, the proposal to the voters on April 27, 1969, was for a reform of the structure of regional government and for the abolition of the French Senate as a legislative chamber. The regional reform was represented as a concession to the rebels of May, 1968, who complained that far too much power was held in far too few hands in the capital; in fact, the changes proposed were minimal. The legislative reform was designed more crudely to do away with a body which had always mustered a majority of opponents to the Gaullist regime and which had been headed by Gaston Monnerville, a black lawyer born in French Guiana; he was not only an irreconcilable enemy of de Gaulle's but was also his legal successor in the event of any unforeseen vacancy at the Elysée Palace.

The technique of popular referendum had been used on four previous occasions by de Gaulle. Each time he had made it a test of popular support in himself, and each time he had been accused of demogoguery; but each time the referendum had been concerned also with a real political problem. The first was the adoption of the constitution of the Fifth Republic, two more concerned the settlement of the colonial war in Algeria, and the fourth instituted direct election of the President by universal suffrage in place of nomination by the country's "notables."

In April, 1969, by contrast, it was evident that the proposed referendum was merely a pretext for demanding a vote of confidence, and though General de Gaulle tried to frighten the electorate by warning of the awful consequences that would follow his defeat, his warnings cut no ice. It was too evident that he had not foreseen or prevented the May Revolution, that at the worst moments it had been Georges Pompidou who had been the government's only bulwark against anarchy, and that it was Georges Pompidou who had won the victory in the ensuing general election. Pompidou became the favorite son of the Gaullist party, and his influence was if anything increased by his dismissal from the premiership after the general elections. There was no doubt who would lead the Gaullists if the General left office, or that he would be an effective successor; indeed, even before the referendum he dropped clear hints that he would lay claim to the presidency. There was no surprise, therefore, when the referendum was voted down and General de Gaulle duly announced his resignation.

Although a majority of the French people had decided, with remarkable calmness, that they could get on perfectly well without General de Gaulle, his resignation marked the beginning of a stampede into marks that dwarfed even the November rush. Things really started to get hectic on April 29, when Franz-Josef Strauss, who must have had something else on his mind at the time, chose to say publicly that the Deutschemark was undervalued and that it might be possible to envisage a revaluation of eight to ten percent if a new international monetary conference were to be called. During the next ten days foreign exchange flooded into Frankfurt in unprecedented quantities: on almost every one of those days the Bundesbank had to buy more than 250 million dollars; at the peak, on May 9 it took in over 1.3 billion dollars; and between April 28 and May 9 inclusive its foreign-exchange reserves rose by a total of 4.2 billion dollars.

On May 4 Strauss tried to undo the damage caused by his reference to revaluation by saying that while the government was ready to take part in a multilateral conference on exchange rates, a unilateral revaluation of the mark was out of the question. But it was already becoming evident that Strauss was not an authoritative spokesman for the German government, since the coalition was deeply split on the revaluation issue.

The German Bundesbank had become more convinced than ever that revaluation was the only realistic policy, for domestic even more than for international reasons. As the guardian of monetary stability in the German economy, the central bank had already in March forced the government to take deflationary measures, and in April it had raised the discount rate from three to four percent. But inevitably anti-inflationary moves could only increase Germany's export surplus, while credit restrictions could only make it more difficult to offset the trade surplus by exporting capital.

## THE SECOND BONN CRISIS

In November, 1968, Professor Karl Schiller, the Minister of Economics and a leading light of the Social Democrat party, had vied with Strauss for popular acclaim as the defender of the mark's parity. Early in 1969 he came around to the Bundesbank view, and in May he became the most powerful political figure to oppose Strauss over the revaluation issue. On May 5 an inconclusive cabinet meeting was held, with top members of the Bundesbank present; it appeared that the government was still prepared to consider revaluation, provided it took the face-saving form of a multilateral realignment of exchange rates (presumably with France as one of the participants), for the deputy government spokesman Conrad Ahlers said afterward: "We have no partner," and added that international monetary cooperation "depends on a nation over which we have no influence." But the following day he said publicly that a decision on whether or not to revalue the mark should be taken soon, "and it could fall either for or against revaluation."

But with foreign exchange pouring into Frankfurt at an accelerating rate, the German government could not sit on the fence for very much longer. On May 9 the cabinet held another four-hour session, at the end of which Schiller's proposal for a seven-percent revaluation was ruled out. The decision, said Ahlers afterward, was "final, unequivocal and for all eternity," and the government "hoped and expected" that its decision would bring speculation to an end.

What had finally decided Chancellor Kiesinger against revaluation was the advice of the Bundesbank that a single revaluation would not end Germany's chronic trade surplus. It took the view that Germany's competitive advantage against other countries was steadily increasing year by year, and that international stability could be assured only if a moderate revaluation in 1969 was followed by regular but small revaluations of one or two percent every year. This was too much for the party of the industrialists and the farmers, and it used its weight as the senior partner in the coalition to overrule Schiller.

The hyberbolic terms in which the Bonn government announced that its decision was valid "for all eternity"—"immer und ewig"—were not enough to give it credibility. It was clear that the mark was undervalued: the November adjustment in taxes levied on exports and imports had made a slight dent in the trade surplus during the early months of the year, but this backdoor revaluation had not gone far enough to reduce it to internationally manageable proportions. It was also abundantly clear that the coalition was split, with Schiller and the Social Democrats advocating revaluation and Strauss and the Christian Democrats opposing. The German government had withstood foreign political pressure and two speculative onslaughts, but many people predicted that it would not have the determination to stand up to a third wave. Far from accepting that the decision was valid "for all eternity," the market assumed that it might remain in force until the general elections on September 28, but could well be reversed shortly afterward. Accordingly, the dollars which had poured into the coffers of the Bundesbank so rapidly in the days preceding May 9 were a great deal slower in flowing out the following week, and the big-time foreign-exchange operators arranged their affairs so as to be in the starting gate again in September.

The market's assumptions were rapidly confirmed. On May 13 Professor Schiller, who did not apparently accept the finality of the government's decision, again publicly advocated revaluation at a session of the Bundestag (the German parliament), and again clashed with Strauss. A month later the government forecast that the trade surplus would reach 3.5 billion dollars in 1969, not much less than in 1968, and the Bundesbank was again obliged to tighten credit and raise the discount rate to five percent in another attempt to curb the inflationary pressures in the economy. On July 7 Professor Schiller proposed that the export tax and import rebate should be raised from four to six percent, but was rebuffed by Chancellor Kiesinger. On July 14 he again publicly called for revaluation, and ten days later announced that revaluation might become necessary in the autumn or winter. When it is recalled that the combined German Economic Institutes had published a report on April 28, representing revaluation as inevitable, and that on July 14 another independent economic committee had advocated revaluation, it is not surprising that the money operators remained unimpressed by the permanence of the government's decision.

Politically, however, there was no doubt that Kiesinger's obstinacy impressed popular opinion at home and created something of a sensation abroad. When Strauss emerged undefeated from the November meeting, German newspapers carried banner headlines announcing "We're Number One," and sober observers wondered whether the crisis had not marked a significant shift of power in Continental Europe. West Germany had long been the most powerful economic unit in Europe, but in the postwar era it had been inhibited from making full political use of its strength. It was scarcely credible that it would forever be content to take a back seat, and many people had long predicted that after General de Gaulle's departure Germany would really emerge as Number One in Europe. Now it looked as though the sleeping giant was beginning to stir.

General de Gaulle, long accustomed to lording it over the Ger-

mans, was perturbed as much by the political implications of this
turn of events as by the money aspects. In March he sent his Foreign Minister, Michel Debré, to Bonn to tell the Germans that
they were getting too powerful. It was never quite clear what
Debré expected to achieve merely by saying it, but there is no
doubt that that is what he went there to say.

It all really depends what one means by a shift of power. The
Germans had learned to imitate the negative aspects of General
de Gaulle's conduct of international affairs, and in that sense one
can say that the mark conflict marked a spread of negativism
across the Continent. But there was no suggestion that the Bonn
government wanted to use the mark issue as a lever to gain other
political ends on the international scene—it was simply a question of political infighting at home—and there is no evidence that
it aspires to the leadership of Europe. That may yet happen, but
it has not happened yet.

## FRANCE ON THE DEFENSIVE

French aspirations to lead Europe, on the other hand, though
still vivid in the mind of General de Gaulle, had been seriously
damaged by the 1968 upheaval. The loss of confidence in the
franc and the hemorrhage of gold from the reserves meant that
the General had lost his major weapon in the war against the
dollar; so during the year France gradually started patching up its
relations with Washington. Even as early as March, 1968, before
the outbreak of student riots, came the first thaw when de Gaulle
publicly praised Lyndon Johnson's decision to stop the bombing
of North Vietnam, and Johnson returned the compliment by
choosing Paris as the site for Vietnam peace talks on May 3. By a
curious coincidence, that was the day the May Revolution broke
out.

After the revolution, which had forced de Gaulle to negotiate a
1.3-billion-dollar credit with foreign central banks, it was hardly
surprising that his semiannual press conference, in September, for
the first time contained no allusion to the evils of the gold exchange standard. The November crisis saw France once more
obliged to seek financial support from the United States and
other foreign governments, but the pill was sweetened by John-

son's warm approbation for General de Gaulle's refusal to devalue.

De Gaulle had not entirely abandoned all hope of seizing some sort of victory on the monetary front out of the jaws of defeat, and his hopes were roused by the prospect that the new American President, Richard Nixon, would be even more anxious to make peace with France. Moreover, Nixon's Treasury Secretary, David Kennedy, made some politically naïve remarks in the closing days of 1968 which suggested that he was encouragingly open-minded about an increase in the official price of gold, still a subject that was close to de Gaulle's heart. But the new administration had barely taken office before it was clear that the Johnson-Fowler line on gold was being assiduously followed by the Nixon-Kennedy team, and de Gaulle was in no position to shift it.

The same kind of downturn characterized General de Gaulle's defense policy in the course of 1968. Over the years he had progressively dissociated himself from Western military integration in NATO, and had engaged in the slow and painful development of an independent French nuclear deterrent, with its own arsenal of Mirage IV bombers, miniaturized hydrogen warheads, land-based medium-range ballistic missiles, and Polaris-type missiles. This policy of military independence reached its peak when General Ailleret, chief of the French defense staff, propounded a new strategy in which the deterrent would be targeted on all points of the compass, and not, as previously, on the Soviet Union alone. In January, 1968, this strategy of "tous azimuths," as it was called, was publicly endorsed by General de Gaulle.

The theoretical justification for this strategy was that France was not in fact facing a real military threat from the Soviet Union, and that therefore there was no reason to point the rockets east rather than west. Six months later, however, this justification collapsed when the Soviet Union and its Warsaw Pact allies invaded Czechoslovakia, and at the annual meeting of NATO foreign ministers, France endorsed a communique which contained a veiled warning to Moscow not to go too far. In December the Defense Minister, Pierre Messmer, announced that France would remain in the Atlantic Alliance—there had previously been much speculation that France might leave in 1969 after the statutory twenty-year period of membership had elapsed—and confirmed

that the economic difficulties and budget cuts would entail a two-
to three-year delay in the completion of a fully operational nuclear strike force. In March, 1969, General Fourquet, the new
chief of the defense staff, revealed that the "tous azimuths" strategy had been dropped and that France had been converted from
a policy of massive deterrence (long abandoned by the United
States) to the NATO policy of flexible response. The implication
of this change was that France was now committed to the initial
use of ground troops and tactical weapons in any conflict in Europe and would therefore have to base its planning on the idea of
cooperation with its NATO allies. Indeed, already by the end of
1968 it was reported that France had started talks with the
United States on the supply of tactical nuclear weapons. A wholly
French strategic nuclear deterrent remained a long-term Gaullist
objective, but for most practical purposes France was having to re-
consider its policy of semineutralism.

On the Common Market, however, General de Gaulle remained inflexible throughout 1968. He stood fast by his veto on
British membership and was apparently unmoved by the attempts
of the Five to create separate political links with Britain. In
reality, the French were more than a little worried by these stir-
rings of independence in their Common Market partners, and
they did their best to crush the various plans launched by Holland
and Belgium. In the beginning of 1969 de Gaulle reacted by making a final desperate bid to remodel Europe after his own image.

### THE SOAMES AFFAIR

On February 4, shortly before a meeting between Britain and
the Five, de Gaulle summoned Christopher Soames, British ambassador in Paris, and put forward a three-point plan for the entire reconstruction of Europe. First, NATO and the Common
Market would be done away with; second, a loose European free-
trade area (without independent institutions or federalist aims)
would be created, in which Britain would be allowed to take part;
and third, the whole edifice would be crowned by a four-power
political directorate composed of France, Britain, Germany, and
Italy. (The French afterward claimed that de Gaulle had not
made any formal proposal, but was just thinking aloud, and had

certainly not expressed his thoughts as categorically as this. There seems no doubt, however, that this was the core of his remarks, for he was not known for simply rambling on aimlessly.)

It never became clear whether he seriously expected these ideas to be accepted. The British, who had never wavered in their support for NATO, seemed very unlikely to change course at the drop of a hat. But Charles de Gaulle may have reckoned that they were so desperate to gain access to the economic advantages of a wider European market that they would be ready to make considerable sacrifices. An alternative interpretation is that de Gaulle, knowing his political career was fast running out, was making a throwaway proposal on the off-chance that it might be accepted. The third possibility was that he was deliberately setting a trap for the British: if he could inveigle them into secret bilateral discussions on his plan, he would be in a position to destroy their standing with the other Common Market countries by revealing what had been going on behind their backs.

After rapid consultations in London, the British government plumped for the third interpretation. It had no intention of abandoning NATO, and it knew that there was not the slightest possibility of persuading the Five to scuttle the Common Market. The gap between what de Gaulle had offered and what was attainable or desirable was so large that prolonged negotiations would be needed to reach any agreement; and long, secret negotiations with General de Gaulle presented an unacceptable diplomatic risk. Within a few days, therefore, Christopher Soames told the French government that the British application to join the Common Market was still on the table; that the British government would be happy to have further talks with General de Gaulle; but that since the other members of the Community were vitally concerned in these issues, they would be informed of the Franco-British conversations. Indeed, more by accident than design, the British informed the German government a few hours before Soames had conveyed his message in Paris; Harold Wilson was by chance on a visit to Bonn that same day, and on a sudden impulse he revealed to Chancellor Kiesinger what had been going on.

The French were livid at being outmaneuvered in this way, but for two weeks longer the affair remained a close secret in the seven capitals. Then someone in Paris could contain himself no longer, the story started leaking out into the French press, and the Foreign Office in London immediately consolidated its position by giving a full briefing. Europe was scandalized at what General de Gaulle had been up to—it needn't have been, since his proposals corresponded precisely with his known views—and France's reputation took a sharp nose dive. The British had responded to the French ploy with unusual brutality, but after the ten years of Gaullism, diplomatic brutality had become the order of the day. Above all, the clumsiness of de Gaulle's initiative suggested that the old man had lost his touch, and the implication that he was betraying dangerous signs of senility may well have contributed to his defeat at the referendum two months later.

## THE FRANC GOES DOWN

The diplomatic setback was, however, the least of France's worries at this time. The Banque de France was continuing to lose reserves, and the deflationary program introduced in November was not apparently having any effect in slowing down the economy or curbing imports. Yet in view of the wage negotiations scheduled for March and the referendum fixed for April, the government felt unable to take the risk of introducing additional unpopular measures. General de Gaulle's abrupt resignation on April 28 brought further delay, for France was immediately plunged into a presidential election campaign, and it was not until the end of June that President Pompidou could form his new government.

During the election campaign, Georges Pompidou had endorsed General de Gaulle's decision not to devalue the franc, and in his first policy speech to the National Assembly the new Prime Minister, Jacques Chaban-Delmas, pledged that the parity of the franc would be maintained. Two weeks later, however, on July 16, Pompidou decided that the franc would be devalued, but the decision remained a close secret, shared only by seven other men in Paris. Three weeks later, out of the blue, the rest of the cabinet was informed of the decision and that same afternoon, Friday, August 8, 1969, it was announced. At the same time, the new Finance Minister, Valéry Giscard d'Estaing, revealed that the published loss of reserves during the previous twelve months was way below the true figure, which was no less than 4.7 billion dollars; to all intents and purposes French reserves were back where they started in 1958, only a few months from total exhaustion.

Though the decision to devalue the franc was a reversal of General de Gaulle's policy, the manner in which it was carried out was thoroughly Gaullist. Under the rules of the IMF, a member state may devalue or revalue its currency only if it consults the Fund. Under the rules of the European Community, too, a member state must consult its partners before changing its parity. Neither the Fund nor the European Community was informed of the French decision, let alone consulted about it, until it was publicly announced. Indeed, it so happened that on July 17 Giscard and the other finance ministers of the Six met in Brussels to adopt a new agreement that members of the Community would in future hold prior consultations before taking any economic measures that would have a Community-wide impact. The French decision to devalue was taken on July 16, but it was kept a dark secret from the Five.

The French had reasons for their cavalier behavior. They claimed that consultations had in fact taken place the previous November, at the crisis meeting of finance ministers of the Group of Ten in Bonn, when it had been accepted that the franc would be devalued by 11.11 percent—this was precisely the amount of devaluation. (As usual, there was at first some ambiguity in the press about the amount of devaluation, since it can be expressed two ways: the amount of gold or dollars required to buy one hundred francs had been reduced by 11.11 percent, while the number of francs required to buy a given quantity of gold or dollars had been raised by 12.5 percent. On French television Giscard announced the devaluation as 12.5 percent because it's easier to say than 11.11 percent.) Secondly, the French claimed that secrecy was essential to avert the risk of speculation; in the light of their own spoiling tactics at the time of the British devaluation in November, 1967, they had good reason to know just how damaging speculation could be. Thirdly, they argued that the devaluation decision had only been taken "in principle"; the consultations would take place immediately afterward in Brussels and Washington.

Apart from these phony "consultations," the immediate consequence of the French devaluation was a sharp setback for the
Common Market's farm policy. Almost five years earlier, when the
Six were still relatively optimistic about the prospects for economic integration in the Community, they had adopted a set of
common farm prices which would be valid throughout the Common Market. They needed common prices because they wanted
to be able to allow free trade in farm products as well as for
industrial goods. But since none of their currencies was absolutely
stable, they defined the prices in terms of a "unit of account,"
which was equal to a dollar's worth of gold.

In practice, of course, the farmers were paid in their national
currencies, not in dollars, gold, or the fictitious unit of account.
But the almost automatic consequence of a devaluation of the
French franc in relation to gold would be a corresponding increase in prices paid to French farmers. Unfortunately, this would
have disastrous consequences in France: it would add to the inflationary pressure on prices and incomes, and it would also add to
the Community's mountainous agricultural surpluses. The butter
situation was already catastrophic: the unsold stocks amounted to
300,000 tons at the beginning of the year, and by the end they
were expected to reach more than 500,000 tons—with only
450,000 tons of storage space in the whole Community. Other
products were also on the way to producing unsalable surpluses.

The alternative to an increase in French farm prices would be a
reduction in the value of the unit of account. This was a way out
that was catered for in the rules. But since it would have meant a
reduction in the prices paid to the farmers in the other five countries, it was obviously unacceptable on political grounds, especially in Germany, where the general election was less than two
months away. So the Commission invented a new rule, that the
unit of account would be devalued in France alone and would
only return to its normal level after two years. In effect this meant
that the Community was abandoning the principle of common
prices and free trade for farm products.

The French devaluation thus demonstrated definitively the lesson that had been emerging so clearly over the previous fifteen
months: the Common Market was not producing the economic
results hoped for, because the six member states were unable or

unwilling to coordinate their economic policies. The May Revolution had been a bolt from the blue, but it only aggravated the underlying monetary and economic tensions in Europe. Had General de Gaulle never existed, it is possible that the Community would have made much more progress in ironing out these economic tensions. But the lessons of Gaullism had been learned only too well in Bonn, and even after the French devaluation, the Deutschemark still remained undervalued in relation to the majority of other currencies.

This was the more important because during the first decade of the Common Market's existence the national governments gradually lost their ability to control the speculative movements of capital. To a large extent this was because they voluntarily gave up most forms of exchange control on money-flows; the British retained severe and permanent restrictions on the freedom of their own nationals to secure foreign currency, and the French reintroduced controls after the May Revolution. But both countries were an exception to the general trend.

## THE HOT MONEY SPONGE

A much more significant factor was the growth of the Euro-dollar market, which was rechristened by conservative Swiss bankers the "hot money sponge." In the first ten days of May, 1969, the Bundesbank bought about four billion dollars, but the other central banks had lost only two billion; the remaining two billion came from the Euro-dollar market. At the time of the November, 1968, crisis the Group of Ten had started talking of setting up an antispeculation procedure, by which a central bank that received a flood of speculative (or "hot") money would automatically send it back where it came from—on loan. Inevitably, this "recycling" procedure proved very difficult to set up. The Germans wanted these loans to be labeled in marks, but nobody else wanted to incur debts in a currency which they believed would, or at any rate should, be revalued. By February the central bankers had got no further than agreeing to meet again at short notice in the event of a crisis—which they would have done anyway.

But when the next crisis did erupt, in May, it was evident that the recycling agreement was not very much use. The Bundesbank did channel a certain amount of money back to Britain, France, and other countries, but there was nowhere to channel the Euro-dollar back to. The Bundesbank did shovel large quantities of dollars out into the Euro-dollar market, but it was quite likely to find that these same Euro-dollars were being used once more to speculate on a mark revaluation, and were flooding back in just as fast as before.

Moreover, the Euro-dollar market was also having the opposite effect on a number of other countries. The high interest rates and the heavy demand for banking funds in the United States were drawing funds out of France, Belgium, and Italy into the Euro-dollar market, and from there they were passed back to New York. So serious was the outflow from Belgium and Italy that these two countries had to impose restrictions on foreign-currency lending by their commercial banks, while the French introduced blanket exchange controls. In other words, the fast and fluid movements of funds through the Euro-dollar market were highlighting the economic and monetary tensions, not merely within Europe, but also between Europe and the United States. Because the U.S. Congress had been slow to take adequate fiscal measures to control the inflationary boom in the United States, almost all the weight of anti-inflation measures had to be concentrated on interest rates and credit restrictions. And because the Euro-dollar market transmitted these tensions across the Atlantic, Europe had to pay for the lack of prompt action by Lyndon Johnson and the foot-dragging of Wilbur Mills and other congressmen. Similarly, the European economies had to pay for the failure of their governments to operate in harmony. The West was facing the drawbacks of moving toward ever-freer trade and payments without at the same time making any significant coordination of economic policies. When things got tough at home, it was just too easy for politicians to say: "To hell with the rest of the world."

And, of course, for nobody was it easier than for the Germans. It was perfectly clear that the Deutschemark ought to be revalued, but no one could force the German government into a revaluation against its will, and it was equally clear that the coalition government led by Chancellor Kurt Kiesinger and the Christian Democrats was certainly not going to revalue before the general elections due on September 28.

As this date drew near, however, speculators began pouring funds into Frankfurt once more, though not on the same scale as in May, partly because many of them had held onto their marks ever since. They received additional encouragement by the public-opinion polls, which forecast substantial gains for the Social Democrats (the party favoring revaluation) and even held out the possibility that they would overtake the Christian Democrats as the largest party in the Bundestag. In fact, the Christian Democrats maintained their position as the biggest single party, but the Social Democrats did make significant advances, and they rapidly reached an agreement on the terms of a coalition with the tiny Free Democrat party. A revaluation of the Deutschemark thus seemed to be assured.

But well before the new government could be installed and take the necessary decision on revaluation, the Deutschemark had already started moving away from its official parity—in a way that was entirely contrary to the rules of the IMF. Three days before the general elections, the Bundesbank stopped buying dollars in exchange for marks and closed the foreign-exchange markets in Germany. Since the German authorities alone are responsible for maintaining the official parity between marks and dollars, this meant that the mark was free to find its own level in other foreign-exchange markets. In other words, it had started to float and its IMF parity was in abeyance.

The morning of Monday, September 29, immediately after the elections, was confused because no one was entirely clear whether the exchange markets would be reopened or not, while at the same time it seemed almost inconceivable that the outgoing government under Kiesinger would be prepared to make a revaluation decision in its last two weeks of office.

After some urgent telephoning between Kiesinger, Schiller, and the Bundesbank, it was decided to compromise by reopening the markets, but to allow the Deutschemark to go on floating. The irony of this decision to suspend one of the principal obligations of IMF membership was that it was taken while all the leading finance ministers and central-bank governors were assembled in Washington for the annual meeting of the Fund, at which they were expected to discuss the pros and cons of a more flexible approach to exchange rates.

A growing number of economists had begun to argue that the causes of the monetary upheavals which had rocked the world for well over two years lay not only with the economic policies of national governments, but also with the rigidity of the IMF exchange-rate system itself. They maintained that in a system of fixed exchange rates any changes became excessively charged with political emotions. The British and French governments had each in turn postponed its devaluation for reasons of misplaced national prestige, while the Germans had repeatedly argued that it was not they, but the rest of the world, which was out of step. A more rational approach, it was held, would be to defuse the political tensions, and at the same time to avoid the stresses of sudden changes in exchange rates, by allowing all currencies greater freedom to move up or down according to supply or demand. The more daring economists proposed that all currencies should be completely free to float in any direction; the more prudent felt this would give rise to wild and destabilizing swings in the relative prices of different currencies, and would make it difficult for international traders to know how much to charge or pay, and proposed merely that the fluctuations permitted under IMF rules should be widened from one to two percent on either side of the official parity. A third school suggested that currencies should be enabled to move gradually in small steps, say, once a month, either at the decision of the national government or (more automatically) in line with the average price paid in the foreign-exchange markets during the preceding period. Nobody expected any of these different formulas to be adopted at the Washington meeting of the Fund, but in the weeks just before the meeting it did look as though a number of countries, including the U.S., would have the courage to propose an examination of more flexible exchange rates. When the meeting finally opened, the finance ministers agreed on such an examination, though they were a good deal more cautious than had been expected. But by this time the Deutschemark was already floating, and seemed certain to be revalued one way or another, and much of the pressure for a wholesale revision of the exchange-rate system had evaporated.

The behavior of the foreign-exchange markets after September 25 was taken by the "free floaters" as a triumphant vindication of their theories: there were no wild swings in the rate, and international trade was able to go on perfectly smoothly while the mark found a new rate. In fact, the four weeks during which the mark floated proved very little. Everyone knew that the rate was only being allowed to float temporarily, until a new parity could be fixed by the incoming government, and the foreign-exchange operators were only concerned to see the rate move to the level at which the new parity would be fixed. Indeed, the mark wasn't floating freely at all: the Bundesbank remained in the market, just below the level at which dealings were actually taking place, and by gradually shifting its offering price upward, it was able to nudge the market rate slowly upward too. At the same time, a series of semi-official pronouncements by a number of leading personalities gave the market a clear hint that the revaluation was likely to lie in the region of seven to nine percent. In fact, when revaluation was finally announced on October 24, it turned out to be rather larger than expected, a 9.29-percent change from 4 Deutschemarks to the dollar to 3.66. But by this time the Bundesbank had nudged the floating Deutschemark to 3.69, which was just inside the IMF margin for the new rate, and it stayed there pretty well unchanged for several weeks.

The floating mark, like French devaluation, caused major problems on the farm front. The Germans refused to cut their domestic farm prices, and introduced border taxes to bring imported food up to the level paid to their own farmers. In a fit of madness, the Common Market Commission tried to force the Germans to fix a new parity quickly, by banning any food imports during the floating period, a move which would have rapidly brought Germany to the verge of starvation. Fortunately common sense prevailed, after an undignified bout of legal squabbling, and as the mark floated upward Germany was allowed to raise its border tax from five to six percent.

After the new parity was fixed, however, the Bonn government was obliged to remove the import duty, despite the fact that France had been authorized to offset its devaluation for two years by means of border taxes. There was no logical reason why Germany should be forbidden to take safeguards analogous to those introduced in France. There was simply the pragmatic reason that if France and Germany were both insulated from the common-price system, the common-price system would virtually cease to exist. Instead, the German farmers were restricted to getting help from compensating subsidies—virtually all of which were paid by Bonn.

Naturally, the immediate consequence of the German revaluation was that a great deal of the money that had flowed into Frankfurt in search of a profit flowed out again. During October the German reserves declined by 2.2 billion dollars, and the outflow reached a peak of 400 million dollars on one day in December alone. After having been for so long the world's leading supplier of credit for deficit countries, Germany presented the unusual spectacle of having to draw 1.05 billion dollars from the IMF in November and December, 1969. But though German industrialists were vociferous that the revaluation had been fixed far too high for their comfort, there was little immediate sign that the long-standing German trade surplus was about to be eliminated. Revaluations, like devaluations, always take time to produce their effects.

## SPECULATION

Speculation is often depicted by the popular press and by politicians as a shady and unpatriotic activity carried on exclusively by a malicious conspiracy of foreign bankers. The real world is very different from this convenient myth. Currencies are traded every day in large quantities, for importers and exporters are in constant need of foreign exchange to finance world trade, now running at more than 230 billion dollars a year. Speculation is merely what happens when the world loses confidence in the value of one currency and therefore sells it in abnormally large quantities, or believes that another currency is likely to become more valuable in the future and therefore buys it in unusually large quantities.

If the market for foreign exchange were completely free, the heavy sale of a currency would tend to drive its price down, as happens with any other commodity. But under IMF rules, the market is not completely free: governments are obliged to maintain the price within one percent of the rate registered with the Fund, and most European governments limit the fluctuation even more narrowly than this. When the price of the French franc falls near its floor, the Banque de France has to step in to prop the price up by buying francs in the market in exchange for other currencies (usually dollars). This is how speculation causes a drain on countries' gold and foreign-exchange reserves. But because the foreign-exchange market is strongly influenced by confidence or lack of confidence, central banks will often try to make their currencies seem stronger than they really are by supporting the price well above the IMF floor, though they always try to conceal their buying operations as much as possible.

As confidence returns to a currency, and the price rises again in the market, the central bank can take in foreign exchange. But as in other walks of life, it is much easier to lose confidence than to regain it.

This confidence game is complicated by the fact that the major currencies are not simply traded for cash. The leading foreign-exchange dealers, of which the London banks are by far the biggest, also buy and sell packets of currency which are to be handed over at some future specified date, such as thirty days, sixty days, ninety days, and so on. Depending on the needs of the commercial concerns, these "forward rates" may well be either weaker or stronger than the "spot rates" for immediate delivery. Finally, the prices fixed in the foreign-exchange markets will also reflect the cost of borrowing different currencies; that is to say, the forward exchange rate between pounds and Deutschemarks is likely to be influenced by the difference in interest rates in Britain and Germany.

Basically there are three types of speculators. First, there are the banks and foreign-exchange dealers themselves, who trade to make a profit and who constantly adjust their prices so as to remain on the winning side. To some extent these banks are operating with their own funds, for they must always be in a position to supply foreign exchange to their clients at the best possible price, and they are constantly on the lookout for opportunities to switch from pounds into Euro-dollars, for example, or from francs into Deutschemarks.

But the banks are also operating on instructions from their customers. A company which regularly imports goods from Germany, for example, and which foresees that the Deutschemark may be revalued and that German goods will therefore become more expensive to import, will inevitably take precautions by buying marks well ahead of time. Similarly, a German corporation which regularly imports from France and which expects either a revaluation of the mark or a devaluation of the franc will delay making payment as long as possible in the hope that the goods will become cheaper in terms of marks.

This double process of accelerated and delayed international payments, which is known in the jargon as "leads and lags," may seem on the surface a minor and temporary wrinkle in the normal pattern, but it can make an enormous difference to the strength or weakness of individual currencies. Britain exports about sixteen billion dollars' worth of goods every year, while its reserves (excluding all its debt to central banks and the IMF) amount to only about 2.4 billion dollars. If all Britain's overseas customers delay payment in the belief that the pound is about to be devalued, then within only two months the entire British gold and foreign-exchange reserve would be exhausted. Few other countries have such a low ratio of reserves to trading turnover, but all of them can be acutely vulnerable to the impact of a heavy swing in the leads and lags.

The third type of speculators are the companies, banks, or private individuals who have, or can borrow, spare cash, and who invest it wherever it looks like bringing the greatest rewards. If the mark looks ripe for revaluation, they move it into Germany in the hope of a quick capital gain; if the franc looks like being devalued, they switch out of France; and if the gold price seems to have a good chance of being doubled, they buy gold. In the 1968 gold rush, American firms in Europe were thought to be among the major gold buyers, despite a U.S. law which bans gold holdings by private organizations or individuals. This certainly seems to correspond with the popular image of "speculation" as an unscrupulous way of "making" money instead of "earning" it. But transpose this activity to the trading that takes place every day in national financial centers among stocks, shares, bonds, government securities, bank deposits, and other monetary instruments, and it looks just like the normal activity of an efficient and fluid capital market. The only real difference is that in one case the trading takes place across national frontiers, and it is then convenient for politicians to portray the speculator as someone who is evil and unpatriotic.

In Britain it has been fashionable at moments of crisis to blame the weakness of the pound on the malice of a mythical race known as the "gnomes of Zurich." To be sure, Zurich bankers sell sterling when they lose confidence in it, but much of their selling is likely to be undertaken on the orders of British businessmen sitting in their London offices. Similarly, General de Gaulle, who blamed the May uprising on an international totalitarian conspiracy (for which there was not the slightest evidence, as he well knew), attributed the flight of capital from France to the work of "odious speculators." As on so many other occasions in France's history, these odious speculators were ordinary Frenchmen who had lost confidence in their own currency and wanted to preserve the value of their money by changing it into something else.

Naturally, the foreign-exchange market is made up of a very mixed bag of people, just like any other random group, and it certainly includes shady operators and gamblers, just as it also includes sober and cautious businessmen who are merely concerned to protect themselves or their shareholders against loss. And in the real world, the only way of being able to avoid loss is to maximize the chances of making a profit. If the foreign-exchange markets are allowed to operate freely, there is no way either of restricting them to people whose motives one feels he can approve or of excluding the rest.

What the politicians really dislike about the foreign-exchange market is that it expresses a crude and inarticulate judgment on their economic policies. Foreign-exchange operators are not necessarily any better at predicting the future than other people; while they are extremely sensitive to what other foreign-exchange operators are doing and thinking, their judgment on broad economic or political questions may well be no better than average. But they are in business to make predictions about the future, and politicians dislike finding that their own claims and predictions are treated by the money men as so much misleading claptrap.

If 1968 witnessed an unprecedented series of international monetary crises, it was also the year which saw the first major improvement in the system since Bretton Woods. This was an agreement to create an entirely new form of international money, known as Special Drawing Rights or, more commonly, "paper gold," which would take its place in official reserves alongside gold, dollars, and other forms of foreign exchange.

Unlike the closing of the Gold Pool and the Basel arrangements to guarantee the sterling balances, which were also agreed in 1968, the Special Drawing Rights plan was not an emergency fire-fighting measure undertaken in the heat of the moment to avert disaster. It was the culmination of over five years of laborious, and at time acrimonious, negotiations, and it marked a major breakthrough toward a more rational organization of the international monetary system. For the first time the world would be able to add to its reserves by a process of deliberate and conscious decision-making, and would not depend solely on the accidents of gold production or on the mixed blessing of U.S. balance-of-payments deficits to increase international liquidity.

# CHAPTER 8

# The Fight Over "Paper Gold"

As with virtually every other major political issue on the international scene, negotiations for the "paper gold" plan were centered on a bitter confrontation between France and the United States. The Americans were determined to secure changes which would help take the heat off the dollar, while the French were equally determined to prevent any easing of the American position.

To begin with, France's partners in Europe were also reluctant to fall in with Washington's wishes, largely for reasons of conservative central-banking orthodoxy; they distrusted the idea of any fundamental changes in the monetary system, and they feared that the changes proposed by Washington would actually make things worse. In time, however, the majority of Continental European countries came to accept that some way must be found of creating new reserve assets. Caution and hesitation were still their watchwords, but they did agree to make plans for the future.

The French, however, were never moved by objective concern for the health of the international monetary system as a whole. Their only aim, throughout most of the 1960's, was to get the Americans. When their partners in the Common Market started being won over to Washington's point of view, the French tried to win them back by holding out the hope of a truly European policy on international monetary affairs, and for a while the ploy succeeded. But the European alliance was a castle built on sand; France was interested in it only as a way of defeating the Americans, and when the Five had to choose, they preferred to side with Washington on the creation of "paper gold," so the French were left to fight their war alone. It was only when France herself got into economic difficulties that the French saw the advantages of the "paper gold" plan.

From the beginning of the 1960's the Americans had argued that the world was in danger of running short of reserves and that some new form of reserve must be created. The French, suspecting with some reason that Washington was much more worried about the level of its own reserves than about those of the rest of the world, fiercely opposed the American argument. The U.S. balance-of-payments deficit was producing a drain on the American reserves, while the European creditor countries were becoming reluctant to take many more dollars. The French believed, therefore, that the U.S. demand for a new form of reserve asset was intended merely to make it easy for Washington to go on running a deficit, regardless of European wishes. The French argued that instead the problem was quite the reverse of what the Americans said—not too little international liquidity, but too much. The international monetary system was being glutted with surplus dollars through the American balance-of-payments deficit, and the only change needed in the system was to end the U.S. deficit. In 1965 General de Gaulle carried this argument to its logical conclusion, as we have seen, by demanding that in future the international monetary system should be based solely on gold.

## PARIS, WASHINGTON, AND NEW "MONEY"

The argument was able to continue between the two countries for five years because there is no agreed and objective criterion for measuring the world's reserve needs. In the absence of any accepted rules, it was inevitable that every country would put forward arguments that fitted in with its national interest. France and the other European creditor countries were steadily increasing their reserves, and they certainly felt no shortage of liquidity. The Americans, on the other hand, could see their reserves falling and their dollar debts to foreign countries rising, while the British were in an even tighter squeeze.

The French argument was not entirely watertight, however. It might be true that the Americans were primarily motivated by national self-interest, but it was also true that the total size of world reserves had for many years been growing much more slowly than the total volume of international transactions. International trade, for example, had grown twice as fast since the war as world reserves. This did not prove that there was already a shortage of international liquidity (that is, a shortage of reserves), since there was no way of knowing just how much liquidity was needed to finance a given amount of trade. But if trade continued to grow much faster than world reserves, then sooner or later the world was likely to run short of liquidity.

As we have seen, countries need reserves as a sort of emergency ration, against a rainy day when their balance of payments runs into deficit or when their currencies lose the confidence of the foreign-exchange markets. If all countries were able to maintain a perfect and perpetual equilibrium in their balance of payments, their theoretical need for reserves would be negligible. But in practice few countries are able to maintain such an equilibrium for very long, and none can be sure that it will not run into a balance-of-payments deficit next year or the year after. They all try to maintain a reserve position which is well above their immediate needs, and if their trade rises fast, they are anxious to keep their reserves rising in step.

From their different points of view, therefore, the French and Americans had strong cases: the French were comfortably off because they were able to build their reserves faster than their trade, while the Americans and the British were badly off because their reserves had declined while their trade had increased. In the end the Americans prevailed, not merely because world reserves had grown much more slowly than world trade but also because the other European countries preferred, when it came to the crunch, to line up with Washington against Paris. Political pressure did much more than rational argument to push negotiations forward to their final conclusion.

The French and the Americans did not fight over only the *amount* of reserves the world needed; they also battled over the *kind* of reserves. Under the existing rules of the system, there were essentially three different kinds of liquidity. First, there was gold, which was a wholly owned reserve asset—"wholly owned" in the sense that it did not represent a debt to anyone else. Secondly, there were dollars, which represented a U.S. liability but which were to some extent under the control of the United States. And thirdly, there were drawing rights on the IMF, which had to be repaid within a limited number of years and which could be subject to conditions imposed by the Fund.

Predictably, the Americans were anxious that any new form of artificial asset should be wholly owned and free from conditions or repayment obligations, for they could see their own gold reserves dwindling. Equally predictably, the French opposed the United States and tried to ensure that any new form of reserve would help the Americans as little as possible. First they proposed a device—Giscard d'Estaing's "cru"—which would be equivalent to an increase in the price of gold, and when that was turned down they demanded a credit type of asset, similar to drawings on the IMF, which would have to be paid back and would be ringed around with conditions and restrictions. In the end the negotiations produced an apparent compromise between the two sides: the name of the new reserve asset, Special Drawing Rights, corresponded to the French wishes, but the meat of the "paper gold" plan strongly favored the U.S. point of view.

## THE TEN INTO ACTION—BUT SLOWLY

The establishment of the General Arrangements to Borrow in 1961–1962 was a halfway step toward the creation of additional liquidity, for the members of the Group of Ten were in fact guaranteeing to provide the IMF with six billion dollars' worth of lendable curencies, over and above what it had received through ordinary quotas. But it was clearly not a permanent solution to the problem of liquidity shortage, and the United States, constantly having to improvise new techniques to make sure that its dollar debts were not converted into gold, was anxious for more radical measures. The creation of the Group of Ten did, however, provide an ideal forum for holding negotiations, since it included all the richest countries but was—in theory, at least—small enough to make progress.

The French, and to a lesser degree the other creditor countries in Europe, still refused to admit that there was any danger of a fundamental shortage of world reserves. Before negotiations proper could begin, therefore, it was necessary to reach some agreement on the nature of the problem: was the American deficit (and to a lesser extent that of Britain) the root of the world's monetary difficulties, or was there a potential shortage of liquidity? For the next three years the Group of Ten set up one study group after another to try to hammer out this basic issue, without making any startling headway. In 1963 a "working party" was charged to examine the "outlook for the functioning of the international monetary system," but after a year's deliberations it could do no better than to report that the time might come—one day—when new liquidity might have to be created. Accordingly the Group of Ten set up another study group, under Rinaldo Ossola of the Bank of Italy, to examine different methods of creating artificial liquidity; but after another twelve months of talking it got no further than listing a series of alternatives, without being able to agree which was preferable. Even to have got so far was progress from the American point of view, but it was very slow progress. The French fought the study groups every inch of the way and insisted that their work was purely theoretical. Nothing that emerged from them, they claimed, implied any commitment to action.

It was not until 1965, with the establishment of yet another study group under Otmar Emminger of the German Bundesbank, that the first signs of at least a consensus began to emerge. Agreement was still a long way off on the type of reserve asset that should be created, and France refused to take part in the drafting of the Emminger report. But by the summer of 1966 the other members of the Group of Ten were prepared to agree that the time had come at least to start making contingency plans for the creation of new liquidity.

Why did France's partners change their minds and come around partway toward the American point of view? For some of them there were psychological reasons: in 1964, when Italy ran into sudden balance-of-payments difficulties, the United States had been quick to provide substantial financial aid, whereas the Common Market countries did little to help apart from offering stern reproofs to the Italians for having mismanaged their economy. The Italians had long been among the most imaginative and constructive members of the IMF; now they had reasons for something akin to gratitude toward the United States. It was hardly surprising that Italy was the first Continental country to abandon the hard-nosed attitude toward U.S. demands for artificial-liquidity creation. When the French in their turn got into balance-of-payments difficulties, in 1968–1969, they too started showing interest in the distribution of reserve assets—after the "paper gold" plan had already been agreed to by their partners in the Group of Ten.

A more important factor was the gradual realization that Europe's moral sermons to the United States, though heart-warming for the Europeans, were not having any practical effect. So long as the American deficit continued, the European surplus countries were faced with an unpalatable dilemma: either they would have to go on accumulating dollars, or they would have to convert these dollars into gold. By 1966 total reserve holdings of gold had started to fall, and the American deficit was providing the only significant sources of additional world reserves. To refuse the dollars would be to refuse any increase in the world's money supply, despite the continuing growth of world trade, and to convert the dollars into gold would lead to a net reduction in the world's reserves. There might be disagreement over precisely how much money the world might need at any given moment, but a reduction in total reserves was almost bound to lead to a shortage of liquidity sooner or later. The weakness of the dollar gave the Americans an additional bargaining weapon, and it was primarily for this reason that 1966 saw the turning point in the negotiations which finally led to the Special Drawing Rights plan.

## THE PAROLE BOARD

The Europeans had not put all their faith in sermonizing, however. In an effort to put additional pressure on the Americans to get rid of their deficit, they had insisted as far back as 1961 that a new and permanent group should be set up in Paris, in which the deficit countries would have to explain what they were doing to put the situation right—a sort of parole board. The group, which was a special working party of a twenty-one-nation intergovernmental institution called the Organization for Economic Cooperation and Development, had almost exactly the same members as the Group of Ten, and frequently the same officials attended the meetings of the two groups. In 1964 the working party, known as "Working Party Number Three," was moved by the Europeans into the front line. In return for agreeing to a study of possible ways of creating new liquidity in the Group of Ten, they demanded that the Working Party should carry out an examination of the problems involved in avoiding either deficits or surpluses. Significantly, however, the report on adjustments in countries' balances of payments took twice as long to complete as the parallel report on liquidity creation, and its conclusions were, to say the least, inconclusive.

The trouble was, of course, that it is impossible for all countries to be in surplus at the same time. If some countries are in surplus, then others must necessarily be in deficit. In the aggregate, surpluses must be mirrored by deficits. The European countries did not entirely abandon the idea that surpluses are signs of virtue and deficits proofs of moral laxity—indeed, German politicians to this day openly endorse this Manichaean view of international economics—but in the reports of the OECD Working Party, they were forced to concede that part of the responsibility for getting rid of imbalances in international payments rests with the surplus countries.

But in other respects the prolonged and theoretical ruminations of the Working Party contributed nothing of practical significance to a solution of the British and American deficits, and the continued growth of the German surplus in succeeding years showed that even the moral concession on the sharing of responsibility was little more than an empty phrase. The Germans were not prepared to take the necessary steps to reduce their own surplus, by faster domestic growth and inflation, and they renounced the conversion of dollars into gold. Since they were not prepared to go on taking dollars indefinitely, they were almost obliged to accept the argument that an alternative form of liquidity must be created—sooner or later.

Like the Germans, all the other Europeans continued to insist on having the moral satisfaction of exercising what became known as "multilateral surveillance"—which meant putting the deficit countries on parole and making them give an account of themselves every few weeks. But at the same time, they effectively gave way before the realities of the situation: it is almost as hard for surplus countries to force debtors to move into surplus as it is for debtors to force creditors to end their surplus. Whether or not the United States moved into surplus, it was going to be necessary to look for some new form of international liquidity, to supplement (and perhaps eventually to replace) dollars and gold.

The 1966 report on contingency planning for the creation of new liquidity also appeared to have marked a turning point of a rather different sort, though in this case appearances were later to prove deceptive. When discussions first started, at the beginning of the 1960's, the majority view—that is to say, the view of the European countries—was that the international monetary system needed only extra borrowing facilities, at least in the foreseeable future. Heavy drawings on the IMF by Britain had left the Fund seriously short of Continental European currencies, and it was in order to make available an additional supply of these currencies that the Group of Ten had set up the General Arrangements to Borrow. By 1964 it was evident that the GAB was not enough to solve the problem. But so long as the European countries took seriously American claims that the U.S. deficit would shortly be eliminated, they might reasonably believe that the shortage of European currencies in the Fund, and the glut of dollars in national reserves, would prove to be temporary. Accordingly, the Group of Ten concluded in 1964 that the need for additional international liquidity could be met by an expansion of credit facilities, at least in the first instance. Only in the longer run did they think that it might "possibly call for some new form of reserve asset."

Two years later their thoughts had swung from credit facilities (like IMF borrowings) to wholly owned reserve assets (like gold), largely because of the contraction in the world's official gold holdings. For while dollars are almost universally accepted in the finance of trade, and have the advantage of bearing interest when invested in American securities, they are in the last resort an American debt which can be redeemed only by being exchanged for gold. So long as America's gold reserves comfortably exceeded its dollar liabilities, European countries had no qualms about holding dollars. But when U.S. dollar liabilities outstripped the U.S. gold stock, the Europeans began to have second thoughts about the reliability of the dollar.

Gold, by contrast, was the only form of reserve asset which did not represent a debt by one country to another, and the drain of monetary gold from official reserves into the hands of private speculators persuaded the Europeans that any new liquidity should take the form of a reserve asset that would be as unconditional as gold. They therefore concluded, in the Group of Ten's 1966 report, that: "Most of us favor, as part of a contingency plan, the creation of a new reserve unit by the limited group" of countries having "particular responsibilities" for the operation of new international arrangements and for the "financial backing for any newly created reserve assets." This was a major breakthrough for the United States and Britain, though it was ironic that the victory was largely due to the U.S. deficit and to distrust of the dollar. But still the French were opposed to the whole affair.

## FRANCE COUNTERATTACKS

By 1966, then, most European countries had come around to the view that, while it was not necessary to create any new form of liquidity in the immediate future, it was desirable to start making plans. But not France. French policy on the international monetary situation, never explicit, was superficially strikingly inconsistent. Three quite different proposals were put forward by Paris at different times, and on occasion alternately; the only common thread that bound them together was the desire to prevent the establishment of any new arrangements which could make life easier for the United States.

The most frequently heard proposal from Paris was that the international monetary system should be "reformed." It was a familiar French theme in the early 1960's, and it was still being repeated (on a note of desperation) in 1968 on the eve of the majority decision in the Group of Ten to press ahead with the "paper gold" plan; but actual "reform" was never spelled out. But the long-term political objective was never in any doubt—to deprive the United States of its privileged role as the source of a reserve currency, and to make it impossible for American business to swallow up European industry on the basis of finance that depended ultimately on Washington's ability to print dollar banknotes.

The second proposal, which was put forward by Giscard d'Estaing at the annual meeting of the International Monetary Fund in 1964, was at once more explicit, more subtle, and (at least superficially) more constructive. The French suggested the creation of a new paper reserve asset called the composite reserve unit, or "cru," which would be distributed to, and used by, a limited number of the leading industrialized countries for the settlement of their surpluses and deficits. As we have seen, the most important feature of this proposal was that the units would be allocated in the first instance to the participating countries in proportion to their gold holdings, and that the settlements of accounts between the participating countries would take place in the same mixture of gold and "crus."

From the international point of view, the merit of the "cru" plan was that France appeared to be making a constructive proposal for once. But its merits from General de Gaulle's point of view were considerably greater. The double link with gold, in both allocation and use of "crus," meant that the plan as a whole would amount to an increase in the dollar price of gold by the back door—and this was the reason why the French "cru" proposal never secured much international support.

In any case, the status of the "cru" plan was seriously thrown into question at General de Gaulle's press conference on February 4, 1965, in which he demanded that the gold exchange standard set up at Bretton Woods should be abandoned and that henceforth the world's monetary system should be solely based on gold.

It was not entirely clear, even to Giscard d'Estaing, whether the "cru" plan had been swept away by General de Gaulle as half-hearted tinkering where only radical measures would do, or whether it simply had been expressed in more forceful terms. The probability is that de Gaulle suspected his Finance Minister of a weakness for wishing to remain on working terms with the rest of the world and that he wanted to preempt any possibility that Giscard might be inveigled into serious and constructive negotiations with the United States. Yet a week later Giscard delivered a lecture at the Paris Law Faculty in which he appeared to be trying to ride both tigers at once, and by midsummer both Britain and the United States were taking a more positive interest in the "cru" scheme, as being less of an evil than the idea of a return to a gold standard.

If there was indeed any possibility of a compromise centering on some version of the "cru" in 1965, it disappeared forever in 1966. Partly because of the apparent failure of his domestic anti-inflation program, but partly also because of his suspected readiness to work for an agreement with the United States, Giscard d'Estaing was removed from the Finance Ministry by General de Gaulle in January, 1966. At the same time, the senior French official responsible for international monetary negotiations at the

Rue de Rivoli, André de Lattre, was shunted aside to a dignified but harmless post as Deputy Governor of the Banque de France.

The new Finance Minister, Michel Debré, was an unreconstructed hard-line Gaullist, and he rapidly dismantled the position established by Giscard. On March 7 he pigeonholed the "cru" scheme for good, and two days later, at a meeting of the Group of Ten, he reverted to the demand that the monetary system should be based solely on gold and to the argument that there was no need for any additional liquidity. For most practical purposes the "cru" scheme would have given gold a new lease on life, even if it did not necessarily imply the elimination of dollars and pounds from national reserves. But the bare fact that the other European countries had swung toward the idea of a new unit, and that the United States was starting to take a serious interest in the "cru" as the basis for discussion, made it imperative that the French should drop the scheme entirely, if they were to avoid getting drawn into negotiations, when negotiating was the last thing that Debré wanted to do. When the Group of Ten met that summer, the other nine countries agreed not only to start on contingency planning, but also that the plan should consist of a new unconditional reserve asset, rather than a form of credit. The French opposed the whole operation, and Debré further isolated himself at the IMF annual meeting in September by again banging on about the virtues of gold, and by demanding, in November, that the Group of Ten carry out a study of the role and price of gold in the international monetary system.

Though this study was, after a certain amount of undignified public bickering, in fact carried out, it was crystal clear that none of the other members of the Group of Ten had the least intention of agreeing to a return to the gold standard or was in favor of an increase in the gold price; several central bankers and finance ministers said so, in terms almost as aggressive as those employed by General de Gaulle. It was also beginning to look increasingly obvious that they would set up a contingency plan for new liquidity, despite French objections, and that the French government's only practical option was to cut its losses by trying to ensure that the scheme finally adopted would give the United States as little satisfaction as possible.

## THE EUROPEAN ALLIANCE

By the end of 1966 it was too late for the French to hope to do this alone, for they had largely lost credibility as constructive members of the international monetary system. But their key card was membership in the European Community, and by appealing to the institutional loyalty of their Common Market partners they succeeded in forging a European alliance in the monetary negotiations. It was a precarious alliance, since the political aims of the French were quite distinct from those of their partners, and at no time did the Common Market countries see eye to eye on the liquidity issue. In the circumstances it was surprising that the French appeal for Community solidarity carried any weight at all in the other European capitals; after all, France had just boycotted the Brussels institutions for seven months and had attempted to force through a weakening of the Community's treaty rules. But the Five remained susceptible to such appeals long after experience should have taught them that General de Gaulle was incapable of a change of heart on any major political issue. The new alliance was forged in The Hague in January, 1967, at a meeting of the finance ministers of the Six.

The French succeeded at this meeting, and at another in Munich three months later, in persuading the Five to give up the idea of a new wholly owned, unconditional reserve unit (like gold), and to go instead for a system of credit creation. After this, it might have been possible for Washington to go on pressing for a unit-based scheme. But it was rapidly recognized that French participation in the negotiations was worth making some sacrifices for, and experience had shown that agreements between the Six were usually reached with such difficulty that there could be little prospect of persuading them to change their minds. The essential features of the Special Drawing Rights plan thus began emerging in the spring of 1967, and though the struggle between Paris and Washington continued without interruption well into 1969, it took place inside the framework of a consensus for a definite drawing-rights plan. Naturally, both sides did their best to extract concessions on the details of the plan, but the essential point was that the Group of Ten was now negotiating in earnest on the

creation of artificial liquidity, and that the French, however reluctantly and obstructively, were taking part—most of the time.

This French participation was not simply a one-sided surrender
to the momentum established by the other countries, however,
and the alliance with the Five was not simply based on an emotional appeal for Common Market loyalty. On one point the Six
were united by a common interest: that European creditor countries deserved a bigger say in the management of the IMF, in proportion to their real weight in the world's monetary system. When
the Fund had been set up, the United States had been incompar-
ably the dominant country, and its quota (and therefore its voting rights) in the IMF was far larger than that of any other
country. The dominant position of the United States had been
diluted by the admission of newly independent countries, but in
1966 it still had over twenty-one percent of the votes, whereas the
Common Market countries together had only a little over sixteen
percent.

By contrast, the gold and foreign-exchange reserves of the Common Market countries now far exceeded those of the United
States, and the Six had become far the most important source of
foreign exchange for countries in need of credits, whether through
the IMF in the normal course of events or with the additional use
of the General Arrangements to Borrow. All the Common Market
countries believed that this situation entitled them to a greater
say in the Fund, and it gave some of them, notably the French,
an additional reason to criticize the Fund as the tool of Washington.

The question of voting rights was important, because some of
the most important decisions could be taken only with an eighty-
percent majority; this meant that the United States had a veto
right, but the Six had not, even if they voted together (which
they had not always done). In practice this difference in status
might not have made very much difference. For so long as the Six
were the biggest holders of reserves, it was virtually inconceivable
that the United States would think of attempting to introduce
any major changes in the Fund's rules without their agreement,
or at the very least without the agreement of most of them.
Whatever the voting outcome might be, no new scheme could
work unless it was supported by the European creditor countries.

Nevertheless, as a matter of principle, the Europeans considered that the balance should be put right. The most obvious method for this would have been for the Common Market countries to raise their subscriptions to the Fund, and the Americans repeatedly urged this course of action on them. Some European countries, like Germany, did make special quota increases in 1965. But the French, as we have seen, had only agreed with the greatest reluctance to fall in with the twenty-five-percent across-the-board increase in IMF quotas in 1965, and most European countries felt that they had already done the equivalent of a unilateral increase in their quotas, by lending funds to the IMF through the General Arrangements to Borrow. The French therefore proposed that the loans made under the GAB should be transferred to the IMF and added to the national quotas, since this would have given the Common Market countries more than twenty percent of the IMF voting rights.

This idea interested some of the other European countries, especially the Belgians, who for cultural and historical reasons tended to find it difficult to oppose the French openly. In April, 1965, the Belgians put forward a rather broader proposal on the lines originally suggested by the French: the General Arrangements to Borrow would be wound up as part of a special increase in the positions of the Common Market countries in the Fund, and at the same time drawings on the Fund would be made rather more liberal. The drawback of this plan was that the liquidation of the GAB would have removed all practical reasons for continuing the Group of Ten as the influential inner ring of leading IMF members, and for this reason the Franco-Belgian scheme was not pursued very hard or very long by any of the other Community countries.

Once the Europeans had discarded the various methods of increasing their stake in the IMF, their only alternative means of strengthening their voting position was to press for a change in the voting rules themselves and insist that the blocking vote should be reduced from twenty to fifteen percent. So long as they voted as a group, the Community countries would thus join the Americans in having a veto over unacceptable changes in the operations of the Fund. And this is precisely what they did press for (though they might not have done so if they had not been pushed into it by the French), and it was the foundation of the fragile solidarity between the Six.

The voting issue was not, however, simply a question of principle and prestige. From the beginning the French had opposed any negotiations on the creation of new liquidity, even in the form of contingency planning, for they foresaw this as the first step on a very slippery slope. Once a contingency plan had been drawn up, it would prove very difficult to prevent its being put into effect. Nor, indeed, were the French alone in taking this cautious view at the beginning; but gradually the other Continental countries came around to the view that new liquidity might be necessary within the foreseeable future and that some contingency planning was therefore desirable. The difference between France and the Five on this issue was that General de Gaulle was not in the least concerned with technical considerations of an economic or monetary nature, and he was not therefore interested in the argument that the world might be facing a real shortage of international liquidity. As it turned out, French foot-dragging was fully justified: the process of negotiating the new system acquired such momentum that it was put into effect almost as soon as the details were tied up.

But France's partners were genuinely concerned (as were the responsible officials in the French Finance Ministry) that a contingency plan for the creation of new liquidity must not be used simply as a dodge to allow the Americans to go on running unlimited balance-of-payments deficits. Throughout most of the negotiations they insisted on an overriding condition, that the new assets should be created only after the United States and the United Kingdom had ended their deficits, since they believed that the world would really start to run short of liquidity only when it stopped being supplied with surplus American dollars. By 1968 France's partners softened their stand on this point, for the gold rush had reduced the world's unconditional monetary assets, and instead of demanding the complete elimination of the U.S. deficit, they insisted only on a substantial improvement in the U.S. balance of payments as the precondition for the release of new artificial assets.

Nevertheless, they continued to insist that the Common Market countries must have a veto right in the IMF rules. They were afraid that, regardless of the conditions agreed in the Group of Ten, the United States would round up support from all other members of the IMF and push through the new plan over the heads of the Common Market countries. At the same time, they were also afraid that if the Americans were defeated in a vote on the new reserve-asset plan, they might attempt to secure the same result by putting forward quite different proposals under the IMF's existing charter. Neither of these fears was realistic, as we have already pointed out, since the European participation was vital for any new liquidity deal; but Europe sincerely felt they were, and the Common Market countries demanded the simultaneous introduction of a fifteen-percent blocking rule, both in the Fund and in the new asset rules, as part of an overall package deal. On this issue they remained united right until the end.

In one sense, the Common Market countries' fear of being outvoted and outmaneuvered was not entirely unfounded, for the rest of the world was becoming increasingly impatient for a free handout of new reserve assets. In the early 1960's a number of the countries in the Group of Ten had started from the idea that the new liquidity should be restricted to the Group of Ten, on the grounds that these were the countries who effectively acted as the world's bankers and had special responsibility for making the international monetary system work. This idea was an essential element in the French "cru" plan, and, as we have seen, was adopted by all the other members of the Group of Ten (apart from France) in the report published in 1966.

## CREDIT, MONEY—OR AID?

But it gradually became obvious that a restricted scheme would not be at all popular with the rest of the world. In real terms the less-developed countries were in much greater need of finance than the members of the Group of Ten, and they exerted considerable political pressure on the industrialized countries to broaden any new liquidity scheme to cover all IMF members.

This development only reinforced the determination of the Common Market countries to exact a controlling voice in the activation of new liquidity, and helped to strengthen the French demand that it should take the form of credit rather than unconditional assets. Motivated by the stern principles of banking orthodoxy—it was easy for them to take a severe line, since they were so rich and so flush with reserves—the Europeans tended to look upon the less-developed countries as either financial incompetents or spendthrift profligates who would simply and immediately *spend* the new reserve assets allocated to them; in other words, the developing countries would treat a new asset as though it were outright development aid. If the Europeans were worried that the Americans and British would use a liquidity scheme to perpetuate their balance-of-payments deficits, they were also quite worried at the prospect that the developing countries would follow suit. The object of any new liquidity plan was not to provide spending money which would make it easier for deficit countries to stay in deficit, but to add to the total volume of international liquidity so as to lubricate the world's economy and allow it to go on expanding smoothly.

The less-developed countries did, indeed, need more development aid. But according to "sound" banking and monetary doctrine, this aid (which amounts to the transfer of real resources from the rich to the poor) should be provided out of taxation in the industrialized countries, and not through the inflationary device of printing a new international money.

Politically, it proved impossible to exclude the less-developed countries from the distribution of new reserve assets. The Group of Ten had been discussing the problem for so long that even the most backward country had grasped the idea that there might be handout money, and none of them intended to be left out. In February, 1966, thirty-one of the leading less-developed countries set up a special propaganda group to campaign for a share in the creation of any new liquidity. At about this time, the Americans made an attempt to satisfy all parties by proposing a two-tier arrangement: the members of the Group of Ten would create, solely for their own use, a new wholly owned unit, while the rest of the world would be accorded the more limited benefits of a relaxation of the rules governing drawings from the IMF. In other words, Washington was suggesting the distribution of an asset with the characteristics of gold to the rich, "responsible" countries, but only conditional credit for the also-rans. The two-tier plan proved unnecessary, however. For when the Six reached a joint agreement on liquidity creation at Munich in April, 1967, they decided that there should be only a form of conditional credit, without any new wholly owned reserve units. There was thus no longer any reasonable pretext for excluding the less-developed countries from whatever plan should finally be adopted by the Group of Ten.

Though this Munich agreement was the essential prelude to the "paper gold" plan which was eventually adopted, it concealed bitter differences of interpretation on the rules which should govern the new liquidity. The French proposed a system of Special Drawing Rights in the International Monetary Fund (in order to wean their partners away from unit-based schemes), but they insisted at first that these drawings must be repayable in full and that they could not be transferred from one country to another. In other words, they wanted nothing more than an extension of the drawing rights available in the existing IMF rules. A drawing right which does not need to be repaid is effectively an unconditional addition to liquidity, and a drawing right which can be freely transferred from one country to another is effectively equivalent to a unit or wholly owned reserve asset.

To some extent the Germans (who have yet to give any evidence of political backbone in Common Market negotiations) were prepared to humor the French. But the Italians and the Dutch (the most liberal of the Six on the liquidity issue) fiercely opposed the two conditions put forward by the French, since they knew they would be unacceptable to the Americans; in addition, they were more ready to be persuaded that the drain on gold must be compensated by the creation of unconditional assets which could play the same role as gold.

Thus by the spring of 1967 the negotiations over liquidity creation had been narrowed down to six major issues within the framework of a consensus on drawing rights: (1) transferability of the new rights among countries; (2) repayment of drawings, or, as it was called, "reconstitution of drawing rights"; (3) the quantity of drawing rights that should be created; (4) the circumstances in which the drawing-right scheme should actually be put into operation, or "activation," as it was called; (5) voting control over the drawing rights; (6) the reform of the existing rules of the IMF, including the question of voting rights.

After a short time, the question of transferability started to fade from the center of the negotiations. The French continued to press for a minimalist interpretation, but it soon became obvious that this was not a real issue. Unlike ordinary IMF drawing rights, which are a claim on the Fund's currency pool, it was agreed that SDRs, or Special Drawing Rights, would be a purely paper asset, not backed by contributions to the IMF, either in gold or currencies. Countries would be able to make use of their SDRs by handing them over to other countries in exchange for spendable foreign exchange. In other words, the transferability of SDRs was to be an intrinsic part of the new system.

Many of the negotiators were afraid that if certain countries remained in deficit for prolonged periods, they would automatically settle their external accounts as painlessly as possible—and that all the new "paper gold" would thus end up in the coffers of the surplus countries. The safeguard that was finally adopted was that drawings of SDRs could take place only under the supervision of the IMF and that no country could be obliged to accept more than twice as many SDRs from its partners in the Fund as it had already received in the original distribution. If Germany's initial allocation of "paper gold" had been one hundred million dollars, for example, it had to accept up to two hundred million dollars' worth of SDRs from other countries in exchange for Deutschemarks, if asked to do so by the IMF. But it could refuse to take any more than that.

Repayment (or "reconstitution," as the negotiators called it) was a much tougher nut, for this was the element of conditional credit in the new plan. The Americans opposed any form of repayment, since they wanted SDRs to be as wholly owned as gold, but the Six all argued that the use of SDRs must carry with it at least some obligation to repay. However, since the new assets were not going to operate in the same way as ordinary IMF drawing rights, it was impossible for repayment to work in the same way either. The members of the Fund were to receive a regular distribution of SDRs each year for five years, and the Europeans insisted that no country should spend its entire allocation every year. They were quite prepared for individual countries to be able to draw heavily on the SDRs when they were really in balance-of-payments difficulties, but they did not intend the new reserve asset to be used for the financing of chronic and uncontrolled deficits. They therefore argued that if a country really needed to spend all its "paper gold" in one year (or even two or three years in extreme cases), then it ought to be taking corrective measures to eliminate its balance-of-payments difficulties, so that it would be in a position to spend fewer SDRs in following years, or even to buy some back with gold and foreign exchange. It would not draw any "paper gold" in these years. In other words, most European countries wanted SDRs to be partly a permanent and wholly owned addition to reserves, and partly an emergency ration for temporary difficulties.

Naturally, the French went furthest, and insisted that only half of the SDRs allocated over a five-year period could be a permanent addition to reserves. If a country used all of its entitlement during the first three years, then it would not only be forbidden to use any during the next two years, but would actually have to buy some back, so that its average use over the five years amounted to no more than fifty percent.

By August, 1967, however, the compromise on this issue was already in sight, and as one might expect, it lay almost exactly halfway between the French and American positions: any country could use up to seventy percent of its allocation on average over five years, but if it went above that level it would have to "reconstitute" its holdings of the new asset by buying some back with gold or foreign exchange.

By August, too, the first signs of a consensus were beginning to emerge on the quantity of SDRs that should be created, lying in the region of one to two billion dollars a year for the first five years, distributed among all the members of the Fund in proportion to their existing IMF quotas. This consensus appeared to remain in force for the next eighteen months or so, though with minor variations aimed at maximizing the acceptability and credibility of the new asset. The main drawback of the SDR plan was its novelty, and despite all the protracted and detailed negotiations which had already gone into its preparation, it was impossible to be sure that governments and central banks would really treat them as reserve assets on a par with gold and foreign exchange. If "paper gold" should be treated as an inferior asset, everyone would want to pay with it, and no one would want to receive it, and the new plan would rapidly lose credibility and would thus fail to provide any usable new liquidity.

Most people believed that credibility would be achieved only if a regular supply of "paper gold" was distributed every year for five years, on the grounds that central bankers, being men of habit and tradition and like other bankers concerned primarily with the value of the assets in their vaults, would take some time to put their faith in the new liquidity. Others, like Otmar Emminger, believed that one to two billion dollars would represent such a small percentage increase in the world's money supply after being divided among all the members of the IMF that it would not have any practical effect on the attitudes of the central bankers. He argued, therefore, that it was essential to start the plan off with a bang, by distributing a really large amount, say five billion dollars a year, for the first two or three years, tapering off to smaller and more normal annual allocations after that.

By the end of 1968, however, it became clear that the "consensus" on a figure in the range of one to two billion dollars did not represent a real agreement between the United States and the European countries. By being moderate on the question of the amount during the crucial stages of the basic negotiations, the Americans had avoided making too many concessions. Once they had secured agreement on the basic principles, they were free to press for expanding the plan above what had originally been "agreed."

In theory there was no particular sense in arguing over figures at this early stage, since the negotiations were concerned—at least in appearance—only with the legal rules under which the new plan would operate when it was put into action. The Europeans had long pretended that they were engaged only in contingency planning, just so that the world would be prepared for the day when a shortage of liquidity should really emerge, and that the establishment of a scheme and its formal adoption into the charter of the IMF were quite distinct from its activation. According to this view, it was conceivable that many years might pass after the SDR rules had been agreed on before it should prove necessary to put them into effect; by that time, the world's requirements for new liquidity might be very different from the one to two billion dollars being discussed in 1968.

In reality it was already apparent, despite the screams of the French, that the political momentum (or impatience) which had been built up over the previous five years was too great to allow any significant delay in bringing the horse to the starting gate. By the time the Group of Ten had reached broad agreement on the outlines of the plan in the spring of 1968, most of them accepted that it would be put into action almost as soon as it had been formally approved and ratified by the members of the Fund. In other words, the French had been right in thinking that the only way to block the creation of artificial liquidity was to delay every stage of the preliminary negotiations as long as possible.

## HOW, AND HOW MUCH?

In any case, as soon as the "paper gold" plan had been safely approved by the members of the IMF, the Americans returned to the attack on the numbers front, demanding a very much larger initial distribution of drawing rights than had previously been discussed, and advancing arguments by (American) economists which set out to prove that the minimum quantity of new liquidity required lay in the region of five billion dollars a year for five years—the equivalent of about twenty-five percent of all existing quotas in the IMF in each of those years. Such a figure would have been regarded by the Europeans as little short of scandalous if it had been pressed by the United States in 1967 and the early months of 1968. It continued to be resisted by them subsequently, but it did not seem quite so scandalous, for in the intervening months the world had had such a surfeit of monetary crises—the pound, the gold rush, the collapse of the franc, and then the Deutschemark rush—that it was plain there was something seriously wrong with the existing international system. It became more plausible to argue that if SDRs were to be created, it made sense to create them in big enough quantities to make a real difference.

Voting control was the last major issue in dispute as the negotiations came into the homestretch in the summer of 1967. That the Six would insist on, and would secure, an eighty-five-percent majority rule on the SDR scheme was a foregone conclusion. But at the IMF annual meeting that autumn in Rio de Janeiro the French also demanded that the eighty-five-percent rule, as well as a number of other minor changes, should be introduced simultaneously into the existing Fund charter. In the head-on clash between France and the Americans, Michel Debré was backed by the German Economics Minister, Karl Schiller. The French failed to secure satisfaction, and though the meeting ended with a decision to press ahead with the legal drafting of the "paper gold" plan, it contained only a vague reference to other IMF reforms.

Karl Schiller may have believed that by supporting the French in Rio he would secure a more cooperative attitude from them in succeeding stages of the negotiations. As usual, he was mistaken. The final full-dress meeting of the ministers of the Group of Ten, in Stockholm on March 28, 1968—which took place against a backdrop of anti-Vietnam demonstrations by Swedish students— was intended to hammer out agreement on all the "political" issues which had defeated their deputies. But it was used by Debré for a wide-ranging protest against the whole scheme and against the Machiavellian maneuverings of the other countries. In short, he threw a tantrum, lasting three days. He claimed that in the months since Rio the scheme had been twisted out of all recognition, demanded much tighter restrictions on the activation and use of "paper gold," and for good measure argued that the whole scheme should be postponed. First, there should be a profound reexamination of the existing monetary system, which was sick and ought to be replaced by a new system based solely on gold and credit. His colleagues solemnly agreed with him that there was much that was wrong with the international monetary system, but suggested that this was not the moment to start at the beginning again.

It was here in Stockholm that the solidarity between the Six finally broke down. General de Gaulle had been enraged by the decision of the remaining Gold Pool countries on March 17 to shut off the supply to speculators, and the Five had been thoroughly alienated by the General's strong-arm attempts to break the gold-dollar system. Both in private meetings of the Six beforehand and in the plenary sessions, the Germans and the Italians attempted to act in Stockholm as mediators between the

French and the Americans. But they left no doubt that in the last resort they would side with the United States against France in favor of the "paper gold" plan.

At this stage in the proceedings France had only one bargaining weapon against SDRs: to threaten not to take part when the plan was put into operation. It was a serious threat, since the refusal of an important country to accept "paper gold" in payment could reduce its credibility as an internationally valid currency, and there was a strong possibility that France would be able to persuade its client states in Africa to opt out too. But it was not a fatal threat, provided no other major country followed suit, and after a prolonged battle the rest conceded to France the right to opt out of the whole operation if it wanted to. Nevertheless, Michel Debré still refused to endorse the final package deal, and his government refused to approve it at the following ministerial meeting of the IMF in Washington that autumn. Significantly enough, however, France failed to rally the support of all its associates in the franc zone; they had too much to gain in cash terms to be swayed by purely political arguments.

Once France's nine partners in the Group of Ten had agreed on the broad lines of the plan, there was little left to do but tie up the loose ends in proper legalese. Nearly all of the finance ministers must have been certain that the formal approval of the new monetary deal by the required majority of the member countries in the IMF and the subsequent distribution of artificial reserve assets were only a matter of time.

Like every previous phase in the negotiations, the Stockholm agreement was hedged around with provisos that "paper gold" would be activated only after an improvement in the U.S. balance-of-payments position, and after a consensus had been reached that there was indeed a real shortage of liquidity. But in fact it was already clear in the spring of 1968 that these conditions were just paper safeguards to appease the French and—to a lesser extent—the other creditor countries, and that activation was a foregone conclusion. The only question that remained to be fought over was: How much?

In this sense, and in this sense only, the French suffered an outright defeat at Stockholm. But in virtually every other respect, the honors of battle were so evenly divided that both the Anglo-

Americans and the Europeans could claim a victory in a revolutionary improvement in the international monetary system. For one thing, the agreement avoided all the explosive words which had been at the heart of so much bitter argument: credit, reserve asset, reserve unit, conditional, unconditional, loans, repayments —all these loaded terms were rigorously excluded, and their place was taken by a new and obscure jargon: "facility," "allocation," and "reconstitution."

But the agreement was not merely the result of semantic acrobatics on the part of the finance-ministry officials. "Paper gold" really is a new kind of animal, which has some of the characteristics of money and some of the characteristics of credit, but isn't exactly like either money or credit, and even has some characteristics quite different from those of any existing reserve assets.

## "PAPER GOLD" IN PRACTICE

Special Drawing Rights are usually described as "paper gold." In fact, an SDR is not a piece of paper, and it has relatively little to do with gold. Though its value is defined in terms of the precious metal, it is an entry in a special set of accounts kept by the IMF. When the plan is put into action, each participating country is credited in the accounts with a certain number of SDRs, in proportion to its existing stake in the IMF. On the other hand, "Special Drawing Rights" is also a misleading name, for the new asset is quite different from ordinary IMF drawing rights.

As such, SDRs cannot be spent directly; they can only be transferred in the ledger from one participating country to another, in exchange for convertible currency which can be spent. In effect, therefore, the plan creates the possibility of temporary redistribution of foreign exchange to countries which need it most, either because they have fallen into deficit or because for some other reason they have suffered a drop in their gold and foreign-exchange reserves.

Of course it is not enough just to write down a number of entries in a ledger. The plan can work only if the SDRs are regarded by all participating countries as a "sound" form of reserve asset, on a par with and complementary to gold and foreign exchange. As we have said, if governments were to believe that

SDRs are somehow inferior to, or less valuable than, their other reserve assets, they would be anxious to get rid of them, and the whole plan would break down.

In the long run the proof of the pudding is in the eating. Complete acceptability can be achieved only after experience has shown that "paper gold" is in fact accepted in exchange for foreign currencies, and countries become convinced that it will in future continue to be exchangeable for foreign exchange. That, after all, is the basis for the confidence private individuals put in their national currencies. The law may decree that the coins and notes issued by the central bank are "legal tender" and must be accepted in commercial transactions. But if inflation gathers momentum, public confidence in the legal currency starts to fray at the edges, and people prefer to spend their money quickly in exchange for durable goods or real estate, before prices go up any more. And if inflation gets completely out of control, as it did in Germany between the two world wars, public confidence in the currency disappears entirely, and transactions with money are likely to be replaced by barter. Once social confidence in the relative stability of money has evaporated, it doesn't matter very much what the law says.*

But until experience has established the acceptability of "paper gold," formal rules for their operation are essential, and the SDR plan is built on a network of incentives, controls, and restrictions. Countries have an incentive for holding "paper gold," in the sense that they carry a gold-value guarantee and that, unlike gold itself, they earn interest. At the other end of the scale is the restriction that no country can be obliged to accept more than twice as many transferred SDRs as it originally received in the initial allocation.

But most important are the controls, which are exercised by the IMF. Any country can decide to make use of its "paper gold," though it will be expected to do so only if it is in balance-of-payments difficulties or if it has lost reserves. But it cannot decide to which country it will transfer its SDRs; that decision can be taken only by the IMF, on the basis of a series of agreed criteria. Broadly speaking, it will channel transfers of "paper gold" to countries which have large gold and foreign-exchange reserves or a

* See "Special Drawing Rights," pp. 210-211.

strong surplus on their balance of payments or which have previously made extensive use of their own SDRs. Over a period of time the Fund will try to ensure that there is a fairly even distribution of "paper gold" among the participating countries. Finally, as already explained, there is a strict limit to the use that any one country can make of its drawing rights. If it spends them very heavily in the first two or three years, for example, it may have to buy them back, so that its average use over any five-year period does not go above seventy percent of its allocation.

Money or credit? One answer would be that the first seventy percent of allocated SDRs are virtually equivalent to money, but that the last thirty percent are virtually equivalent to credit. Unlike credit, they do not represent a debt to any one institution or government and do not need to be redeemed (provided only seventy percent are used). Unlike money, they cannot be spent directly on goods or services, they need not be accepted above a certain limit, and they can be used only under the supervision of the IMF. Unlike gold, they are created at the stroke of a pen and do not have to be painfully acquired by digging holes in the ground or by selling other assets like foreign exchange.

Nevertheless, the French were probably right in thinking that the new facility would be more like money than credit—that is what most other countries wanted—even if they were probably wrong to object to it on these grounds. Yet though they refused to approve or ratify the scheme, they continued to take part in the subsequent negotiations on the activation of "paper gold." Not because they thought they could modify the terms of the scheme —it was far too late to do that—but because they hoped that they might exact some compensating concessions. Predictably, they attempted to slow down the negotiations on the volume of SDRs by tacking on a whole series of other issues which they claimed must be settled at the same time, including the question of South African gold and the future of the ordinary IMF quotas. They abandoned the gold problem quite rapidly, for lack of support from their colleagues, but they stuck fast to the quota issue.

This should have been a good pretext for delaying the creation of "paper gold" for months, if not years, for IMF quotas must be reviewed once every five years, and the next review period did not come up until 1970. As a delaying tactic this proved, however, to be a failure, for the other members of the Group of Ten agreed to settle the question of ordinary quotas in the IMF well ahead of time. But as a bargaining gambit, it could be turned to good account in the service of the French preference for credit-type liquidity, provided the French could strengthen their position by resurrecting a negotiation alliance with the other members of the Common Market. Like the Dutch and the Germans, the French could oppose American demands for a really massive distribution of "paper gold," but they could be sure of forcing the Americans to give ground (and of maintaining a common front between the Six) only if they were prepared to offer a large increase in the lending powers of the IMF.

The irony of this was that the French proposal was doubly inconsistent with everything they had previously stood for. At the previous review period, in 1965, the French strenuously opposed any increase in IMF quotas, objected vehemently to the dodges employed to protect the American gold reserves, and only tagged along with the twenty-five-percent increase voted by the other members of the Fund after it was clear that their objections would go entirely unheeded. Yet now it was they who were pressing for bigger IMF quotas. The inconsistency is underlined by the fact that Giscard d'Estaing, who had been Finance Minister in 1965, was back at the head of the same department in 1969, and that Georges Pompidou, who had been Prime Minister in 1965, succeeded General de Gaulle as President in 1969; the only change which took place between the two periods was that General de Gaulle himself had resigned.

The second inconsistency is even more paradoxical. In 1967, when the European countries had been loudly demanding a bigger say in the affairs of the IMF, in proportion to their real contribution to its lending capacity through the General Arrangements to Borrow, the Americans had always retorted that the easiest way to achieve this result would be for the Europeans to increase their contributions to the Fund: an extra boost in the quotas of the Common Market countries would automatically increase their voting powers. But at that time the Europeans refused to take up this suggestion (on the grounds that they were already contributing heavily through the GAB) and demanded—successfully—a change in the IMF's rules that would give the Six a blocking vote. By July, 1969, however—after this change in the rules had already been agreed—the European creditor countries were ready to do what they had refused two years earlier. At a meeting in Paris they agreed not only that there should be a large increase in IMF quotas but also that the creditor countries—most European countries and Japan—would make bigger increases than the deficit countries like Britain and the United States, and the Six would thus get over twenty percent of the votes in the Fund.

At the same time, they compromised with the Americans over "paper gold" by agreeing that the plan should be put into operation at the beginning of 1970, that a total of 9.5 billion dollars' worth of SDRs should be distributed, but that these distributions should take place over three years only, not five as had originally been agreed in 1968. Though the Americans were forced to make do with a smaller allocation and a shorter period than they had wanted, their concessions had been virtually painless. For if you added together the allocation of SDRs and the increase in IMF quotas, the total increase in international liquidity would not be very far short of five billion dollars a year for three years, even though part of this increase would be in the form of conditional or credit-type assets.

The immediate consequence of the link between "paper gold" and the increase in Fund quotas is that the surplus countries like the Six not only will secure a bigger stake in the IMF but also will receive a proportionately larger allocation of the new drawing rights. In the first year, 1970, the allocations are based on existing Fund quotas, which means that the Six get nearly eighteen percent. But once the Six have increased their share of Fund quotas, they will also be entitled to a bigger share of "paper gold." This suits the French, of course, since it means that the Americans will get proportionately less of the new artificial reserves and will therefore have less scope for using them to finance a continuing balance-of-payments deficit. But it should also improve the prospects that SDRs really will acquire the status of valid reserves. If one excludes the Bank for International Settlements, which pays its dividends in gold francs and has always had a weakness for the virtues of gold, reticence about "paper gold" had been strongly felt in France, and only to a very much lesser extent in some other European countries. If the surplus countries were prepared to accept large initial allocations of the new assets, it meant in arithmetical terms that their obligation to accept transfers of "paper gold" from deficit countries would be that much greater too.

In fact, French arguments that SDRs would relieve the United States from any obligation to reduce its deficit were little more than hysterical scare-mongering. Between 1959 and 1968 the American deficit amounted to sixteen billion dollars, as measured by the fall in gold holdings and the rise in foreign debts, or an average of about one billion dollars a year. The present American quota in the Fund is about twenty-four percent, so that of 3.5 billion dollars' worth of SDRs created in 1970, the United States will receive about eighty-four million dollars' worth of them. But over a given period, the United States can spend only seventy percent of its allocation, which means that its usable drawing rights will amount to about 588 million dollars. To a small extent this may ease the problem of the American deficit, but it certainly will not permit the United States to go on for the next ten years as it has for the past ten. In any case, it represents only an addition of just over five percent to the American gold stock (somewhat over ten billion dollars) and leaves wholly untouched the problem of the dollar liabilities to foreign countries, which amount to over seventeen billion dollars.

It is conceivable, of course, that the Americans will continue to run a deficit on the same scale as in the past. If that happens, other countries may simply resign themselves to accepting yet more dollars, or they may protect themselves (and the United States) from a further accumulation of official dollar liabilities by pushing the dollars onto the Euro-dollar market. But SDRs by themselves will not enable the United States to finance a large and prolonged deficit, unless much larger amounts are created in the future.

When the liquidity negotiations started, the orthodox Europeans opposed a worldwide distribution of assets, on the grounds that it would be treated as development aid by the poor countries. Once again, the facts do not support this kind of argument. On the basis of a total distribution of 3.5 billion dollars' worth of SDRs, the less-developed members of the Fund would get about 970 million dollars, of which the spendable seventy percent would amount to some 680 million dollars. Yet their total imports run at about forty-seven billion dollars a year, so that "paper gold" would give them only 1.5 percent of extra spending power. Similarly, even if the developing countries were to treat their SDR allocations as aid, to be spent immediately on goods and services, it would not add very much to what they already receive from the industrialized countries. In 1967 the total flow of official aid reached just under seven billion dollars, and the total flow of private aid just over four billion dollars, a total of slightly over eleven billion. Against this order of magnitude, an allocation of 680 million dollars' worth of spendable SDRs represents an increase of about six percent—a noticeable and welcome addition, no doubt, but less than the increase in aid flows from 1966 to 1967.

"Paper gold" should provide less-developed and industrial countries alike with a small but steady increase in liquidity, which will make it easier for any of them to get through periods of temporary deficit. It is small, because 3.5 billion dollars' worth of SDRs represents well under five percent of the free world's total reserves, if one counts gold, foreign exchange, and IMF drawing rights, and at this rate reserves will continue to grow more slowly than international trade. But smallness should be partly compensated by regularity. Countries which are short of reserves—or, much more important, countries which *feel* short of reserves—are reluctant to run their economies at a high rate of expansion if it looks likely to lead to a balance-of-payments deficit and a further drop in reserves. But if they feel confident that they can count on a regular inflow of reserves through "paper gold," they are much more likely to contemplate a temporary deficit with equanimity. That, at any rate, is the purpose for which the new reserve assets are being created. It is still too early to say whether it will operate exactly as planned.

"Paper gold" represents the most significant improvement in the international monetary system since World War II. In practice it may well prove to have some imperfections and require periodic adjustment. But the essential feature of the plan—that liquidity will no longer be dependent either on the arbitrary characteristics of gold production and distribution or on the balance-of-payments deficits of rich countries like Britain and America or the ad-hoccery of credit arrangements between central banks—is a major step forward. We cannot yet say the liquidity will be created in the future on purely rational grounds, since there is no agreement on precise liquidity needs, and decisions on numbers are bound to reflect a compromise between conflicting political pressures. But we can say that in future liquidity will be created as a result of systematic negotiations and deliberate international agreement.

In reality, the shortage of liquidity is one of the least of our international worries, and it is the most easily solved because it has the least effect on the freedom of countries to run their national economies as they see fit. "Paper gold" provides no solution to the more serious underlying problems of economic management, it does nothing to eliminate large and chronic balance-of-payments surpluses and deficits, and it leaves entirely untouched the question of exchange rates. A thirty-page study on the adjustment of balance of payments, which emerged after two years of discussions in the OECD, resembled the philosophy of the Greeks, which, according to Bacon, "must be acknowledged puerile, or rather talkative than generative—as being fruitful in controversies, but barren of effects."

## SPECIAL DRAWING RIGHTS

Special Drawing Rights are a new form of international reserve asset which are to be included in reserves alongside gold, dollars, pounds, and other foreign exchange. The broad lines of the new rules governing SDRs were agreed by the Group of Ten at a meeting in Stockholm in March, 1968. In July, 1969, the Group of Ten agreed to put Special Drawing Rights into operation, with a distribution of 3.5 billion dollars in 1970, three billion dollars in 1971, and three billion dollars in 1972. On each occasion the Special Drawing Rights would be distributed to each participating country in proportion to its current IMF quota.

Though SDRs, or "paper gold," are defined in terms of gold and earn a small amount of interest, they are a wholly artificial form of reserve asset, created solely by a majority decision of the members of the Fund, and exist solely as bookkeeping entries in a special ledger kept by the Fund in Washington. As such, SDRs cannot be spent directly on goods or services, but they can be exchanged with other countries for usable foreign currency.

Normally a country should draw upon its SDRs only if it is in deficit or is losing reserves, and on average it may only use seventy percent of its SDR allocation; if its spending goes higher than this, it must reduce its drawing in subsequent years, and may have to buy SDRs from other countries in order to get back under its seventy-percent ceiling.

Every participating country is obliged to provide currency in exchange for SDRs if it is requested to do so by the IMF. But it can refuse to accept any more SDRs once its total holdings rise above three hundred percent of its initial allocation.

For purposes of comparison, the total volume of gold held in Western reserves is thirty-nine billion dollars; the total volume of dollars held in official reserves is 15.8 billion dollars; and the total of quotas in the IMF is 21.2 billion dollars, probably to rise to 28.2 billion dollars. The initial distribution over three years of SDRs will amount to 9.5 billion dollars.

Just about the only thing on which people who know something about the monetary system can agree is that it ought to be improved. Reform of the Bretton Woods agreement—indeed, calls for a "new" Bretton Woods—are now almost standard in the vocabulary of would-be monetary sages. Reform is in fashion and many of its advocates seem to believe that if only their ideas were adopted, the world would have seen the reform to end all reforms.

Yet the trials and tribulations of the Bretton Woods system during the past twenty-five years show the folly of thinking that any reform of the monetary system is final. After a decade largely devoted to patching up the Bretton Woods agreement, there is clearly a need for reform. But it must be a continuing reform, accepting its own long-term inadequacy in advance.

There are more plans for reforming the monetary system than there are problems—from the Triffin plan to the Bernstein plan to the Stamp plan to the Rueff plan and scores of others. Many of them are technically superb. But monetary reform is too important to be left to the technicians. Any one of a number of plans might work well; there is

CHAPTER **9**

# What Next?

no reason to believe that the Bretton Woods conferees might not have come up with an equally good but totally different arrangement. But no plan can be certain of operating properly unless people and governments have confidence in it, because no international authority exists to encourage or force them to follow its rules. Confidence can result only from the strength of the international consensus about any monetary system and the action—the political action—taken by governments to buttress that consensus.

Each government must decide what it wants and what it should do to get what it wants. These are, of course, political decisions. Based on the experiences of the last decade, both the United States and Europe are faced with a number of choices which will do much to shape the future world monetary system and, not incidentally, the future world.

## THE CRISIS OF AMERICAN LEADERSHIP

Ever since the British learned at the time of the Bretton Woods conference that they no longer could call the shots in international economic affairs, the United States has dominated. At first, no one could question the American right to this role, because it was the chief economic benefactor of many nations and possessed an unusually large share of the world's wealth and power. The United States still occupies the position as leader, but this role is no longer unquestioned, nor, in the eyes of some abroad, is it completely justified.

American leadership in monetary affairs has been based on the ability of the dollar to serve as the international trading currency as well as forming a major part of the reserves of most nations. In other words, both the private sector and central banks have willingly accepted dollars. The private sector, at least, continues to do so willingly; the central banks settle with each other in dollars, because they realize that refusal under present circumstances to do so would lead to economic chaos and collapse of the monetary system. Thus American leadership is no longer based on a position of strength.

In view of this changed situation, to obtain the kind of monetary reform that would suit American interests, the U.S.

government faces a series of decisions affecting both national policy and foreign policy. Because both sets of decisions involve setting priorities and choosing among options that could determine the nation's future course, the government is grappling with essentially political issues. The technicians of monetary policy can only suggest the various methods to achieve desired goals; they cannot prescribe the goals. Of course, policies should be adopted because they are worthwhile of themselves and not merely as monetary palliatives.

## THE CHOICES IN NATIONAL POLICY

Military programs, foreign economic aid, international trade, and foreign investment—these four factors have had the greatest impact on the deteriorating American balance of payments and hence on the weakening of the dollar and on American leadership in monetary affairs. As we have seen, all too seldom did Washington policy-makers take into account the "side effects" of major decisions in these sectors on the U.S. monetary position. Naturally, monetary considerations are not the only ones that matter, nor are they always worthy of highest priority. But they are not, on the other hand, so peripheral that they can be completely ignored. If the United States makes sacrifices in its balance of payments, say, for military-assistance programs abroad, this means that it cannot do other things abroad. It is not simply a question of raising additional revenues to finance additional programs. The United States cannot pump an unlimited amount of dollars into the world. Other nations may agree to hold the dollars they receive without turning them in for gold, but they will not do so forever and for an ever-increasing amount. So long as there is an overall balance-of-payments deficit, the United States must take steps to limit those programs which cause the greatest number of dollars to flow out.

Of course, the situation would be markedly different if the United States were running a consistent balance-of-payments surplus. But in order to get to that point, the United States would still have to limit programs which drain dollars out of the country in excess of what it can reasonably expect to earn and receive from abroad.

As we have seen, American foreign military programs have been a continuous and sizable drain on the dollar. Many of them are necessary, not simply because of U.S. commitments to aid in the defense of other nations, but because such military alliances also are vital to the defense of the United States. Military programs provide national security, and many if not most Americans believe that there should be no quibbling about the cost of defending the nation. But they may not realize that if no attention is paid to the cost of any one program, its scope may in fact prevent the establishment of other programs equally vital to national security.

The United States has accepted its overseas military commitments on a relatively ad hoc basis. American troops are stationed in all corners of the world, arms and matériel are shipped to every continent. In Vietnam, sums that would have seemed astronomical ten short years ago are now spent with careless abandon.

Naturally, we cannot define in an offhand manner what specific foreign military programs should be created, maintained, or canceled. But we can accept as a given fact that U.S. troops will continue to be stationed in Europe. As a result, dollars will continue to flow into the coffers of those very countries which have a diminishing need for them and thus are tempted to convert them into gold. To prevent this kind of pressure building up on the dollar, the American government is forced to seek each year agreements with European nations which will cause the dollars to be channeled into purchases of American arms or U.S. Treasury bonds. This is a sort of charity given by the Europeans to the Americans in return for the U.S. forces stationed in Europe. Naturally, these forces are there as much in the American interest as in the European interest, and consequently the United States should foot part of the bill. But, instead of annual negotiations, it would seem wise for the United States to press for the adoption of some formula by which a European contribution to their costs would be possible. This would not necessarily be a compensatory expenditure in the United States by the country receiving dollars. It might well be direct contribution to the cost of maintaining the forces. The cost could be reduced if the European country in question decided to increase the size of its own armed forces, making it possible to withdraw some American troops. After all, if the Atlantic Alliance has any meaning, it is that troops of all

NATO nations are committed to the defense of the region. NATO agrees on the necessary overall level of forces, but there is no reason why the strengths of the national contingents making up NATO forces could not be altered.

The debate over American intervention in Vietnam has acquired major moral overtones, and monetary considerations pale in importance beside them. The government is committed to a withdrawal of American forces from that country, but it has never undertaken a commitment to reduce expenditures there. If Vietnam costs are not cut, the United States must recognize that the dollar drain, which some estimate to be as high as four billion annually, will continue to reduce flexibility in American foreign policy, simply because the United States will not be able to spend an unlimited amount of dollars freely, even if it had them to spend. In addition, the United States depends, as we have seen, on the goodwill and cooperativeness of other countries to maintain the strength of the dollar. But their patience and willingness to help may grow thin if the United States makes little or no progress in extricating itself from the Vietnam conflict, of which many American allies disapprove. Vietnam is a monetary albatross around America's neck. While monetary considerations cannot alone determine U.S. policy toward an ultimate settlement there, they obviously cannot be ignored.

The foreign aid program, as we have seen, has been less of a burden on the American balance of payments in succeeding years, thanks to a gradual cutback in aid outlays. Reductions in foreign aid were not made, of course, in order to spare the American gold stock. Funds for economic development assistance were in fact cut because many in Congress felt that the program was failing to meet the objectives they had set for it. In the short run, it may be expected that foreign aid should mean that a recipient country will assume a friendly attitude toward the United States. For those in Congress who believe that this is the purpose of foreign aid, there have been some indisputable disappointments. If they choose to reduce this aid because it has not fulfilled short-term goals, they do in fact provide short-term assistance to the American balance of payments.

But in the longer run, the reduction of foreign economic aid will do no service to the American balance of payments and may also worsen the climate of international monetary negotiations. Foreign aid may be seen as part of an effort to build up the economies of nations around the world. Admittedly, even when their economies are stronger, these countries will not be guaranteed allies of the United States. But, if the case of Europe after the Marshall Plan is any indication, they should be better customers for American production and perhaps even open new opportunities for American investment. The ties created by trade and capital movements are likely to bind countries more closely than the relationship between donor and recipient. In addition, more countries with stronger economies and possibly stronger currencies will be able to play some role in the reform of the international monetary system. With more countries participating in the system and contributing to it, the sacrifices demanded of any single one of the current members—including the United States—are likely to be reduced. Without the kind of intellectual and financial contribution that other countries can make to the system and its reform, the existing members will have fewer options and less latitude for seeking solutions to their problems. Of course, no one should harbor the illusion that the day is near when the poor countries can contribute to the health of the international financial community. But it won't get any nearer without some effort to speed the process of economic development.

Foreign trade has always been a source of support for the American balance of payments. Traditionally, the United States sells more abroad than it buys from foreign countries. Now, however, the United States is trading more, but enjoying it less. Trade surpluses have dwindled to the point where they have almost disappeared. A tide of protectionism, fairly well held back for the last thirty-five years, is threatening to burst through the limits placed on it and dominate U.S. trade policy.

The protectionists argue that the only way to improve the trade balance once again is to reduce drastically imports from abroad, while maintaining a high level of exports. They correctly perceive that U.S. imports have risen far faster than exports in recent years. They believe this increase in purchases of foreign goods is due to a competitive advantage enjoyed by other countries, for example, in the form of lower labor costs. As a result, they argue that

American protection should be increased to slow the inflow of these foreign-made goods.

But the protectionists are wrong on two points. American imports have risen at an alarming rate. This is not due to the cut-rate pricing of foreign goods, but because American goods have become inordinately expensive as a result of inflation. More expensive American products are naturally less desirable to foreign consumers. In order to cut the flow of imports, then, it is far more important to reduce domestic inflation than to slap controls on imports from abroad. The protectionists also fail to reckon with foreign retaliation against increased American protectionism. After all, other governments must think of their trade balances just as much as Washington.

If the United States wants to prolong its unbroken string of trade surpluses dating back about a century, chances of success are far greater if it tries to boost exports. Admittedly, in order for another country to acquire the dollars it needs to buy more from the United States, it may well have to sell more to the United States. But American exporters have shown themselves to be astute judges of the market, able to provide goods not obtainable elsewhere, particularly those which result from the latest technological developments.

Americans have never considered their country to be a trading nation in the way the Dutch, the British, or the Germans do. Their countries must sell a large part of their production abroad or they cannot survive economically. This is not true for the United States, where exports account for only about four percent of the gross national product. Though this figure is not particularly impressive in relative terms, let's take a look at its absolute level. With a gross national product of more than nine hundred billion dollars, the goods and services which are exported would be valued at thirty-six billion dollars—more than the entire national product of the Netherlands. This means that it would be unwise to think solely in terms of the relative importance of trade and wiser to recognize that thirty-six billion dollars in exports creates hundreds of thousands of jobs and represents the sale of production that might be superfluous in the U.S. market. In other words, it would be appropriate to think of the United States as a trading nation.

At the present time, American policy does not do as much to stimulate exports as is the case in some European countries. Special tax incentives, easier credit terms, and an increased effort to publicize American products are all desirable measures. By gradually shedding some of its remaining protectionist policies, the United States would be in a stronger position to attack the protectionism of other countries.

American investment abroad has borne the brunt of the criticism of U.S. policies which led to the dollar drain. As we have seen, such criticisms are not completely justified in that American investment has been an important factor in the economic growth of the countries in which it has been particularly intense. Yet the Johnson and Nixon administrations have been forced to conclude, however reluctantly, that stringent controls had to be placed on investment abroad in order to cut the dollar outflow.

Government controls on American investment cannot continue indefinitely because they represent a form of official restraint on the economy which is contrary to the American tradition. The business community is bound to become increasingly restless with the existing controls, and the administration is committed to their removal at the earliest possible date. But once controls on direct investment abroad are removed, there is no assurance that the flows will not be of such magnitude as to endanger once again the U.S. balance of payments. Instead of being forced to contemplate the reintroduction of controls on dollar outflow, the government might consider attaching a few conditions to renewed freedom to invest abroad. For example, corporations might be required to invest a certain number of dollars in the high-risk, less-developed countries for every few dollars invested in the low-risk, highly developed countries. This requirement would probably be in the best interests of business which stands to gain a high rate of return on its investment in the developing nations. Dollars invested accordingly would not only make money for the investor, but would help serve the aims of American foreign policy, which is only fair in view of their potential effect in increasing the dollar drain and the threat to the American gold stock. Investment in the poorer nations is, in any case, unlikely to grow without the government encouraging or forcing it. The Nixon administration has said it favors increased private investment in these countries to take over part of the development burden formerly assumed by the foreign-aid program. Putting together all these factors, it seems to make good sense to channel some direct investment to the developing countries, not merely by permitting it when it is restricted in other countries, or by asking corporations to do their part, but by requiring it.

The kind of domestic measures we have just been discussing represent the major part of a constructive effort to strengthen the U.S. balance of payments and the American position in international monetary affairs. They will probably be more successful than American exhortations to other countries to help the United States deal with its monetary problems, though, of course, they should. Naturally they do not relieve the American government of the immediate task of reducing inflation.

The United States has now had ample time to learn that there are no politics of gratitude, that memories in other countries may be far too short for Americans to count on these countries repaying their moral debts, much less their financial ones. On the other hand, now that the economic and monetary interdependence of Europe and the United States is an established fact, there is nothing to be gained by taking delight in other countries' difficulties. A cooperative and constructive American attitude, designed to promote confidence among the countries participating in the monetary system, still seems to be the best approach.

## THE AMERICAN APPROACH TO MONETARY REFORM

By putting its own house in order, the United States will be in a much improved position to seek the kind of reforms in the Bretton Woods system that will suit its interests. Long-term American goals probably remain much the same as they were twenty-five years ago: relative exchange-rate stability, wider convertibility of currencies, and an effective reserve pool which can enable countries to overcome short-lived balance-of-payments difficulties.

Attention in recent years has come to be focused on parities among the world's leading currencies. Governments have been overcommitted to maintaining the exchange rate of their money in terms of the dollar. They take this position of ironclad adherence to fixed and stable exchange rates partly to discourage speculation against their currencies and partly because they believe that their electors will accept nothing less than a last-ditch defense of the exchange rate because it symbolizes the relative international standing of their countries. When devaluation and, less frequently, revaluation become unavoidable, they appear to be catastrophic political events indicating that the nation is in imminent peril of going under for the last time.

A number of ideas are now under study which would help take the sting out of devaluation and would prevent governments from waiting until the last minute to decide that their countries' balance of payments were in "fundamental disequilibrium"—hopelessly out of balance. The IMF's Pierre-Paul Schweitzer, apparently speaking with the assent of most of the Fund's executive directors, has suggested that there is nothing in his organization's rules which would prevent more frequent changes in the parities of the currencies of its members. In effect, he said that the IMF would not object to more regular and less earth-shaking decisions to devalue or revalue based on a belief that such a measure was inevitable sooner or later, but if done sooner might be limited in scope.

Many experts do not, however, believe that there is sufficient flexibility in the Bretton Woods "rules of the game." They would prefer some form of regular, small, and semi-automatic changes in the parities of currencies. One proposal calls for a "wider band" of permissible fluctuation in exchange rates. Under the current rules, a currency's parity cannot be allowed to move more than one percent above or one percent below the established exchange rate with the dollar or gold. But the band could be extended to any limits from two to five percent on either side of the official rate. A second proposal calls for a "moving peg," whose very name suggests both revision and stability, a neat trick. According to this proposal, a government could make small, frequent changes in the exchange rate amounting to one or two percent annually on the basis of balance-of-payments performance and prospects. A third proposal calls for a "dynamic peg" (more motion, but still the stability of a peg), also known as a "crawling band" (pretty slow-moving). As might be guessed, this proposal combines the features of the first two. The exchange rate of a currency would be raised or lowered on the basis of a moving average of the actual exchange rates that have prevailed within a relatively wider band than is now used. Thus, if the exchange rate were normally near the top of the allowable zone of variation, the official exchange rate would be increased to this level and a new band established. This proposal would encourage speculation because monetary gamblers could guess in advance when it looked like the parity of a currency was due to be changed.

All of these proposals are now under study, and some experts even envisage the creation of freely floating exchange rates, which would mean the end of any semblance of imposed stability. It is hard to see how floating rates or even some of the flexible-parity proposals would work, and there is no guarantee that they would work better than the existing flexibility in the IMF rules. Yet all the proposals contain the common element of depoliticizing the decision to alter exchange rates; this is probably all to the good. Because changes in parities have become such major political decisions, they have been made only reluctantly, after periods of speculation and often of considerable stress on the monetary system. This can and should be avoided.

The United States is involved in this debate only to the extent that it is the leading member of the IMF. These proposals would not affect the dollar, which is, in fact, the currency against which the exchange rates of other moneys are calculated. But the United States can throw its full weight behind a thorough study of the alternatives and a possible trial of the most attractive of them by at least some countries. Even now, Chile and a few other countries are taking advantage of the flexibility in IMF rules and are devaluing their currencies regularly, as needed. Naturally, the Americans cannot encourage other governments to give up political control of the fate of their currencies. Governments can, however, adopt a general line of policy and then leave the actual execution of it to technical experts, probably central bank officials. This kind of reform of the IMF "rules of the game" would probably prove helpful in ensuring its continued ability to serve the changing needs of the international community.

The main problem with these proposals for new ways to make short-term and small changes in parities easier and less painful is the underlying belief that a single reform is all the tonic that the monetary system needs. If there is one lesson that the past quarter-century should have taught, it is that IMF members must be willing to accept continual reform of the Fund and the Bretton Woods system, that none of the "givens" that seem so sure today can be counted upon to be certain tomorrow. Consequently, even while endorsing the exploration of various proposals for flexible rates, the United States should not delude itself into believing that such a reform would be the last. Nor should it become complacent about reform, just because of a lull in the monetary storm.

Sooner or later, the problem of the dollar's international role will have to be examined. There is little doubt that it will continue to be the major currency for commercial purposes and, what's more, that dollars used in this way are not really a threat to the American gold stock, especially since the closing of the Gold Pool. They must remain in circulation to serve their purpose.

For monetary purposes—exchanges of reserves among central banks—the dollar is already to share the place of privilege it held beside gold with the newly created "paper gold." The chief virtue of this new monetary instrument is that its creation and growth are not based on gold production, but on IMF quotas. These quotas, subject to regular review, themselves reflect the relative economic, monetary, and political importance of IMF members. As a result, "paper gold" is similar to Keynes's *bancors*, though it is based on more factors than a country's share of world trade. And the quotas which underlie them are the fruit, not of some automatic rule, but of negotiations among governments. Such negotiations are the best way of taking account of intangible, political factors in making an important monetary decision.

It is still too early to know if the world will give its confidence to "paper gold." If it does, the amount of these Special Drawing Rights may be expanded, thus further reducing the relative importance of gold and dollars. It is not inconceivable that "paper gold" might one day be as acceptable for commercial transactions as the dollar is now.

Such developments could force the United States to revise fundamentally its view of the monetary system and the dollar's place in it. They do not mean that the American position of leadership would necessarily be undermined. Because they are not merely pipe dreams, though they may take place in the relatively distant future, they do require that Americans begin thinking of the dollar in different terms. There is nothing sacred about the dollar being pegged to gold at the rate of thirty-five dollars an ounce. A great weight could be lifted from American shoulders if the defense of this parity were not an article of faith in the ability of the United States to keep its commitments. It is quite conceivable that gold's place in the monetary system will decline to a point where no currency, including the dollar, can be usefully tied to it. After all, gold is only a metal and the dollar is only a piece of paper. What *is* important is the purposes they serve, and there is no reason to insist that they must always serve the same purposes as they "always" have served.

The present role of the dollar is not necessary for the maintenance of the American position of leadership in the monetary system. As long as the United States can maintain its strong and growing economy and its political leadership in the world, it can be certain of being a leader of the monetary system. And, by gradually freeing itself of the straitjacket of the current parity of the dollar to gold, the United States may actually be able both to strengthen its domestic economy and to have more discretion in its international activities. This is, at least, something worth thinking about.

## EUROPE'S MISSED OPPORTUNITIES

In the past ten years the biggest European export to the United States has been advice. With a certain smug self-satisfaction, the Continental European countries have talked throughout the 1960's as though it was all Washington's fault: the world would return to normal just as soon as the Americans paid some attention to the opinions of the Old World, stopped fighting wars in the Far East, and started practicing the solid virtues of discipline, modesty, and balance-of-payments equilibrium. Michel Debré's young assistant was speaking for a whole segment of European society when he compared the Americans to the imperial and domineering Romans.

By contrast, it was almost unheard of for any European politician to admit publicly that Europe should bear some of the responsibility for the continuing crisis in the international monetary system. As far as General de Gaulle was concerned, the Americans were intolerable and the power of the dollar was unbearable, and that was all there was to it. As far as the Germans were concerned, the American deficit was proof of inadequacy and the German surplus was proof of economic virtue; but somehow these two phenomena were regarded as totally unrelated. At no stage did the Continental Europeans even begin to recognize that the international monetary crisis highlighted a whole series of political choices for Europe which could not be avoided.

This blinkered attitude of otherwise responsible Europeans can be partly excused by extenuating circumstances. The United States had not followed a particularly constructive policy in the international monetary sphere, and long seemed almost oblivious of the real strains being set up in the international system. General de Gaulle was so obviously attempting to play the role of Samson in the temple that it was not entirely surprising that the other Continental countries attached their highest priority to propping up the pillars of the system, while at the same time exerting a restraining influence on the worst excesses of the United States. Yet it is curious that the Europeans should have gone on believing for so long, like the Americans, that the international monetary crisis was just a little local difficulty which would shortly disappear, and allow the world to return to the good old days of the mid-1950's.

Since 1969, however, the scope for self-deception and excuses has been considerably reduced. General de Gaulle is no longer there as the front man for those who are attached to old-fashioned monetary nostrums or who secretly share his nostalgic obsession with the virtues of the wholly independent national state. During the first ten years of the Common Market, political deadlock between the Six was offset by virtually trouble-free economic prosperity, but since 1968 the political strains within the Community have been matched by economic strains. By remaining divided, the Europeans have had little option but to leave most major initiatives to the United States. The multilateral force in NATO, the Kennedy Round of tariff cuts, the creation of artificial reserve assets, were all ideas that came out of Washington, and the policies of the European countries have been formed only incoherently as a reaction to those of the United States.

In retrospect, the balance sheet of European-American relations has been broadly positive. The Atlantic Alliance has continued to function after a fashion, and the MLF was fortunately dropped; the Kennedy Round was a very successful negotiation, even if it was nothing like as successful as President Kennedy would have wished; and the Special Drawing Rights agreement is potentially the most significant improvement in the international monetary system since Bretton Woods. But one cannot assume that the imbalance of power between the United States on the one hand and the rag-bag of disunited European states on the other will always produce such positive results for Europe; it is time that Europe made up its mind whether it wants to have an effective voice in world affairs.

The one thing that is certain is that it will not have an effective voice so long as it remains disunited. General de Gaulle tried to magnify French influence by an aggressive policy of freewheeling neutralism, but like the frog in the fable, which tried to swell up as big as a cow, he only succeeded after ten years of huffing and puffing in blowing himself up. The other Continental countries, by and large, were content to tag along behind the United States, but the British continued to nurse the hope of being able to wield a modestly independent influence in the world (and particularly in Washington) long after it had become little more than a costly illusion.

Now, most European countries may feel entirely free from any desire to put the rest of the world to rights. The Germans are still recovering from the scars of the Hitler regime and are quite clearly reluctant to be even suspected of throwing their weight about. The Italians and Belgians are currently having a hard enough time maintaining internal political cohesion without worrying too much about what happens on the other side of the world. But even if the European countries don't, in general, have ambitions to be laying down the law outside Europe, the plain fact of the matter is that the world is now too small for any country or group of countries to think that it will do just fine if it is only allowed to cultivate its back garden in peace. As the world's largest trading bloc, the Common Market has a vital interest in the way the world is run, and if the Common Market countries don't get together to defend their interests, no one else will do it for them.

For brief periods and on limited issues, the six members of the European Community have got together to work out a concerted stance. But as we saw in the case of Special Drawing Rights, their common policies were arrived at only after bitter fights and therefore tended to be precarious and short-lived: their alliance over international liquidity lasted only fourteen months, from January, 1967, until the crunch in March, 1968. If they really want to defend their interests in future, they will have to do better than that.

The institutional machinery is all ready for the six Common Market countries to work out common external policies in most areas. They have frequent and regular meetings of foreign ministers, economic and finance ministers, agriculture ministers, and central-bank governors, not to mention almost permanent sessions of official committees. But in practice the Six have proved unable to reach durable agreements on foreign-affairs issues and have taken refuge in ad-hoc compromises which had to be hammered out in response to some U.S. initiative.

The Common Market's disarray on external affairs is the direct result of the internal tensions between the member states, who have not yet reached a consensus over the kind of Community they want. To a large extent the responsibility for these tensions and the lack of any significant progress in the development of the Common Market in the past four years can be laid at General de Gaulle's door. He was so determined to resist any erosion of French national sovereignty that he was prepared to precipitate any number of conflicts with the other member states to defend it.

Over a period of time his example proved contagious: the Dutch blocked progress on the coordination of transport policies, in the defense of Dutch national interest, and blocked cooperation on technology, in the name of European integration; the Italians helped to destroy the Community's program for the development of peaceful nuclear power simply because they felt they were paying more into the program than they were getting out directly; the Germans balked at their treaty obligations to submit all their foreign trading relations to an overall Community policy because they wanted to be free to use trade bargaining as a diplomatic weapon in their dealings with the East European

countries. (French attempts to evade or break their treaty obligations are altogether too numerous to mention.) In short, the
Common Market countries have lost the so-called "Community
spirit" of the very early years.

One consequence of this deterioration in relations among the
Six is that they now have a lopsided Community. They have
removed all tariffs on internal trade in industrial products and
have harmonized their customs duties on imports from the rest of
the world at the same level all the way around their external frontiers, but they have done nothing to coordinate the management
of the six economies. This means that an export boom by one
member country is almost inevitably achieved, in the first instance, at the expense of one or more of the other member countries, because they have no tariff protection against additional
imports. In normal circumstances this might not matter very
much, for one would expect the member states to fluctuate back
and forth between surpluses and deficits, and in the long run the
swings would tend to balance out. But when one of the member states is in heavy and chronic surplus because its currency
is undervalued, like Germany in 1968 and 1969, and when another is in heavy and apparently fundamental deficit because its
currency is overvalued, like France in 1968 and 1969, then the
strains on the Community can be very serious.

As we have seen, they were particularly serious for France, because they produced a heavy flight of capital from Paris into
Frankfurt, but they could also be serious for other member states.
Belgium and Holland, which depend on trade for about forty percent of their gross national product, do more than half this trade
with their partners in the Community; after France devalued in
July, 1969, they were inevitably caught in a vortex between
French exports, which had just been made eleven percent
cheaper, and German exports, which had long been too cheap.

## TOWARD A EUROPEAN MONETARY UNION

The Common Market Commission, the Community's executive body, had long foreseen the need to avert this kind of
situation by matching the customs union with progress toward an

economic union. As far back as 1963, the Commission had been urging the Six to start coordinating their economic policies, so that their currencies wouldn't get out of line with each other and set up serious economic strains within the Community. A whole series of committees was set up, at whose meetings officials of the Six were meant to discuss and coordinate monetary policy, budgetary policy, short-term economic policy, and central-banking affairs. But the proof of the pudding was in the eating—the German and French governments consistently refused to run their economies in accordance with the advice of the Commission, their currencies did get out of line, and economic union was as far off in 1969 as it had been five years earlier.

In some ways it was even farther off. In the middle 1960's the Six set up a new Community-wide farm policy which was intended to parallel the industrial customs union by opening the door to free trade in agricultural goods between the member states. This farm policy maddened the farm lobby in the United States, because it was considerably more protectionist toward farm imports. But the sacrifice of American interests would have been worthwhile if the farm policy had proved successful.

In fact it proved an abysmal failure. The fixing of common farm prices in terms of gold had been partly intended as a way of dragging the Six faster along the road to economic and monetary union, and some observers predicted that it would make parity changes by the Six impossible. But when the crunch came, the member states were not prepared to make the sacrifices of national sovereignty necessary to make the farm policy work. During the first half of 1969 the common price system broke down by accident because French francs could be bought so cheaply that German importers of grain could undercut the minimum Community price by about ten percent; after the franc was devalued in July, 1969, it was deliberately abandoned because the French refused to accept the consequences of common prices fixed in terms of gold. According to the rules, they ought to have raised the prices paid to French farmers by 12.5 percent in terms of francs, so as to keep them on the same level as the farmers in the other member states. But they felt that the French economy could not stand this extra inflationary pressure, and they preferred to abandon the principle of free Common Market trade in farm products. For the following two years the French agricultural market would be partly insulated from the rest of the Community.

In addition to the farm policy, the Commission proposed a number of measures which were intended to bring the Six a few steps closer to economic union. These proposals included the creation of a new type of European company statute, which would open the door to cross-frontier mergers and the harmonization of different forms of company taxation in the Six. But each time they were brought up short by doctrinaire objections from de Gaulle, who opposed anything which appeared to infringe French national sovereignty.

At the beginning of 1969, however, Raymond Barre proposed that the Six should set up a permanent network of multilateral credits which could be drawn on automatically by any member state that got into balance-of-payments difficulties. This proposal was intended as a cautious first step toward the establishment of a European monetary union, in which the members would pool part or all of their reserves and might one day create a common currency.

Very wisely, Barre linked his plan to a procedure of consultation between the member states, which would have to be ready at all times to hold joint discussions of economic measures which could affect their partners, and which would be obliged to submit their economic policies to the approval of their partners whenever they drew on the network of credits. The idea of a partial pooling of reserves was fine, but it would be no use in the long run if it were not accompanied by greater coordination of economic policies than had been customary in the past.

The French reaction to the Barre plan was characteristic. Being themselves in serious balance-of-payments difficulties, they were the first to welcome the notion of an automatic credit network; but they wouldn't hear of any obligation to discuss their domestic economic policies with their partners. When Georges Pompidou replaced de Gaulle at the Elysée Palace, and Giscard d'Estaing replaced Michel Debré at the Finance Ministry, they changed their tune, and accepted both parts of the package. But they still did not inform their partners of their devaluation plan before it was announced to the world at large, let alone discuss it with them.

Naturally, they were able to produce explanations, justifications, excuses for their behavior, but it was not a very auspicious beginning to the post-Gaullist era in Community affairs.

The early enthusiasts of the Community believed that the expansion of internal trade in the customs union would inevitably lead to closer economic integration at all levels, and that economic and monetary integration would lead to closer political union. Walter Hallstein, first president of the Common Market Commission, was fond of saying, "We are not in business, we are in politics," and he was right, in the sense that every Community decision was a political decision. But later years were to demonstrate that there was nothing automatic or inevitable about the process of integration. Rather, the record since 1965 has shown that political disunity can prevent economic integration, regardless of what the Common Market treaty says, and when Hallstein claimed that "We have passed the point of no return," as he did every time a major decision was taken by the Council of Ministers, he was only giving himself a pep talk.

The European Community today is a bit like Christianity: it's not that it's failed, but that it's never been tried. The Europeans have so far failed to meet the challenge of political and economic integration, but they still have the opportunity to make up for lost time, and the departure of General de Gaulle should make it a lot easier for them to do so. Their summit meeting in The Hague in December, 1969, certainly seemed to promise a new readiness to move forward on several fronts. As a result of it, new financial rules for the Community were quickly negotiated, which hold out the prospect of a more federal and more democratic structure in the future. The Six undertook to prepare for membership negotiations with Britain and the other candidate countries by the middle of 1970, and they agreed to make plans for much closer monetary and economic union by the end of that year. In fact, they are aiming at joint representation in the IMF. Enormous problems still remain, especially on the agricultural front, for the mutual hostility fostered for so long by General de Gaulle cannot be dissipated all at once by a simple declaration of good intentions.

In January, 1970, the Barre plan got off the ground. The Six agreed to make one billion dollars available for short-term monetary aid to each other. In addition to this relatively automatic assistance, one billion dollars more could be doled out if the lending countries wished. Though this arrangement adds little to existing "swap" accords, it demonstrates a European desire to strengthen their own monetary links.

With the mark revalued, the first priority for the Six is to ensure that this kind of fundamental imbalance could not recur, or that, if there should be another cataclysmic event like the May Revolution in France, they would be properly equipped to deal with it smoothly and efficiently. One way of ensuring that the Common Market currencies do not get wildly out of kilter with each other would be to adopt more flexible exchange rates, possibly with one of the variants of the "moving peg," so that parities would be changed more frequently, in smaller jumps than at present and with less political hysteria on all sides.

The Bundesbank has been in favor of such a "moving peg" system for the Deutschemark, since the discrepancy between the mark and other currencies has shown a steady tendency to widen all the time. Guido Carli, governor of the Bank of Italy, has proposed that all the Common Market countries should move over to more flexible exchange rates for a period, as part of the adjustment process necessary for enlarging the Community to include Britain. The Commission, on the other hand, is not merely opposed to more flexible exchange rates, but would actually prefer to see even the day-to-day fluctuations permitted by the IMF eliminated between the Common Market currencies, which would then move only as a block up or down in relation to the dollar.

In the long run, the Commission's approach is nearer to the ideal of Community integration. A true European monetary union would inevitably play a bigger part, and should play a more constructive part in the international monetary system. But it will probably remain an ideal until the Common Market countries have got a lot closer to the unification of their economies than they are today. The "moving peg" approach, by contrast, which could be useful in the meantime, would almost inevitably mean that the Community would have to abandon the present system of common farm prices indefinitely, and not just temporarily, as was done in July, 1969, for France alone. In any case, the adoption of a system of more flexible exchange rates would not by itself dispose of the problem of economic harmonization between the six member states. The governments would still have to take the decisions necessary to maintain the Community's economy on an even keel, and they would have to take these decisions together in the framework of the Common Market institutions. Flexible exchange rates might prove to be a useful technical device, but they certainly could not be a panacea which would exonerate the governments from facing up to their economic and political responsibilities.

If the Common Market governments feel a revival of confidence in the all-round and equitable advantages of pooling their sovereignty in the Community institutions, then the way will also be open for them to perceive their community of interest in external affairs, too. Without a common attitude at home, they can scarcely be expected to have a common policy abroad, and without a shared approach to economic integration, where their joint self-interest is so apparent, they can hardly hope to reach a common attitude to, say, defense, where there is rather more room for argument.

But whatever steps the Six may take to resolve the economic tensions inside the Community, they can only have the strongest interest in making sure that the international monetary system works smoothly. As a major industrial, commercial, and financial grouping, the Community needs to avert all the different restrictions on trade and payments which have sprung up on both sides of the Atlantic in 1968 and 1969. It will always be easy to blame the Americans for what goes wrong, or whoever happens to be the scapegoat closest at hand, but it will never be particularly productive.

Externally, the most immediate long-term monetary problem now facing both Britain and the Common Market is the fact that the world is effectively operating on a dollar standard. The role of gold in the monetary system has been circumscribed, probably forever, and the piling up of American liquid liabilities abroad means that the U.S. obligation to convert dollars into gold is now little more than a polite fiction—not to say a joke. The pound is still a reserve currency, but only just, and its importance as a trading and financing instrument will almost certainly decline.

Yet the growing internationalization of business and the continuing expansion of trade means that the world needs a suitable international currency, and at the present moment this need can be supplied only by the dollar. The Euro-dollar market is now a truly international capital market, and its astonishing growth in the past two years is due not only to the American credit squeeze and the pulling power of the big American banks, but also to the fact that there is a very large commercial and industrial demand for a capital market of this type.

The dollar standard is not an unmixed blessing, however, for it poses serious problems both for the European surplus countries and for the United States. European surplus countries dislike being forced to accept the U.S. deficit and the accumulation of dollars, but with the end of gold convertibility they have little choice; their only alternative would be to ban exports to America, and that would be even less advantageous than taking dollars. But the situation is liable to get worse as the U.S. credit squeeze ends, for then Euro-dollar rates will come down and it will become more difficult for European central banks to pump surplus dollars into the Euro-dollar market.

Of greater significance is the fact that the world is on a legal dollar standard too, in the sense that all other currencies are valued in terms of dollars under IMF rules. This means that the classic remedy for a chronic deficit—devaluation—is not open to Washington, since a change in the dollar price automatically means an exactly similar change in all other currencies. At some distant date it may be possible to peg currencies to something other than the dollar, say SDRs. But this will be a practical proposition only if SDRs cease to be a purely central bank asset and start being traded in foreign-exchange markets, for it is there that central banks intervene to stabilize the value of their currencies.

**O**nce upon a time, there lived a wise, old King. He was loved by his people, whom he had ruled in peace and harmony for many years.

Now, the King had a beautiful daughter, the Princess Felicity, but he had no son to follow in his footsteps.

One day he decided he must seek a successor. He proclaimed that there would be a contest on Midsummer Eve. The winner would succeed to the throne and would also be given the hand of the fair Felicity.

On the appointed day, the palace courtyard was thronged with hundreds of contestants. When they were assembled before his throne, the King warned them that all who failed would be condemned to sit in the stocks for forty days and endure the public scorn. When they heard this piece of news, all but three of the contestants withdrew.

The first to come forward was a rich Prince, who was followed by a score of servants carrying a massive, brass-bound coffer. Opening the lid with a flourish, he said to the King: "Sire, I have here a vast store of a precious, yellow metal. With this, the Princess and I will have everything we need to ensure forever the happiness and prosperity of your subjects."

# The Would-be King

235

The second to come forward was a learned professor, who was followed by a band of students dragging a cart loaded with heavy, dusty tomes. "Your Majesty, these books," he said as he lovingly fondled the first volume, "contain the rules of the game. With them, the Princess and I will have everything we need to govern your subjects and guarantee their prosperity."

The third to come forward was a young man, who appeared to be carrying no gift at all. "Sire," he said, "the most valuable gift I can offer is common sense. No precious metal can ensure happiness and prosperity. No rules will work forever. With common sense, the Princess and I will have everything we need to perpetuate the peace and harmony of your Kingdom and the people's confidence in their rulers."

The wise King took less than a moment to make his choice. "Young man," he said, "you shall have my daughter's hand. You shall be King."

The young man and the Princess were married the next day, and they and their subjects lived flexibly ever after.

# INDEX